JURISPRUDENCE AS IDEOLOGY

How can universally valid legal principles possibly exist in a manifestly unequal world? In *Jurisprudence as Ideology* Valerie Kerruish examines how a progressive law may be possible. She presents jurisprudence as a paradigm of legal ideology, unravelling the unjust social dynamic within which law operates and which, she argues, law helps to create. Central to Kerruish's argument is her illuminating concept of 'rights fetishism: the mystification of the value of law for persons occupying subordinate positions in social relations'.

The author creatively engages with contemporary issues in socialist, feminist, and critical legal theory, while linking these issues to debates in jurisprudence and the philosophy and sociology of law.

SOCIOLOGY OF LAW AND CRIME
Editors:
Maureen Cain, *University of the West Indies*
Carol Smart, *University of Warwick*

This new series presents the latest critical and international scholarship in sociology, legal theory, and criminology. Books in the series will integrate the sociology of law and the sociology of crime, extending beyond both disciplines to analyse the distribution of power. Realist, critical, and postmodern approaches will be central to the series, while the major substantive themes will be gender, class and race as they affect and, in turn, are shaped by legal relations. Throughout, the series will present fresh theoretical interpretations based on the latest empirical research. Books for early publication in the series deal with such controversial issues as child custody, criminal and penal policy, and alternative legal theory.

Titles in this series include

CHILD CUSTODY AND THE POLITICS OF GENDER
Carol Smart and Selma Sevenhuijsen (eds)

FEMINISM AND THE POWER OF LAW
Carol Smart

OFFENDING WOMEN
Female Lawbreakers and the Criminal Justice System
Anne Worrall

FEMININITY IN DISSENT
Alison Young

THE MYTHOLOGY OF MODERN LAW
Peter Fitzpatrick

JURISPRUDENCE
AS IDEOLOGY

Valerie Kerruish

London and New York

First published 1991
by Routledge
11 New Fetter Lane, London EC4P 4EE

Simultaneously published in the USA and Canada
by Routledge
a division of Routledge, Chapman and Hall, Inc.
29 West 35th Street, New York, NY 10001

First published in paperback in 1992

© 1991 Valerie Kerruish

Typeset by Michael Mepham, Frome, Somerset
Printed and bound in Great Britain by
Biddles Ltd, Guildford and King's Lynn

British Library Cataloguing in Publication Data
Kerruish, Valerie *1943–*
Jurisprudence as ideology
– (Sociology of law and crime)
1. Jurisprudence
I. Title   II. Series
340.1

Library of Congress Cataloging in Publication Data
Kerruish, Valerie, 1943–
Jurisprudence as ideology / Valerie Kerruish.
p.   cm. – (Sociology of law and crime)
Includes bibliographical references and index.
1. Sociological jurisprudence.   2. Law – Methodology.
3. Law – interpretation and construction.
4. Deconstruction.
5. Effectiveness and validity of law.   I. Title. II. Series.
K370.K47   1991
340'.1 – dc20   90-9018
                                                          CIP

ISBN 0–415–08857–7

In Memory of My Mother and Father

CONTENTS

SERIES EDITORS' PREFACE

As Series Editors we constantly find ourselves preparing prefaces for books we wish we had written ourselves. This is most certainly the case for Valerie Kerruish's *Jurisprudence as Ideology*, because, while this book is in some senses a new departure from the series and the discipline, in another sense it epitomises what the series stands for.

Jurisprudence as Ideology is a departure from the series because, quite simply, it is not about women. Yet it is a work which addresses some of the central issues of feminist theory in the field of the sociology of law. It shares feminist concerns for the oppressed, including not only women, but also aboriginal peoples, working and poverty-stricken peoples, and all those, as Kerruish describes it, on the 'down-side' of society as presently structured, and seeks to discover what a theory and practice of law would and should look like from their standpoints. It is a book which skates over none of the problems, yet remains full of hope. While taking the individualist eighties on board, this is a text for the 1990s.

The book epitomises what the series stands for because it is gender conscious rather than gender blind, and because in its argument it displaces and transcends disciplinary boundaries. Kerruish is lawyer, jurisprude, philosopher and sociologist and none of the disciplines or arguments she encounters is given short shrift as she constructs her case for a possibility of progressive legalism.

Kerruish's journey starts with a refinement of the concept of ideology in which she distinguishes negative and positive meanings. The careful distinction enables her to integrate postmodern insights into a postmarxian argument, and re-emerges at the end of the text to form part of her discussion of the contradictory forms of value in rights. Chapters 2 and 3 take us into exegeses of representative jurisprudential theories which are both critical and creative. We emerge knowing much more about Hart, Finnis, and Dworkin. These are scholarly analyses, paying proper respect to some of the major legal theorists of our time, not polemical trashing exercises. As a result, we emerge, too, with a basis for the forward movement of theory on which the author is to embark.

Chapter 4 deals with the legal construction of objectivity, and demonstrates the fallacies and the inadequacies of this internalist enterprise. This chapter may be paired with Chapter 5, which elaborates a concept of the fetishisation of rights which parallels Marx's concept of the fetishisation of commodities. As ever, in this scholarly text, nothing is taken for granted, and Kerruish defends the source of her key concept with a precise and detailed argument which is conceptually consistent with the rest of her discussion. The concept is used to isolate the legalistic notion of rights from rights claims made by oppressed groups, which are historical or specific rather than absolute and abstracted. Fetishisation is revealed as a device which excludes while purporting to generalise.

Here, Kerruish has created a conceptually and theoretically refined way through the vexed issues of the rights debate and the double-faced nature of law. Up until now, both users and social theorists of law have been sucked into the authoritarian vortex of its fetishised groups. Now, at the least, we can fight for concrete rights for oppressed groups with a clear conscience borne of a better understanding of both risks and the gains to be made.

The concluding chapters lead us further into a knowledge of how a progressive law may be possible. The most crucial new conception here is the distinction between points of view and standpoint. Standpoints are relational and shape the ways in which we know and experience reality; points of view cut across standpoints and are available to be used in a more off-the-peg fashion. Thus occupants of many standpoints, owners of variously fractured identities, may work together from a legal point of view, to constitute a progressive legal practice.

Postmodernism has deconstructed law, and largely side-stepped jurisprudence. Kerruish argues that ideologies of, and in, law are real and powerful and obvious appearances, so that criticism of them must take them first on their own terms. Only then will it be possible to understand the ways in which these terms are inadequate, and to construct a jurisprudence for a more hopeful future.

We are proud to offer our readers a jurisprudence of hope and and possibility which is yet prepared to embrace diversity.

Carol Smart
Maureen Cain
May 1990

ACKNOWLEDGEMENTS

I wish to thank Maureen Cain, Ian Duncanson, Judith Grbich and
Alan Hunt for their support, criticism and encouragement of my
work over several years. Jurisprudence and Philosophy of Law
students at the University of Western Australia have stimulated and
challenged my ideas. I have special debts to Uwe Petersen, with
whom the main themes of this book have been discussed and
clarified, and to Joseph and Tim McAuliffe. Research assistance was
given by Ian Oi, and Heather Ghisalberti and Lesley Nesbitt helped
in the production of the manuscript. As the final version of this book
was being written, I stood with Nyungah and other Australian
Aboriginal people in a protracted struggle against the commercial
development of an Aboriginal sacred site in Perth by the Western
Australian Government. I owe thanks to the black people and the
white people whose commitment to that struggle has helped me to
understand better my own ideas.

INTRODUCTION: THINKING ABOUT JURISPRUDENCE AS IDEOLOGY

QUESTIONS OF VALUE

The symbol of law in our society is a blindfolded woman holding evenly-balanced scales of justice. The cover of the English paperback version of a recent book on the philosophy of law by Ronald Dworkin shows a strong human arm holding scales which are tilted towards it. It is common to speak of 'the strong arm of the law', and perhaps the intention of Dworkin's pictorial metaphor is indeed to suggest that the interests of those on the side of the law are weightier. Such interests might be thought of as rights – claims to social goods which are justified by moral and political principle, rather than justifiable in terms of a policy embodying some particular conception of human well-being. Law, magisterially blinded against contingent differences of class, gender and race, holds the instrument of balance, the measure of equality.

The symbolism, thus interpreted, invites two conclusions. Those who are benefited by law may rest content that their claims have been made for reasons of universal validity. Those who are restrained or coerced by its strong arm ought to reflect that the agency of that arm is for a community of free and equal individuals.

This book questions both these conclusions while arguing that they are necessarily part of legal ideology. It questions them because of theoretical disagreement with the idea that differences of class, sex–gender and race are contingent to the forms of law in Western democracies which are thus symbolised. It takes a standpoint for people whose work, or lack of it, is conditioned by the pursuit of profit for others; of those who suffer the devaluation of the feminine; and of races whose civilisation has been denied or destroyed by others. It asks how universally valid principles can be

1

thought to exist in a world where social relations oppose the needs of some to those of others, and it questions the agency of law.

From these standpoints, even Dworkin might admit, some scepticism is warranted. Workers, women, gays and people of colour have had a hard time with the common law of England, at home and on export, and these injustices continue. Yet, he would have it, this is not law's fault. Law is innocent. Law, far from being complicit in social practices which are destructive of human well-being, is, of all social institutions, the one which embodies the ideals and procedures of and for that well-being.

The claim of law's innocence is ideological. It is made within interpretations of our ways of life which give law a particular nature, purpose and value. These interpretations claim their own truth and prescribe their own values in adversarial argument against other ideas of law. They imagine their own most persuasive case and pursue it against those who tell a different story. Their arguments are paradigms of the lawyer's in-court skills; and they prosecute those whose beliefs undermine them with the assurance of one who knows that guilt must be punished if innocence is to survive. The claim of law's innocence is a claim about an idea of law, because given the diversity of legal practices and institutions, 'law' as a term denoting a unitary object can only refer to an idea. It is supported by the knowledge, technique and organisation of the legal profession, and the discipline within which the claim is made, explained and justified is jurisprudence.

There are various schools of thought about law within this discipline. Some seek to persuade us that law, by virtue of offering a coherent set of objective rules which can be impartially applied, is the best possible means of stopping a war of all against all. Others consider it self-evidently true, or at least warrantably assertible on the basis of their own experience, that law participates in achieving social harmony. Others again tell us that law is our culture's integrity. To return to the traditional symbol of law, on some interpretations, the blindfolded woman represents the irrelevance of human agency in law's workings. Neither male, nor sighted, she can have no active role. It is the scales that count. Here the suggestion is that legal culture has found the right instrument for weighing and balancing claims. The rule of law is disjoined from rule by men.

However true it is that jurisprudence has the overall purpose of persuading people of law's innocence, and however much cause there may be for scepticism as to this claim, it would be wrong to suppose that it offers nothing to the understanding of law. Jurisprudence is a source of both understanding and misunderstanding of law. As the most generalised and abstract form of legal discourse it reveals the categories and concepts in which lawyers and jurists think about law. How widely this mode of thought is shared within the practising profession, how influential it is on people in the wider community, whether and how it pervades the study and understanding of law by non-lawyers, are empirical questions which I do not address. Jurisprudence may be a backwater in the faster flow of everyday life and yield little information on the concrete ways in which legal practices and institutions affect particular undertakings. Even so, if we are concerned about the actual and symbolic power to regulate and control human thought and action which is vested by the configuration of technical expertise, market control and coercive power in systems of law, there is reason for studying every aspect of the way in which law appears and is represented. The construction of general concepts and categories of this formalistic discipline, law itself, rights, duties, obligation, authority, validity, legitimacy, is both selective and systematic. It is compatible with the method of abstraction used in the production of legal doctrine and dogma, and it is articulated to ideas about politics, morality and human association.

Moreover, and more practically, if law's innocence is less than self-evident, there will be few who have had no experience of its benefits. Law can and has conferred benefits on people who are subordinated and devalued within existing social relations and it imposes constraints of some kind on dominant and empowered people. These considerations not only give credibility to the claims of law's innocence found in jurisprudence, they are also grounds for not substituting a root-and-branch condemnation of law for the claim of innocence. Law as an unmitigated evil is as overgeneralised as the claim for law's innocence. Both views can only be coherently defended by exclusions and closures of and against other relevant considerations.

The central claim of this book is that the analysis and explanation of jurisprudence reveals a social phenomenon, which I call rights fetishism. A fetish involves the irrational reverencing of a human artefact, and I use rights fetishism in that broad sense. Rights fetishism is constituted by legal practices which regulate and adjudicate particular enterprises and disputes by use of general rules.

What seems to happen is that these general rules somehow cast loose their moorings as deliberately formulated standards for human action and float off to constitute a realm of the sacred. From within this realm, the mundane activities of lawyers, judges, and legislators become invested with a meaning and significance which goes beyond any down-to-earth account of what they are doing. A Constitution, for example, a document drawn up at some time in the past by a group of empowered men which, in more or less convoluted prose, sets out their ground rules for human association, becomes invested with genius after no more than the passage of time. Superior courts go through their business in a ritualised manner, in fancy dress, with people playing out various roles in a distinctive language and by use of an elaborate and highly mannered set of conventions, and this drama is seen as homage to the majesty of the law. This performance has more in common with a church service than with shopping in a supermarket or catching a bus, yet it may be concerned with rights and wrongs arising out of just such everyday activities. Somewhere, between an event that might happen to anyone in the ordinary course of his or her life and these sacred rituals, there is a form of human activity which manufactures these mysteries.

This transformation of the secular to the sacred will have a different meaning for people who do not participate in it on a regular basis, than for those who do. As it happens, in common law countries where Anglo-European culture is dominant – the United Kingdom, the United States of America, Australia, Canada and New Zealand – the legal profession, sociologically, is part of the middle and upper class. It is overwhelmingly white, until the early decades of this century it was exclusively male, and the upper echelons of the legal hierarchy are still, very dominantly, male. Rights fetishism, being constituted by legal practices which take place within configurations of extra-legal social relations such as those of sex–gender and race, mystifies law and makes realistic judgments of its value difficult for everyone. But regular participants in legal practices take benefits from existing institutions and practices which are different in kind from the benefits, real or imagined, which law might be thought to confer on others. For members of the legal profession and the judiciary, law is satisfying work, a salary or wage, a relatively high social status, and a body of expertise which in a technocratic society confers power over those who lack it. Practices which invest Constitutions with genius and

4

law with majesty must seem less at odds with their perceptions of what is valuable in life, than with the perceptions of those from whose life law is remote – whether threateningly or beneficently. This is ground for thinking that the mystification of the value of law which is involved in rights fetishism is at least different and possibly more acute for people occupying subordinated positions within social relations.

Jurisprudence interprets legal practices from a legal point of view. That is to say, it is made up from internalist understandings of law. These understandings refute the hypothesis that nation states are best understood in terms of social relations. Instead, they suppose a dichotomy between 'the individual' and 'the social' to be fundamental to social theory. Consequently, albeit in a variety of forms, the constantly recurring idea in jurisprudence is that conflict between the individual and the state and between free and equal individuals within the society, are given, natural or necessary conditions of social life. Law alone, it is argued, prevents these conflicts from destroying society, and, since the conflicts are supposed to inhere in social life, law gets invested with a foundational necessity.

It should not be thought that common law jurisprudence is contextualised by independently developed social and political theory. The legal paradigm changed prior to the sixteenth century. Within the older paradigm, community of opinion between the common law judges and their senior colleagues at the Inns of Court was necessary to giving an answer to a question of law. Commonly enough, if the judges disagreed, the point went unanswered (Baker 1985). Within the new paradigm, the idea that legal questions had to be answered and a consequent objectification of legal doctrines as statable in the form of rules and principles strengthened. Ideas of the social as explicable in terms of individuals' contracting or internalising norms of reciprocity emerged more or less contemporaneously. The structuring dichotomy of the individual and the social is common to the political, social and legal thought in seventeenth- and eighteenth-century England.

It is, clearly enough, an idea which excludes conceptions of self as connected with others. It also defines political community in terms of the nation state. It thus serves a double purpose. On the one hand it encourages competitive individualism and nationalism. On the other hand the abstract, free and equal individual is a persona to which rights can be attached. The ascription of rights, then, constructs legal identities – landowners and tenants, husbands and wives, employers and employees, principals and agents, etc., and this identity defines a role for which there must be players in a particular form of life.

Rights fetishism is constituted by legal practices. Insofar as legal practices are justified in jurisprudence, the discipline is an exemplary instance of a system of thought pulling itself up by its own bootstraps. Justification involves the application of an independent standard of value. But jurisprudence justifies legal practices in terms of values constructed by legal practices. The ascription of rights to free and equal legal subjects is justified either by arguing that this process is an actualisation of an independently existing reality of entitlements or by arguing that it is a fiction or convention which must be maintained for the good of individuals. There is no reason to doubt the social reality of ascribing rights to legal subjects. That is simply one of the things legislators and judges do in making laws and deciding cases; one of the things lawyers assume in advising clients on a course of action; one of the things which is part of everyday lives – on the street, on the farm, in business and in homes. But the justification of this practice is quite a different question. Despite the linguistic absurdity, it is not inconceivable that the discourse of right is heuristically wrong from the standpoint of working people, feminists and people of colour. Jurisprudence, however, does not entertain such an idea. Law is already justified as necessary to social life through the individualist social theory which it helps to construct, and since law involves the ascription of rights in both its theory and its practice, there is no logical space left for scepticism as to the value of rights. Jurisprudence contributes to and conceals rights fetishism by denying the self-referential character of legal justifications and so arguing their independence.

This is a complex argument. This book is devoted to elaborating and explaining it. But the contribution/concealment function of jurisprudence in relation to rights fetishism is replicated in many instances of ideology. Women, in law and in philosophy, for example, in order to make their voices heard, may adopt the adversarial mode of argument which dominates both discourses (Bender 1988; Moulton 1983). In so doing they deploy intellectual power according to rules and conventions formulated and lived by men. The consequence is to strengthen the paradigm if this participation in it is justified by recourse to universalistic notions such

6

as necessity. Such justifications exclude challenge to the adversarial mode of argument as a means of furthering knowledge and understanding. The subjective intention of such participation may well be to subvert the paradigm. But success in operating with it brings its own rewards – forensic success, a job, even a tenured job, professional recognition and acceptance. These are benefits which relatively fewer women share. Moreover receipt of these benefits is structured by competition and rationalised by the concept of merit. Incorporation, a process which negates the subversive intention, may take place if competitive practices and meritocratic judgment, coming on top of material benefit, conceal from the actor the way in which her activity constitutes the paradigm (Purdy 1989).

The contribution/concealment function of ideology is general. It has particular modes of expression and jurisprudence is one such mode. A study of it reveals a way in which social relations of exploitation, devaluation and alienation are both basic to legal forms of social regulation and control and are reproduced by those forms.

JURISPRUDENCE: A PRELIMINARY ENCOUNTER

The research object of this study is common law, philosophical jurisprudence. The term 'jurisprudence' has a double sense and refers both to general theory of law (according to the Oxford English Dictionary, to philosophy or science of law), and to the accumulated doctrine and expert knowledge of the legal profession in a given legal system. From this point, throughout this work I shall use 'Jurisprudence' to refer to the first of these senses and 'jurisprudence' to refer to the second. The jurisprudence of a nation state is like a distillate or highly refined abstraction of legal practices. In Jurisprudence, that distillate is written down and justified; fundamental legal concepts are identified and given meaning or interpreted according to the philosophical, sociological and political views of its authors.

No definition and no model of Jurisprudence is offered in this work. Chapter 2 gives an account of three concepts of law elaborated within it. Chapter 3 considers questions of method and identifies issues of agreement and argument in Jurisprudence by considering the dialogic and adversarial relations between the three texts analysed in Chapter 2.[1] Chapter 4, 'The Jurisprudence

Game', considers the legal construction of objectivity. Prior to this more detailed consideration of Jurisprudence, however, some further orientation toward this arcane discipline may be helpful.

Jurisprudence is not confined to general theory of law. Another exercise undertaken within it is concerned with generalised descriptions of particular legal doctrines. Such work, however, either tacitly presupposes a general theory of law or relies on the common sense of the dominant professional legal culture. There is certainly interaction between general theory of law and the middle level theory of particular doctrines or doctrinal areas. For example, a recent essay by Andrew Ashworth, on the justification of punishment, is informed by the revival of natural law and rights theories and reflects the retreat from utilitarian theory in much moral, political and legal philosophy in England during the last decade. The texts analysed for this work, however, are concerned with general theory of law, because, whether this level of abstraction in theory is embraced or eschewed, the effects of that judgment will inform middle order theory (Kerruish 1987).

Practitioners of Jurisprudence will be conversant with the legal doctrine of at least one national state and this will be backgrounded by a broader tradition – Roman law, contemporary civilian law, or, in English language jurisprudence, the common law tradition. The degree of ethnocentricity of the work is partially dependent on the tradition(s) of which it takes account. English language jurisprudence is highly ethnocentric, tending to disregard all but the common law tradition.

Dating perhaps from Blackstone's *Commentaries on the Laws of England* (1770), the site of production of common law Jurisprudence has largely been law schools within tertiary educational institutions where the principal educational objective has been to educate and train for the practising profession.[2] Here it has traditionally been taught as a 'theoretical' subject as distinct from a 'practical' or doctrinal one. It aims to refine and clarify students' thought about and understanding of selected concepts or doctrines, presupposing the technical doctrinal knowledge pertinent to its projects. To ask which concepts, and why these, is important. To ask about the absence of certain concepts in Jurisprudence is equally important and, in the conception of this study, is of primary importance. Jurisprudential silence about ideology is profound. The social relations of class, sex–gender and race and the institutionalised practices of exploitation, devaluation and alienation are hidden in its depths. To return, however, for the moment, to what Jurisprudence is concerned with: 'What is law?' has been said to be *the* question of Jurisprudence (Tur 1976) but we need beg no questions by commenting on that. Sovereignty, contract, property, possession, personality, punishment, precedent and legislation are more specific notions which are frequently examined. In contemporary Jurisprudence, analyses of legal reasoning, rights, obligations, powers, rules and authority stand alongside or within general theories of law and justice.

As well as being informed by legal doctrine and written within the context of a broader tradition, Jurisprudence may draw, both in method and content, from other disciplines, such as sociology, history, anthropology, or philosophy. In writing only about philosophical Jurisprudence, I do not intend to accord it privilege as a paradigm, any more than in writing only about common law Jurisprudence I wish to continue its ethnocentricity. Nor, on the other hand, do I think that other kinds of Jurisprudence do not need to be examined for their ideological form and content. My selection is made merely in order to be specific in what I am examining.

The method of philosophical Jurisprudence is argumentative and interpretive. Modes of reasoning and concepts of rationality differ between its various schools. But one unifying feature of the discipline is the claim that the concept of rationality employed is embedded within the law itself. In that sense, philosophical Jurisprudence is an internalist philosophy of law. It is written from or with reference to a point of view internal to professional legal practices. It draws out a mode of reasoning and system of thought said to be characteristic of the *Rechtsstaat* (the state based on the idea of the rule of law) and, by analysis, interpretation and adversarial argument within the same conceptual framework, develops its general theories of law or pursues its conceptual elucidations.

The only other general observation to be made at this stage about philosophical Jurisprudence of common law jurisdictions brings us on to its mode of presentation in this study. From the eighteenth century three of its main schools have been legal positivism, natural law theory and rights theory. The recent publication of three major texts, all from the University at Oxford in England and each written within one of these schools, is symptomatic of the general terrain if not exhaustive of it. In order to make the argument for Jurisprudence as ideology from grounds more concrete than a generalised model, I have made these three texts my primary focus for analysis and for presentation to the reader of philosophical Jurisprudence. The texts are Herbert Hart's *The Concept of Law* (1961), John Finnis' *Natural Law and Natural Rights* (1980) and Ronald Dworkin's *Law's Empire* (1986). Hart works within the British tradition of legal positivism, Finnis within classical and scholastic natural law theory, and Dworkin is a rights theorist. While there is a sense in which Finnis and Dworkin are both natural law theorists, Finnis remains within the classical school of medieval natural lawyers who, following Aquinas, saw the natural law *as* practical reason. Dworkin continues the more recent tradition of natural rights as discoverable, or in his version, sayable, *through* reason (Stein and Shand 1974). We give too much credence to legal positivism by supposing Jurisprudence to be structured by arguments between natural law and positivist theorists. These texts, in my judgment, present three distinct traditions in their strongest (most coherent) contemporary form.

They do not stand alone in twentieth century Jurisprudence. Two other streams in particular should be mentioned. First, Hans Kelsen's *The Pure Theory of Law* (1970) argues a strong form of neo-Kantian legal positivism which is philosophically divergent from the empiricist tradition which Hart continues. It has been and continues to be an immensely influential text. I have chosen Hart's *The Concept of Law* as a text representative of legal positivism, because the common law tradition is deeply informed by British empiricism as a matter of its cultural production. No judgment of the greater coherence or plausibility of the empiricist development of Cartesian dualism over the rationalist one is made in according precedence in this study to positivist legal theory developed within the former. The selection looks rather to imperial and professional cultural traditions.

The second stream is the pragmatist Jurisprudence which was developed in the early decades of this century by American jurists who called themselves Legal Realists. Their work drew some of its inspiration, both directly and indirectly, from the pragmatic philosophy of Peirce, James and Dewey. It made a wide-ranging critique of formalism in legal theory, that is of representations of law as a system of rules. The effects of this critique have permeated common law Jurisprudence ever since. Hart and Dworkin both incorporate some of its insights, while at the same time, using it as a foil against which to argue their particular formalisms. American Legal Realism, however, was a consciously diffuse and eclectic movement which looked more to the social sciences than to philosophy for an understanding of 'the law in action' rather than 'the law in books' (Llewellyn 1962). It is not a paradigm of philosophical Jurisprudence, and to analyse it as such, as Dworkin does, does not do it justice. It is mentioned here because of the influence it has had on philosophical Jurisprudence.

The results of my analysis of dialogic relations between the three texts chosen for study, or to put that another way, analysis of very basic ideas about law which, being shared by the authors of these texts, give some content to the notion of a discipline of philosophical Jurisprudence, can be summarily stated as follows. Philosophical Jurisprudence presents conceptions of law as norms (that is, as rules or principles or requirements of practical reasonableness). These conceptions are elaborated within theories of society within which the individual is defined in some form of opposition to the social. They are written from or with reference to an internal or legal point of view and they are all concerned to show law's legitimacy. This, then, gives in broad outline the paradigm which is analysed in this study as a form of ideology.

IDEOLOGY IN ITS NEUTRAL AND NEGATIVE SENSES

Analysis of common law, philosophical Jurisprudence as a form of ideology reveals the phenomenon of rights fetishism. An understanding of this phenomenon is important if the value of law to people occupying places on the down-side of social relations of class, sex–gender and race is to be adequately appraised. Ideology is frequently discussed in contemporary social theory. For some socialist, feminist and critical theorists, ideology is a central focus. This interest in ideology is developing a rich and complex interplay of understandings of the multiple ways in which ideas are part of social reality. While it would be quite wrong to take the notion of ideology out of this context of contemporary social theory and attempt to fix its meaning as being this or that, it is necessary to propose precise meanings of the notion where, as here, it is being claimed that something is a paradigm of ideology.

Chapter 1 makes such a proposal. It proposes that 'ideology' be understood as having both a neutral and a negative sense. Ideology in its neutral sense encompasses more or less complete systems of ideas produced in societies whose basic social relations are relations of material inequality. By social relations of material inequality, I mean relations between classes or categories within which one class or category is systematically exploited, devalued and disempowered by the other. In its negative sense, ideology is theories which justify these materially unequal social relations. Social relations of economic class, of sex–gender and of race are the basic social relations of inequality which I have in mind in referring to ideology in the United Kingdom, the United States and Australia.

I do not suppose that the existence of these classes and categories is self-evident. In writing and speaking of them and in assuming that systems of thought within a culture are not independent of them, I am using a social theory. This theory is, itself, ideological in the neutral sense and though, clearly enough, it is not concerned to justify the materially unequal social relations referred to, that, in itself, is no guarantee against its being negatively ideological. What has to be avoided is closure within a theory. The problem is a complex one of theoretical frameworks. It has to be tackled from the premise that all theory is normative. No construction of thought is the bearer of truth. What is the case – we can call it reality or THE WORLD – is the bearer of truth. Human thought and language grasps at it as best it may, knowing, if it imagines and uses an idea of dialectic, that in grasping it will change, if only because thought and language are themselves part of the whole.

Theory offers ways of living within this whole. Whatever it recommends, whatever its enterprise – from metaphysics to chemistry, its message is that we *ought to* understand things as being thus and so. To discuss the way that 'ought' is intended takes us to the heartlands of philosophy and social theory. It might, for example, be intended pragmatically, that this way of conceiving things will get us where we want to go. It might be intended teleologically, that this way of conceiving things grasps the essence of being and becoming. It might assert, by reference to some tests of verification or falsification, that we ought to understand things thus and so because that is how they are.

There are other ways to handle this confusion of very abstract ideas. Ways which are informed by the experience of being exploited and devalued. Awareness that this is *not* a universal experience goes against the legislative or normative tendency of theory. Awareness of rights fetishism as an actual social phenomenon reveals a ground in social reality from which normative thought acquires its tendency to silence. These ideas are explored in Chapters 5 and 6 of this book through an interpretation of Marx's account of commodity fetishism, the drawing of an analogy between commodity fetishism and rights fetishism and an exploration of the normative dimensions of frameworks of thought that perceive secular social practices as giving rise to fetishes.

Two points of great significance to studies of ideology come out of this. One thing is that if theory is not to be ideological in the negative sense it must be trying to find something out. The other thing is that it must be aware that at the very moment of finding, the context changes. One way of saying that is to say that a new horizon of knowledge and understanding is opened. Another way of saying it is to assert the fallibility and incompleteness of knowledge. Either way, what I am endeavouring to convey is the sense in which the getting of wisdom is an ongoing process to which ideology poses a double barrier. This double barrier does not keep politely to a place in the scheme of things. It moves into place against every advance in knowledge and understanding, offering an enclosure to travel-weary thinkers.

In everyday terms that enclosure is familiar enough. It is being stuck in our own ideas. In some contexts this is dogmatism, bigotry and prejudice, in others ethnocentrism and androcentrism. In others again, most notably in the professions and academia, it is a form of chauvinism which spawns inter-disciplinary rivalry and professional arrogance – phenomena which contradict the ideals of knowledge and service espoused by academics and professionals. In terms of theoretical and philosophical discussions of ideology, the enclosure is considered as closure, as silencing, as thought which has become static and false, in each case resulting in mystification, alienation and the reproduction of oppressive and repressive social and psychological tendencies.

The negative sense of ideology dominates all these notions of it. To understand how and why this is so, as well as to understand the social and psychological phenomena of ideology, it is necessary to look at the double barrier constructed by it – ideology in its neutral and negative forms. A realist will construe this task as undertaking to 'trace the way in which *reality appears*' (Barker 1985: 14). He or she will take account of Poulantzas' observation that '... ideology has the precise function of hiding the real contradictions and *reconstituting* on an imaginary level a relatively coherent discourse which serves as the horizon of the agent's experience' (Poulantzas

13

1973: 207). And, aware of an inner struggle and of capacities for self-deception, she or he will consider the power of culturally constructed ways of thinking and being and the ways in which these inhibit self-knowledge (Griffin 1982).

Contradiction and paradox are implicit in all these ways of considering ideology. Ronald Dworkin would have it that contradiction is an 'infertile metric' for grasping a coherent justification of legal culture (Dworkin 1986: 272). If we swallow the immense pretension of talk about a metric in this context, there is good sense in his comment. A coherent justification of legal culture must ignore contradiction and paradox within it. The point Dworkin misses in a casual acknowledgment 'that the shape of the law at any time reflects ideology and power' (Dworkin 1986: 272) is that coherent justifications of legal culture deny or marginalise the hurt and harm which the ideology of dominant social classes and groups inflicts on subordinated people and the environment.

We shall find that our jurists ignore, marginalise and exclude a lot in their texts. Yet there are more spectacular examples of exclusion in legal discourse. A doctrine that is thought by some to be part of Australian law is the doctrine of *terra nullius*. It declares the continent of Australia to have been 'desert and uninhabited' in 1788 when the British laid their first claim to it. On that basis, Australia is assigned the status in law of being a settled colony, with the consequence that both Aboriginal property in the land and sovereignty as a people is denied (Law Reform Commission 1986: 52–7; cp. Reynolds 1986). Aborigines had lived in Australia for about 40,000 years before the British arrived. They were certainly numerous. Contemporary estimates of their number put it at about one million. They tended their lands in a variety of ways – by controlled burning, yam planting and river works. They fought the colonists – almost to a point of extinction in Tasmania, and on the mainland with great loss of life. Yet Australia, in this perverse doctrine, is a land which, two hundred years ago, was inhabited by no civilised people and was peaceably settled by the British.

The pragmatically minded may defend their sensibilities against this doctrine by reflecting that, settled or conquered, the Aborigines would have lost their land by one legal means or another. Those who think that a concept like sovereignty means only or mainly what it meant to eighteenth century European jurists may take no exception to the denial of Aboriginal sovereignty. And eminent lawyers and legal academics working on the Australian Law Reform

Commission's reference on the recognition of Aboriginal customary law were able to declare that the continuing effects of the
doctrine were sufficiently intangible, to leave it in place (Law
Reform Commission 1986). They miss, as our jurists miss, the
violence of discursive exclusion and enclosure. In declaring a whole
race and its culture either non-existent or not worthy of recognition, *terra nullius* is an act of ideological genocide. Aborigines have
survived it as well as having survived being shot, poisoned, raped,
herded onto reserves, imprisoned, and infected with white diseases;
ideology is not co-extensive with social reality. There must, however, be grave doubts about whether a legal culture which spawns
such a doctrine can contribute much to the realisation of ideals of
liberty, equality and real community. Yet these are the ideals of
contemporary common law jurisprudence.

We find here something akin to the way that professional and
academic chauvinism contradicts ideals of service and the pursuit
of knowledge. Again, these ideals are part of the self-concept of
professionalism and academia. Where the ideals are not actually
part of the practice, they function merely to justify privileges and
benefits which accrue to professionals and academics. The point
here is not to question the value of these ideals. Concepts of liberty,
equality, community, knowledge and service (in a non-menial
sense) have been developed in Western culture in answer to questions about the constitution of human happiness and well-being.
The record of answers has been selectively constituted, so as to
silence the voices of subordinated people. Nonetheless, the reason
for taking the record that does exist seriously, is that it tends to
speak for those who do fare well. We should not doubt that they
have some understanding of their own sense of satisfaction. The
trouble is that it does not occur to these authorities on the goods of
life, that it is subordinated people who have that same quality of
understanding of human exploitation and devaluation. Lacking
this dimension, the institutionalisation of these goods through
social practices is deeply flawed.

This is tricky, this ground of the social construction of values,
goods, ideals and virtues, and it is rights fetishism that makes it so
tricky. One caveat has to be entered immediately. The understanding of participants in social practices is necessary to any
adequate theory of that practice. It is not sufficient, it is not univocal
and it is not privileged in terms of its truth value. It contributes a
special dimension to knowledge of the practice of which an ad-

equate theory will be aware. If this caveat is not made, the authority of the normative discourses of systematically empowered groups is enhanced and a perception of certain practices as constituting fetishes is banished. On the other hand, the caveat is necessary to guard against idealising poverty, powerlessness, and. the experience of being devalued. Practical wisdom is not gained in acceptance and celebration of subordination but in resistance to it. That resistance, far from valorising the experience of subordination, has the purpose of ending it.

All thought and theory construction involves abstraction. It is inevitably purposive and intentional. Language, spoken and written, shapes, guides and constrains it but offers, through its polysemy, participation in the ideological struggles of history. The very process of trying to understand those struggles requires theory. We have to abstract from concrete, multiply determined being in order to find out quite down-to-earth things about the persistence of material inequality. That, it seems to me, is just the way it is and I leave it to others to legislate against it. My idea is to try to disentangle the process of valorisation which attends on the purposive and intentional construction of one aspect of our social reality – legal relations, practices and institutions. A particular understanding of ideology is necessary for doing that and so, in the context of law, is the idea of rights fetishism.

THE BASIC CONTOURS OF RIGHTS FETISHISM

Rights fetishism is actual. It is not a matter of having false ideas about law. It is part of the social reality of societies within which the classical Western form of law retains influence and it is constituted by legal practices. A theory of law which draws attention to rights fetishism as part of social reality does not impair the fetish or do away with it. Such a theory can only claim to have explained a social phenomenon which is invisible within other legal theories.

As a social phenomenon, rights fetishism may constitute individuals as fetishists, but this is not a determined process. As individuals we are not all, inevitably, rights fetishists any more than individuals living within a sexist society are inevitably sexist. I make this obvious point because, in order to meet the difficulties in making visible something which is made invisible by the dominant ideology, I want

16

to introduce the notion of rights fetishism by an example of its absence in a response to the legal system.

Several years ago an Aboriginal group living on the outskirts of Perth in Western Australia took objection to the State electricity authority putting a pipe through a brook on land which 'always was sacred, since the beginning of time' to the Aboriginal people. The Aboriginal people's belief is that the Waugal or water-snake 'moved through the area, creating the brook. That is why it is said today, it is the Dreaming Track wherever it moved across the land.' The Aborigines wanted the pipe to be constructed over the brook so as not to disturb the Waugal. 'It was to go over the brook and not down into our Mother the Land.'[3] Negotiations with the electricity authority were initially unsuccessful, but the Aborigines succeeded in getting an injunction against the authority from the Supreme Court. Shortly after reading of their success in court, I met the Spokesperson for the Aboriginal people concerned and congratulated him on the victory. He told me, however, that he and his people regarded the court action as a defeat, not a victory. It would have been a victory, he explained to me, if they had been able to negotiate an agreement with the electricity authority. As it was, they had to rely on the good will of a liberal white judge.

My understanding of the response is that these Aborigines wanted such mutuality of understanding as would have led the planners to respect their beliefs and so accept that the pipe should go over and not through the brook. This was the real benefit they sought and did not get. So far as rights fetishism is concerned, the point is that they were aware – as I was not – that they got only a token of that respect.

When rights are fetishised, the fact that they are tokens for the lived experience of freedom, material equality and community is forgotten. Critiques of rights by socialists, feminist and critical theorists attest the fact that this forgetting is no uniform feature of human consciousness. Yet in Jurisprudence, if the voices of those for whom rights are sometimes wrong are heard at all, the response is invariably to justify rights as mechanisms for human society. At the worst, rights, as the product of (never-guaranteed-to-be-perfect) humanly made rules are said to be the best we can do to avoid the war of all against all. At the best, rights are said to exist as derivations from natural laws of the universe. Liberal theories take up multiple positions in between this hell and heaven of juristic imaginings as to the way we are.

It is this justificatory dimension in Jurisprudence which provides an object for understanding rights fetishism, not because rights fetishism is constituted by Jurisprudence, but because this justificatory dimension derives from legal practices which do constitute rights fetishism. Prior to that it needs to be shown both that this justificatory dimension is part and parcel of Jurisprudence and not merely an optional extra of fashion or theoretical inclination, and that it is backed by particular legal practices. These questions are addressed in Chapters 3 and 4 respectively. My argument is basically that justification of the standards of behaviour thought to be set by legal rules, principles or judgments is inherent in the legal or internal point of view and relies on its exclusion of standpoint.

For the moment, though, let us come back to ordinary understandings of fetishism, that is, to the notion that fetishism involves the worship or faith-based reverencing of an artefact of human construction, and consider both the process of fetishisation and its consequences. The idea that fetishism in this sense is a characteristic of so called primitive societies is mere ethnocentric bias. It is a prejudice of the cultural paradigm established within the social context of the European Enlightenment. The binds and bonds of superstition, mystification and ignorance did not fall away from Western eyes with the discoveries of Galileo, Descartes and Newton. Some did. But the falsely optimistic belief that human intellectual and scientific endeavour had discovered immutable laws of nature so that philosophers could now uncover the foundations of knowledge, signified a displacement of fetishism from the domain of religious belief to domains of secular activity within the then emergent social order.

The idea of fetishism as characteristic of ostensibly secular practices was propounded and partially explored by Marx in his discussion of commodity fetishism. Marx's discussion marks a turn in a critique of the continuing influence of religious dogma in political, scientific and commercial activity extending back to Machiavelli and Bacon (Larrain 1979). It is a powerful idea simply insofar as it suggests the emergence of phenomena characteristic of religious practices and thought into the mundane world of commercial activity *without* the mediation of religious belief.

The idea that some universal value is embodied in human law is affirmed day in day out, when, against what is known to be the case in fact, the legal construction of reality is accepted and enforced. What can answer for the law's preference for its own under-

18

standings against those of history, science and social science in a culture which values those latter understandings as truth, except assertions of either the necessity or the superior wisdom of the law? We need not doubt that law is useful or beneficial to some people some of the time. Indeed it is hard to imagine how legal practices and institutions could have the vitality and persistence they do have if that were not the case. Nor should we imagine that those 'some people' will always be middle or upper class, white and male. But the instrumental value of law in specific undertakings is not ethical or universal value and does not account for the ways in which human law is accorded ethical or universal value within our culture.

GUIDE TO READERS

My purpose is to get around the double barrier that ideology poses to understanding the value of law for people on the down-side of social relations. This cannot be accomplished by staying within the confines of one discipline – certainly not within the discipline of Jurisprudence. The whole enterprise begins from a theoretical disagreement with the individual–society dichotomy which is presupposed by legal thought and by social and political thought that is compatible with it. So we cannot move straight into the accounts and analysis of the texts promised and from there to rights fetishism. The framework of thought within which this whole project has been conceived has first to be made available to the reader. No thought takes place outside some framework, and to pretend that it does is just a ploy of theoretical imperialism. Still, the next chapter is concerned with issues of general social theory and philosophy and may seem remote from Jurisprudence and rights fetishism. Legal readers may be advised to begin with the familiar by reading Chapters 2 and 3 first and then coming back to Chapter 1; but they will need to come back to Chapter 1 if the subsequent argument is to be understood. On the other hand, Chapter 3 is a technical chapter that cuts its way through Jurisprudential agreements and disagreements for the purpose of having a reasonably uncluttered view of the discipline. Social scientists might leave it out, though if they suspect an elision of an important difference between the schools they should refer back to it. Inevitably, because the argument covers several disciplines, many readers will be taken onto unfamiliar ground. I hope they will not find the going there too difficult.

1

A REALIST CONCEPT OF IDEOLOGY

Our knowledge is social, therefore it is relative to our way of life. That is one of the most celebrated conclusions of this century's social theory. It raises a puzzling question for a culture which prizes science very highly. How can we continue to believe in science? How can we continue to think it possible to 'find something out'? Whatever we think or say is the case must reproduce the socially constructed character of our thought and language.

No doubt it must, but that is not to say that our thought and our language stand between us and the world like a brick wall. They mediate our perceptions and conceptions in some way or another which is profoundly significant. If we make that mediation a domain of inquiry we may be said to be studying ideology – ideology, that is, as it is understood to be within a framework of thought that is realist and relational. The use towards which a realist concept of ideology is put, is in developing an approach to the problem of the relationship between thought and reality, where reality is presupposed as that which is what it is independent of thought. To put that another way, a realist concept of ideology makes the relation between thought and reality an object of inquiry. In this work, it does so for a quite specific purpose, the purpose of seeking a practice which will contribute towards getting rid of social relations of material inequality.

Now this is not quite the path that mainstream philosophy has travelled, and the absence of serious concern with ideology in Jurisprudence reflects that. But neglect of ideology in philosophy and Jurisprudence should not be thought to indicate lack of awareness of or concern about the questions raised. On the contrary these are questions of contemporary debate in metaphysics, epistemology

and philosophy of science. They are also touched on in Jurisprudence, mainly in discussions of method.

So this inquiry into Jurisprudence as a form of ideology begins,
in the heartlands of philosophy, with an elaboration of a realist
conception of ideology. Such an elaboration is not just a matter of
explanation of my use of the term 'ideology'. There are strong
philosophical claims to be made in this chapter. They give the
theoretical context for my claim that examination of Jurisprudence
as a form of ideology reveals the social phenomenon of rights
fetishism. We are involved here with realism in some of its many
variants, as well as with the rich texture of competing conceptions
and theories of ideology. Centrally, the argument of this chapter is
that we can handle the undeniably social character of our knowledge, while hanging on to the idea of reality as that which is the
case, by means of a conception of ideology which has both a neutral
and a negative sense. What a perception of rights fetishism does, is
propose a theory of how and why neutrally ideological thought
becomes negatively ideological. But that is a much longer argument
to which the chapters following this one are devoted.

The plan used is as follows. In the first section, having re-stated
what I understand by these two senses of ideology, I ask the
question, 'What does it mean to talk of ideology as neutral and as
negative?' Neutral and negative *vis à vis* what? This will give us an
approach to some popular understandings of ideology. The second
section gives the context of a realist conception of ideology by
mapping out the version of realism being used here. From this
context certain concepts that are basic to a realist and relational
social theory are developed. These are concepts of social relations,
social practices and standpoint. The third section considers the
function of the conception of ideology being elaborated. Using
Barker's formulation that the central problem of ideology is to trace
the way in which reality appears, it explains in more detail what the
problem is, and why and how it arises within a realist theory. The
final section draws these strands of form, context and function
together so as to give the substance or content of my approach to
the relation between thought and reality. So we come to the point
of developing and applying a realist conception of ideology in an
analysis of Jurisprudence.

CONCEPTIONS OF IDEOLOGY

I have already suggested that 'ideology' can be understood as having both a neutral and a negative sense. Within this understanding, ideology in its neutral sense encompasses more or less complete systems of ideas produced in societies whose basic social relations are relations of material inequality. Theories which justify such materially unequal social relations, directly or indirectly, are considered as being negatively ideological.

A bivalent use of the term is part of its history. The term 'idéologie' was coined by the French liberal philosopher, Destutt de Tracy, at the end of the eighteenth century as the name for the sensationalist philosophy of mind he and his colleagues in the Institut National ('the ideologues') were developing. In this original use of the word, there was no negative or critical connotation. On the contrary, it was intended as the name for 'the science of ideas which treats ideas or perceptions, and the faculty of thinking or perceiving' (Head 1985: 32). The intended contrast here was with the pre-scientific metaphysics of the past. Within a few years, as the political relations between the ideologues and Napoleon Bonaparte deteriorated, the term was used by Bonaparte in a pejorative sense to attack those democratic theorists who 'mislead the people by elevating them to a sovereignty which they were incapable of exercising' (Williams 1976: 154).

This two-way use of the term has continued through the nineteenth and twentieth centuries. There is a substantial literature on it in contemporary social theory (e.g. Bhaskar 1979; Keohane, Rosaldo and Gelpi 1981; Larrain 1979; McCarney 1980; Thompson 1984). Within this literature a variety of competing conceptions of ideology and theories of ideology are put forward. I do not argue that there is one true meaning of the term 'ideology'. I accept the contextuality of meanings. In this chapter I elaborate a conception of ideology contextualised by a version of scientific realism.

What motivates this task is the perception of Jurisprudence as a source of understanding and of misunderstanding of law; misunderstanding which, in its failure to make an inquiry into the complicity of legal practices in the reproduction of social relations of material inequality, has become part of that process. To put that another way, Jurisprudence is stuck in the dogma of law's innocence. To free it and ourselves we need a conception of ideology which can cope with the generation of that dogma.

For dogma, like any other form of thought, is produced and its processes of production can and should be examined. It is not enough to assume bad faith, whether in terms of egoistic self-interest, wilful exploitation, misogyny or chauvinism. Insofar as these are phenomena of the human condition there is no more reason to say that they are a natural part of our genetic programme than are the capacities humans have shown for social life – by which I mean simply life with and for others. A very early comment on law is Sophocles' observation in *Antigone* that man has 'found out the law of living together in cities' (Sophocles 1947: 135). This simple optimism is expressed by a chorus celebrating the mastery of the human species over the earth. Yet it is followed by a chorus proclaiming the absolute sovereignty of the gods:

> For what presumption of man can match
>   thy power,
> O Zeus, that art not subject to sleep or
>   time
> Or age, ...

(Ibid., 142)

Antigone bears a simple contemporary interpretation as a drama of the limits of human understanding and capacities. Discoveries of some things in or about social reality, though they may be expressed as true statements or propositions, are always limited in the extent to which they enable us to cope with or change our environment by what we do not know. Though we describe what we know or think we know about social reality in propositional form, social reality is not a collection of isolated facts. It is complex, and if considered as a whole, cannot be known absolutely or infallibly.

This is not only a question of extent. We cannot, even in principle, consider knowledge and understanding as a cumulative process on a linear trajectory toward absolute knowledge. Not only is the physical world constantly changing, but human practical activity is a factor in that change. Since practical activity is intentional, that is, since we act for particular purposes and with particular understandings of how those purposes are to be achieved, human thought and its expression in language and action is similarly participant in the construction of social reality.

A conception of ideology, formulated within this way of looking at things, constructs a domain of inquiry which takes ideas as objects. It may then consider them against some standard of value or consider their generation and effects. Differing notions of and about the value of ideas give content to the senses in which sets of ideas can be referred to as negatively or neutrally ideological. Not surprisingly, therefore, links between different conceptions of ideology and different uses or understandings of the value of ideas can be drawn.

We can begin with a very simply stated position.[1] The value relevant to ideas is truth. Its opposite is falsity. Theories are either true or false. If they are true they are scientific and if they are false they are ideological. The second position is only a little more complex. Truth and goodness are conjoined values, at least where practical reasoning (that is reasoning about what is to be done) is concerned. So theories which are practically ignorant or are indicative of false consciousness are ideological in the sense of irrational.

A third position begins from the idea of knowledge as power and considers ideologies as belief systems or as political consciousness. Ideology, in this context, is a social and political notion rather than an epistemological one. Ideology is conceived as a mechanism or function of power. It will be seen as all-pervasive insofar as power relations are taken as constitutive of social interaction and it may be used in a neutral sense as meaning simply that (inevitable) part of discourses which deals in power, or it may be used negatively as 'essentially linked to the process of sustaining asymmetrical relations of power – that is to the process of maintaining domination' (Thompson 1984: 4).

Ideas are valued then in terms of truth, goodness and effectiveness *vis à vis* the will to power, and differing conceptions of ideology reflect this. Obviously enough, notions of truth, goodness and power are themselves very variably conceived. But at this stage I want only to note that if ideology is used in a negative sense, an elaboration of that sense will involve a particular theory of knowledge, or of practical reasonableness, or of political relations of domination and subordination, or of some combination of these. On the other hand, if ideology is used in a neutral sense, it will be being considered primarily as a social phenomenon.

If ideology is conceived in both a neutral and a negative sense, it becomes a fundamental concept of social theory and philosophy. That is to say, it is a concept which works to place other notions and ideas into relation with each other, presenting a different map of ideas than, for example, one which considers ideology as concerned only with false ideas. The conception which I am putting forward, considers that questions of truth, of how we ought to act, and of the role of ideas in the human construction of social reality, are all relevant to ideology. So it rejects the traditional philosophical construction of separate domains of metaphysics, epistemology and ethics. But it re-forms rather than rejects these traditional philosophical inquiries and arguments. So it does not take the anti-epistemological view of contemporary pragmatist, poststructuralist and postmodernist philosophers and sociologists (e.g. Rorty 1980; Hindess and Hirst 1977; Douzinas and Warrington 1987).

This is why I adopt Barker's formulation of the problem of ideology as being to trace the way in which reality appears. For this formulation takes up a metaphysical and epistemological position in using the notion of reality and in supposing it to be knowable.

SOCIAL RELATIONS, SOCIAL PRACTICES AND STANDPOINT

Two issues addressed in this formulation call for further elaboration. First, what is this metaphysical and epistemological position? It is excessively vague to speak of 'using the notion of reality' and of 'supposing it to be knowable' for there are many traditions which call themselves or are called 'realist'. So it is necessary to spell out the understanding of our social life and of human capacities for knowing intended by it. This is partly a matter of location within a tradition of thought and partly a matter of developing or modifying that tradition. Thereafter the dimensions of *the problem* of ideology can be spelled out. This is the second issue and it calls for further elaboration because it is neither self-evident nor descriptive of any essential function of the concept of ideology. It is a problem which arises within the version of realism being espoused. Outlining its dimensions is thus a further elaboration of the realist conception of ideology with which this chapter is concerned.

The version of realism in question is commonly termed scientific realism (Benton 1984; Bhaskar 1978, 1979; Bottomore 1983; Cain 1986; Keat and Urry 1982; Kerruish 1987; Sayers 1985). There are, however, sufficiently important differences between the theories of 'scientific realists' to put us on notice that little is to be learned from the label. What little there is may be stated as follows. First, it calls attention to the development of these theories having been within philosophy of science and of social science. Second, the label indicates a concern to hang on to the idea of science as a relatively secure form of knowledge of an objective reality. Third, the label is often used to distinguish direct realism and common-sense realism from scientific realism. Direct realism is the view that we have direct access to reality (see Sayers 1985: 58–63). Common-sense realism is the naive empiricist view that there is a real world of sensuously perceptible objects of which we are aware through ideas which correspond to or mirror nature.

A realist framework

The realist theory of this essay falls within the label in all these ways. However, to define it further, and to do so in its own terms, rather than by articulating it to debates with which readers may not be familiar and with which we have no direct concern, I shall list and explain its constitutive assumptions as briefly as possible. Thereafter I shall flesh out these assumptions into basic concepts of a social theory. Debates around realism which do concern ideology are dealt with in subsequent sections.

First there is an assumption (R) that there is a world with a being and nature independent of human consciousness which is knowable through consciousness. This assumption is compatible with philosophical positions as diverse as Platonism and empiricism because that 'independent world' could be forms or ideas – 'transcendent realities directly apprehended by thought' (Flew 1984: 273) or it could be the mind-independent realm of sensuously perceptible objects – the common-sense world of everyday life in which the garden furniture stays in place whether or not anyone is perceiving it.

Platonist realism can be distinguished by qualifying R to assert the mind-independent existence of a *physical* world, but it is also distinguished by supposing (K) that knowledge of this independent realm is indirect, that is, is mediated by ways of thinking already embedded in human culture, and (F) that such knowledge is fallible. The common-sense realism of empiricism is distinguished by a dialectical assumption (D) that human being is to be understood as being in unity and in opposition to nature. Human being is part of nature – as much and as little components of a whole as stones and stars, trees and animals. So the subject–object dualism of empiricism is rejected and with this rejection the basic characterisation of human beings as knowing subjects of a perceived or experienced world is rejected too. Spinoza is said to have conceived nature as thinking (Ilyenkov 1977: 32) and I understand that to mean that it is human beings as part of nature who think. However, in practical activity, human beings intentionally change their physical environment and construct a social environment appropriate to many different ways of life. The oppositional aspect of this relation then gives us a reference for the idea of culture.

What this assumption (D) does is take a relation as the denotation or referent of two concepts, nature and culture. This is in no sense exceptional. A dialectical theory is a relational theory in which all concepts are considered as products of social practices through which human beings relate themselves to their environment. Thus while reality is understood as that which is, independent of human consciousness (so that 'reality' itself is conceived relationally), *social reality* must be introduced as the actual, that is the lived, environment of human being. As a concept, the notion of social reality in use here, participates in both the idea of having been made, that is, of constructedness, and of independent being. This is not incoherent. The independence relation is a relation of individuals to social reality. This comes in because it is individuals who act and who speak. But they do so from within a relation with others and with their physical environment which, however it is conceived, will exert its influence on understandings of self and other. Thus, finally, (SR) social relations are taken as the basic objects of social science.

Social relations

By social relations I mean persistent ways in which individuals and groups of individuals relate and are related to each other within and by a specific natural and cultural environment. 'Individuals' is an ideology-laden term and as we move through the argument of this book I shall move away from using it. For the moment, though, I use it to mean simply those physically identifiable human bodies which act and speak and think and to which intentions are ordinarily attributed. Social relations are not reducible to individuals, but then neither are individuals reducible to, in the sense of being fully determined by, social relations. Thus a realist and relational theory does not deny the being and significance of individuals. It insists, however, that individuals do not exist and cannot be comprehended in abstraction from their relations with nature and with each other (Bhaskar 1979, Ch.2 esp. pp.39–47).

If this is a little difficult to grasp, not the least reason for the difficulty is the recurring and perverse tendency in Jurisprudence and in much social theory and philosophy to suggest that there are only two classical models for understanding society, namely the individualist model and the collectivist model. The individualist model supposes societies to be aggregates of human individuals held together by bonds of will or reason. The collectivist model, on the other hand, considers the social to have an of-itself reality to which the individual and all its attributes are secondary. A relational theory rejects both these models. It works on a third, classical social model, within which the individual and the social are each conceived in terms of the other. As Marx puts it: '... we must avoid postulating "Society" again as an abstraction *vis à vis* the individual. The individual *is the social being*' (Marx 1964: 137–8). In other words, relational social theory rejects the construction of individual and social as antithetical concepts that is undertaken in both individualist and collectivist theories.

In rejecting the antithesis between the social and the individual, relational theory rejects a whole further set of antitheses which are paradigmatically constructions of liberal theory – public and private, altruism and egoism, other and self – as basic contradictions of and in social reality. This is not an argument about whether or not it makes sense to talk of a public sphere as distinct from a private one, or of selves as distinct from others. Of course it makes sense to make these distinctions. Apart from anything else, liberal ideology has, in some degree, constructed social reality according to them. Moreover liberal ideology is powerfully assisted in the Anglo-American and Anglo-Australian worlds by the way in which empiricism has formed our common sense. Flesh-and-blood individuals, bodies, are present and observable in a way that neither societies on the one hand, nor biological and psychological structures on the other, are.

So when, within a culture dominated by common-sense realism, we speak of a relation, there is a tendency to think of it as reducible to the two things which are related. To ascribe reality in the sense of independent being to the relation seems somehow rationalistic or perhaps idealistic. And that intuition may be confirmed by saying that the notion of social relations is what enables us to explain the social and individual in terms of each other without circularity. The individualist (and for that matter the collectivist too) will want to say that this just avoids the issue of which *really* has ontological (or epistemological or methodological) priority.

There are other problems too. Relational social theory finds a popular origin in Marx. While Marx may have been aware that social relations are relations of production and of reproduction, the location of his major inquiry in the domain of political economy encouraged an emphasis on production relations. As received in various versions of Marxism this emphasis became a reduction of social relations to relations of production of goods, and under capitalism, of commodities. In Western cultures, in the course of a century of lower female than male participation in the commodity-producing workforce, this reduction marginalised women. Furthermore, emphasis on relations of production of goods or commodities can edge out the importance of relations of reproduction of species and of their ways of life.

Then there is the problem of free will. How can individuals be considered responsible for their acts if they lack moral autonomy, that is, if they are not constituted as beings having an essential independence from conditioning forces or structures? It is too easy to dismiss the moral autonomy of individual human beings as a construction of bourgeois ethics; as being more concerned with theological dogma than with human psychology; or as a mechanism of disciplining and controlling large masses of people. Ethical individualism, insofar as it involves the premise that individuals can choose how to act, is an empowering notion.

In attempting to escape these problems, theorists have conceived social relations as structures, as structuring structures, as linkages or as forces of established social practices. It seems to me that these are unnecessary complications. When Einstein discovered the relativity of time to the observer's state of motion, he went on to show the transformability of individual observations of a given occurrence, each to the other. Space–time, that is a unity of formerly independently conceived notions, then replaced the concepts of absolute space and absolute time as a real object of scientific thought.

Similarly all that needs to be given up here are absolutist conceptions of the individual and of the social. That is, it should be admitted that neither the individual nor the social is (has being) in and of itself. The question of priority, as an ontological question, is simply a bad question. What enables us to make sense of both the individual and the social is a relation. To think of social relations as persistent ways of relating and being related, rather than as structures, linkages or forces avoids their reification by understanding them in terms of human activity and the physical environment of that activity.

This determination of the basic object of knowledge of society is the work of philosophy. But having come up with the concept of social relation, the question of the content of social relations, is a question for social science. The view which I follow is that in the societies of which I write, that is, in the United Kingdom, the United States and Australia, now and for the past several hundred years, the basic social relations are relations of class, sex–gender and race.

Class relations are property relations considered not in their specific and very diverse content but in their exploitative form, that is, in the circumstance of one party to the relation using the other for its own benefit and its own survival as a dominant class. That is not to say that the exploited party takes no benefit from the relation. Indeed, the persistence of exploitative property relations is partially explicable in terms of some mutuality of benefit. But it is to say that where possession or control of the means of production is differentially located within a population, then that section of the population which has such possession and control has an exploitative capacity which the other section lacks.

Sex–gender relations are relations of power emergent in the co-ordination of action for purposes of reproduction – not only of the human species but of ways of life. They need not be relations of coercive and manipulative power, that is of getting some other to act in conformity with the will or desire of a self by force or trick. Concepts of self and other could be formed simply on the basis of an unevaluated recognition of difference. However, in the societies of which I write, sex–gender relations are inscribed in a form of coercive or manipulative power. They involve the normative or prescriptive construction of stereotypes of sexuality and sexual behaviour which are hierarchically ordered. The consequence is devaluation of the other against the self – a process involving both alienation and chauvinism. Given the historical control of means of coercive power by men, this comes down to us as a devaluation of women, of children and of men whose non-conformity to the going male stereotype marks them as other (Harding 1986).

Race relations, like sex–gender relations, involve differentially evaluated biological difference. They are also, in the countries in which I write, social relations which have emerged through the exploitation of the lands and bodies of non-European peoples by Europeans. They are relations of the production of commodities within which people of colour tend to form a segment of the working class. At the same time they are relations of reproduction of the species and of ways of life. In the result, as a segment of the working class, people of colour tend to be selected for that class's most degraded functions – in particular for having their capacities declared irrelevant in unemployment. Additionally, having had their traditional ways of life dislocated by colonisation and slavery, yet having found, notwithstanding, the power to survive, coloured peoples in dominantly white societies are a focus of resistance which calls down the most brutal forms of repression.

These social relations are alike in their persistence and in their all being relations of material inequality. Each, in its present form, informs more particular, less enduring social relations, not in isolation, but configuratively. So if we take particular property relations – for example, relations of landowner and tenant, proprietor and stranger, licensee and licensor, etc. – we shall find these to be systemically skewed in terms of the benefits taken from the relationship. The characterisation of class relationships as exploitative property relationships, however, should not take the place of analysis of the concrete circumstances of that skewing, that is, of a local and specific analysis of, say, landowners and tenants in explicitly identified locations – legal, economic, geographic, or whatever. Such an analysis may show that women and blacks are more often tenants than white male workers in regular employment. On the other hand, a close look at family relationships may show differences in sex–gender relations related to class or race.

Social practices

The configuration of basic social relations of class, sex–gender and race into more particular social relations takes place through social practices. Social practices are fully intentional in a way that social relations are not. Individuals have no choice as to whether or not they live within basic social relations. They have a degree of choice as to their place within them, but not as to their being within them. There is upward mobility, there is sex-change and gender diversity and it is possible for women and people of colour to adopt the way of life of a white male elite. Such moves are made intentionally and

31

are effected by engaging in various social practices which, having a conventional and institutional character have a tendency or purpose which is characteristic of the practice itself.

It is individuals, social practices and sociologically and legally identifiable social relations which are the least controversial objects of social science. Basic social relations of class, sex–gender and race are identified through more abstract theory – through philosophy and high-level sociology; through 'grand theory' or 'the grand narrative' as some would have it. They are controversial and their being as basic objects of social knowledge is strenuously denied by individualist theorists. So it is important to distinguish this analysis from analyses made in terms of individuals and social practices to which social relations of both kinds, that is both basic social relations, and sociologically and legally identifiable social relations, are secondary.

Dworkin, for example, modifies the traditional individualism of liberal social theory in such terms (Dworkin 1986). He retains the view that flesh-and-blood individuals are the real components of societies but argues that such individuals are essentially associative and so are actors in social practices. In the result he comes up with a theory of the state (synonymous, it would seem, with society, community) as having its being in social practices of thought and language which create and personify it.

This social theory accords well with the common-sense intuition that it is individuals that are the really real components of societies, while also giving due significance to language and interpretive community as irreducibly social. It is attractive to socialist, feminist and critical theorists who are embarrassed by the apparent rationalism or idealism of treating relations as real and who perceive social practices as sufficient explananda of social and ideological struggle and change. The problem with it is that we need the notion of social relations as real social objects to understand individual intentionality (free will) and agency, and to get beyond convention and institutionalisation in explaining social practices.

For what is lacking in such associative accounts of community is an acknowledgement that social practices are social not merely as a matter of convention and institution or tradition but as practices of basic social relations. Consciousness of one's class, sex–gender or race position at a given time is not a constitutive aspect of that position. It can be and frequently is denied. On the other hand, and automatism aside, although a person cannot engage in a

32

practice without being conscious of it, the practice in question may be misunderstood or misdescribed. For social practices have tendencies, which may not lead in directions which individual participants intend. The claim I am making is that basic social relations are at work shaping these tendencies of social practices.

Standpoint

What comes out of looking at societies in this way, as constituted at the object level by social relations and individuals, and as configured and patterned by social practices and individual action, is a particular concept of standpoint. To say that individuals have a standpoint within social relations is pretty much common sense. One is either husband or wife, landlord or tenant, vendor or purchaser, and has, as such, particular interests (Pound 1959: 129–32). Notions of standpoint, however, are also developed in the context of epistemological discussions. As Alison Jaggar succinctly points out '[b]oth liberal and Marxist epistemologists consider that, in order to arrive at an adequate representation of reality, it is important to begin from the proper standpoint' (Jaggar 1983: 370). As a concept concerned with the adequacy of representations of reality, standpoint merges into the more familiar notion of point of view.[2]

But standpoint, as it is used here, is also concerned with the constitution of human individuals as agents for one or other of the classes designated by basic social relations. People are constituted as agents of or agents for some other person or group, by choice or circumstance or both. So the concept of standpoint used here does not just make reference to an individual's position within social relations and assume that a particular point of view flows from that. It refers also to an individual's awareness and will in respect to that place. That is, whether she is aware that her identity is partially determined by her social position and whether she wants to act against or within the limits of that determination. But then, the awareness and will of selves which are social beings will themselves be socially patterned and ideologically influenced.

So standpoint is not just a position in social relations nor is it just an epistemological position. It is a position within social relations and within ideology. It has profound consequences for theories of knowledge (Jaggar 1983) and of method (Cain 1986, 1987). It is also concerned with agency – with the personal and political identity of individuals and groups of individuals who, while having spaces within which to constitute themselves as free and responsible actors, must also understand themselves as acted on by social relations and as participants in social practices. Thus both the personal and the political challenge of standpoint is the ongoing process of finding ways of making and sharing standpoints with others.

TRACING THE WAY IN WHICH REALITY APPEARS

The version of realism I have sketched and the theory of society that flows from it is abstract and elaborate. In these pragmatic days of Western culture the question 'Why bother?' is to be expected.

So why bother? Why construct so complex a problem of ideology as being to trace the way in which reality appears? To begin answering that question it must be admitted that the problem is constructed. The concept of ideology has no essential function. Different ways of conceiving ideology have different functions in different discourses. Very often, for example, particularly in mainstream discourse, the term functions simply to discredit views with which the speaker disagrees. In that case, a very simplistic notion of ideology will be being employed – one which opposes ideology as falsity to science as truth, for example. At the other end of the scale, a serious sociological study of ideology may find a very specific way in which ideology actually does function in a particular social formation. Poulantzas' observation as to the concealing/reconstituting function of ideology (Poulantzas 1973: 207; above: 13), seems to me to be an extremely apt description of a function of Jurisprudence insofar as it is negatively ideological. We should not, however, over-generalise such a finding to constitute a solely negative conception of ideology by supposing that this is the essential function of (all conceptions of) ideology.

So to formulate the problem of ideology as being to trace the way in which reality appears is a functional description of a conception already in mind, a conception that includes ideology in its neutral and negative senses. What then is back behind this conception? What reasons can there be for posing so ambitious a task?

The reasons that there are, are standpoint specific. They make no claim to universal validity. They would not be counted as 'good reasons' by those whose standpoint is that of dominant classes. They rest in that understanding of philosophy which argues that philosophy should be concerned not merely with interpreting the world but changing it (Marx 1976: 8). Feminist theory and socialist theory is committed theory in the sense that what it precisely does not seek to do is 'leave[s] everything as it is' (Wittgenstein 1958: 49e). But it is not just any old change that is in mind here. Feminist and socialist theory looks for ways of changing exploitative, alienating and disempowering forms of social relations at all levels of such relations. That is not to say it imagines that such change can be accomplished by theory alone. What is sought is an effective practice.

Ideology in its negative sense, as theory which justifies existing social relations, confronts committed theories in practical ways. For example, it has a profound capacity to interrupt communication. All forms of ideology provide interpretive schemas within which what we say and do acquires meaning. Negative forms of ideology, however, try to negate polysemy by the imposition of meaning. Rhetorical devices, tendentious arguments, truth claims, claims of predictive or explanatory power, of the sacredness (or utility or success) of a particular tradition of thought, are all verbal devices which are used in ideological struggle for and against the imposition of meaning. It is difficult enough translating meanings from one interpretive schema to another. Negatively ideological thought actively obstructs such translation and when the negative ideology in question is that of dominant classes or voices in a society, the task becomes doubly difficult.

Consider, for example, the difficulty of communicating the idea that it is sex–gender relations of coercive and manipulative power that ground the devaluation of women in our societies, to a chauvinist who sincerely believes that women are less valuable than men. The idea makes a claim about the way in which beliefs come about, which cannot be understood in its form, let alone be critically assessed in its content. It will be heard as an attempt to escape from the 'fact' of female inferiority, and its explanatory dimension, since it cannot rely on conventions of scientific explanation that are themselves androcentric, will be dismissed as pseudo-scientific. There are, in our social life, processes of concealment of the exploitative and chauvinistic character of basic social relations of which negative ideologies are an expressive part. Participants in these processes *cannot* see it this way if they are unaware of the very abstract assumptions which constitute an interpretive schema. And if, being aware of them, they give them the status of absolute truths, then they are closing their and other people's minds to alternative understandings.

So far as individuals are concerned, being a woman, being working class, being black is neither a necessary nor a sufficient condition for seeking a standpoint that is for subordinated people. Negative forms of ideology come in here with stock in hand, to hinder understanding that seeking such a standpoint is a means of self-realisation. A standpoint for others is characterised as altruistic or caring and subtly downgraded to egoism and machismo. Blame the victim – and feel guilty or inadequate about your own sources of unhappiness. Look at the nation's high standard of living, democratic elections, free press and speech – and conclude that feelings of discontent must have personal not social grounds. It is all up to the individual.

If the study of ideology is understood as the study of the relations between our ideas about social reality and social reality itself, its problem is that this is a relation whose form and content is concealed by negative forms of ideology.

But there is a further question. All of this might be admitted in its reference to social reality, for it is indeed old hat that social reality is constructed, in part, by thought. But why bring in reality?

Again, an answer to that question must begin with an admission that there is a difficulty with conceiving reality as that which is independent of, but knowable through, human consciousness. The *idea* of reality, that is the concept constituted by this assumption, is self-evidently part of consciousness. How can we be sure that this idea refers to an independent reality? As soon as we speak of knowing we bring in consciousness and language and the active, constitutive dimension of representations. If we posit reality as independent of consciousness, we seem to be stuck with a thing in itself which is, tautologically, not knowable in itself. This is, roughly, a Kantian problematic and though many contemporary anti-realist theories may be thought to present sociological variations of this problematic, that is an insufficient ground from which to dismiss them (Barker 1985).

Realist philosophers have taken various ways with this problem – from kicking stones to the elaboration of transcendental proofs.[3] However, it seems to me to be in no way damaging to realism to admit that indeed we cannot be sure that our idea of reality comes from and refers to reality itself; that our philosophical framework can and should admit that degree of scepticism. But then such scepticism works the other way too. We cannot be certain that the idea of reality does not come from and refer to reality itself. This then is a point at which the framework is left open. The assumption about reality is an hypothesis not an assertion; a metaphysical claim which being constitutive of a framework of thought is not provable within that framework.

All we can give by way of response to the question 'Why make the assumption?' are reasons which are, again, standpoint relative, for they are reasons given within an ideology – scientific or relational realism – that has been developed in the search for socialist and feminist standpoints. Here, however, a strong, non-sceptical claim comes in: that this form of ideology is neutral. It does not involve cognitive defect, or any provable form of practical unreasonableness. It does participate in ideological struggle because it is a position within ideology which is under constant attack and it both defends and prosecutes its claims in order to maintain itself. But it does not in maintaining itself reproduce patterns of domination and subordination.

It is around each of these strong non-sceptical claims that philosophical debate takes place. Those who consider that philosophy can find certain foundations for knowledge will argue that it is false to say that all sets of ideas produced within Western culture are ideological in the neutral sense. They will deny the standpoint relativity of reason and insist on the possibility of reaching that Archimedean point of view from which representation is fully objective. Those who think that there are principles of practical reasonableness which give one right answers to questions about what to do, deny that there are different answers to such questions for people with different standpoints. These positions are of particular concern in relation to Jurisprudence. Hart, Finnis and Dworkin all argue variants of them. Those who are aware of the negative ideology which has developed around science – the myth of value-free knowledge – and who see claims to know and understand merely as assertions of power, will dispute the claim that such claims can be made without reproducing that ideology.

Realism must maintain its non-sceptical claim against these arguments through practice – including a practice of non-dogmatic argument which de-centres the model of adversarial argument in philosophy and legal theory (Bender 1988; Moulton 1983). Let us go back to our chauvinist and ask what is to be done about him or her. First, there is no point in engaging in adversarial argument.

As a means of testing the different views, such an argument could only be a shouting match because there is no open ground for inquiry. The chauvinist 'knows' that women are less valuable than men and that facts of lower pay, the feminisation of poverty and the drop in status of jobs and professions which become feminised, prove it. On the other hand, as a moral or political argument, adversarial argument must come down to mutual accusations that women or chauvinists are lower forms of life. But something has to be done. Chauvinism in sex–gender relations, in race relations and in international politics is harmful and hurtful and helps to reproduce the social relations of coercive and manipulative power from which it comes.

We should save our wits and energy from such arguments and put them to working out strategies to defeat chauvinism. But which strategies? One strategy is to claim truth for our political theory. Dworkin, for example, argues that '[A]ny political theory is entitled – indeed obliged – to claim truth for itself, and so to exempt itself from any skepticism it endorses' (Dworkin 1985: 350). Alternatively we might say that truth is of no use here. That what we have here are two different narratives about women and we should simply stick to our story and go about the political task of getting most people to think like us. The problems here are that the first strategy justifies closure in political theory. The second strategy, in playing the numbers game, does not give sufficient credence to the strength of the opposition on the tactic of winning hearts and minds. Perhaps it over-estimates itself on this point, or perhaps it secretly relies on right being on its side. Either way, the stakes are too high to permit errors of judgment or reliance on truth and goodness to win the day.

There is another alternative. We can try to work out why the chauvinist thinks this way. We can consider the belief regarding the value of women as produced and try to trace back the process of its production. If we do that, we will come up with a number of different theories. Each of these theories will argue that if we look at chauvinism in a specified way, we will understand it better and so know where to intervene in the cycle of its production and reproduction. We are then faced with a problem of selection – which one to follow in practice.

It is here that reality comes in. It may not be the case that any of these theories is true. Each may have grasped some important dimension of the problem of chauvinism. But I do not see how we can sit on the fence here. We live a life. We have a daily practice which brings us into contact with other people. We can and must do what we feel is right – that is a truism; but we can also be self-conscious and self-critical in that doing by thinking about our practice in terms of a theory. Why do we feel this way? This means questioning the practice in terms specifically related to theoretically identified levels at which the construction of social reality takes place. Does it go to my own chauvinism? For as an individual in a society whose sex–gender and race relations are chauvinistic I am partly formed to their ways. That is the question of individual responsibility. Does it articulate with the anti-chauvinist strategies of other people in my workplace so as to create conditions in which blatantly chauvinistic practices are checked? That is a question of seeking to share standpoints and forging political relations. Does it help me to understand and predict in what latent forms chauvinism will re-assert itself? That is the realist's question because the realist is not content with appearances; is struggling always to discover and deal with those geneses of social reality to which all human consciousness is subjected.

We are dealing with a problem of knowledge here – a problem of the standpoint relativity of knowledge. For we cannot know without thought and we cannot think without following some process of reasoning. It is this that necessitates understanding ideology in its neutral sense. The problem of tracing the way in which reality appears, so far as ideology in this sense is concerned, is the problem of preventing the interpretive schema of our thought and language closing out other representations of social reality. If we take the trouble to follow the process of other ways of thought we can begin a collaborative construction of knowledge that is not limited by one framework and not specific to one standpoint.[4]

IDEOLOGY AND CONCEPTS OF RATIONALITY

The conception of ideology elaborated in the preceding sections argues the possibility of getting beyond the influence on perception and conception of culturally, historically and socially specific ways of thinking, to secure and emancipatory forms of knowledge, by making the way in which human thought interferes with or interacts with reality a problem for investigation. In this sense, the realist hangs on to the idea of truth and to the idea of science as a secure form of knowledge.

Ideology, particularly in its neutral form, confronts us with difficult questions in epistemology and in method. But awareness of ideology in its negative form cautions against attempting to answer those questions solely in terms of norms of 'correct method' or of adequacy claims for our epistemology. On the other hand, I have suggested that we should not treat the problems raised by ideology as political problems to be tackled by slugging matches of adversarial argument or pragmatic strategies for winning hearts and minds. We need to re-think our politics so as to stay clear of egoism and machismo.

In this endeavour, it is important to displace the model of legal argument as a paradigm of principled political argument which liberal moral, legal and political theory has been promoting. Rights theories, in their various versions, represent political and moral argument as being like argument in court where each lawyer's brief is to persuade the court of the truth of his or her client's claims. Dworkin's claim to be entitled and obliged to assert the truth of his political theory is a good example of this approach. Such paradigms of argument are inseparable from paradigms of rationality which accompany them. People qualify as rational by participating in the arguments according to the arguments' conventional rules and practices. They are labelled as irrational when they break these rules.

This brings us then to the point of working out and using a realist concept of ideology in the analysis of Jurisprudence. The conception of ideology in a neutral sense imagines the end of ideology because ideology in this sense is understood as a product of social relations of material inequality. What is imagined, though, is not a Utopia in which there is no further need for scientific inquiry. The problem of tracing the way in which reality appears which would disappear with the transformation of social relations is the problem of oppositional and exclusive models of rationality. It would no longer be necessary to discredit different ways of thinking and acting. Scientific theory and practice would still be directed to tracing the way in which reality appears but it would not be fractured by standpoint relativity. Knowledge, in other words, would no longer be in the service of classes of people whose identity as social classes is constructed by the exploitation and devaluation of others.

This can be put another way. The relation between thought, social reality and reality would change in its form and in its content. But just because the only ways in which philosophy has been able to conceive unproblematic forms of the relation is in theories of direct access or mirroring, is no reason at all to suppose that I am committed to saying that these are the forms into which the relation will change.

I do not know how thought is related to social reality and reality now, let alone in the future. That is why we need a conception of ideology which makes the relation an object of inquiry. But this admission of not-knowing is no disclaimer. Theory is not a product of knowing. It is a product of not knowing. We construct theories of X when there are questions about X which trouble us. And this is precisely what is involved in the conception of ideology set out here and the realist theory which contextualises it. It is proposed as a conception and a theory which enables us to handle the sociality of knowledge within an overall commitment to the idea that there is an independent reality in terms of which the effectiveness of our strategies of intervention is measured.

But this claim is not to be pursued by further philosophical argument. It is to be pursued by analysing one domain of knowledge, Jurisprudence, as a form of ideology – both neutral and negative. We need to acknowledge that we do not know much about how thought refers to reality in order to see the sense of this research programme. The same is not the case when it comes to knowledge of the effects on people and their environment of profit-oriented relations of economic production. The data are ambiguous only from the standpoint of those who benefit from such relations and wish to maintain them. And there is no ambiguity about coercive and manipulative relations of power. The difficulty here is rather with the fact that there is a standpoint within these relations to which their coercive and manipulative character is actually invisible.

Unaided, one cannot see one's own eyes. Dominant sex–gender and racial classes gaze at the world as lords of dominion; a view from above to which all is visible – except the mechanism of its own gaze. Perhaps it is some theoretical awareness of these points – an awareness divorced from political practice but engendered by the curious proclivity of justly ruled minions to revolt, protest, resist and ridicule – that has lumbered our culture with moral, political

41

and legal philosophy so desperately concerned to justify the present and reproduce it in the future.

There is no quarrel here with practical reasoning. The basic question of practical reasoning – 'What is to be done?' – must always be kept in mind. In pursuing this question we should keep in mind that it is a belief of ruling class culture that there are basic goods or values discoverable by reason which guide answers to the question for all members of a political community. It is, moreover, a powerful belief. Articulated either to religious belief or to the humanism of the Enlightenment, and elegantly circumscribing the individualism of liberal social and political theory, it offers universals to guide action in actual social conditions of self-isolation and alienation.

In Jurisprudence these universals are, most consistently, liberty, equality and community. The point here is not to devalue liberty, equality and community as aspirations or ideals, but to show that their fetishisation prevents their realisation for those on the down-side of existing social relations.

2

THREE CONCEPTS
OF LAW

A NOTE ON METHOD: GIVING AN ACCOUNT AND MAKING A RECORD

In this chapter I give an account of three concepts of law taken from three texts of mainstream Jurisprudence. The purpose of presenting these accounts is to give a basis from which subsequent analyses of Jurisprudence as ideology can be followed and critically assessed. I have therefore attempted to place myself within the conceptual framework of each theory so that the account might be as accurate as its brevity allows.

I do not attempt to provide models of the theories discussed. That is why I describe the presentation of the texts as accounts. No doubt it is the case that an account, as much as a model, is a product of its author's judgments of what is significant in and about the text. A model, however, is a maximally abstract representation, and because of this its author's way of thinking – of abstracting from the concrete phenomenon – has a greater constitutive role than where an account is being given. In Jurisprudence, both Hart and Dworkin use the technique of constructing a model of the theory they wish to supersede and demonstrating the superiority of their theory by critique of that model. Such a technique is open to the objection that the constructed model is a man of straw: a weak or tendentious representation of the earlier theory, constructed for the purpose of furthering its author's own arguments rather than for giving a sense of the earlier text. Use of the technique shows a significant continuity between forensic and Jurisprudential argument. It is, however, intellectually unsatisfying for those who come to Jurisprudence with serious questions about the practice and nature of law.

43

Giving an account is not immune from similar objections. Attempting to place oneself within a conceptual framework other than one's own is at least an enterprise fraught with artifice and the possibility of going radically wrong. At worst, there is sense to an objection that it is in principle impossible and that an account can be no more than a clumsy and cluttered model. Ways of thinking are, according to my own premises, part and parcel of ways of life. Inevitably, in dealing with ways of thinking that are products of an opposed standpoint, there are points where sympathy and even comprehension fail. All that can be done at such points is to admit that they have been reached and so begin a record of ideological difference.

These difficulties are standing difficulties in a world structured by opposed standpoints and the interpretive schemas of opposed ideologies. Two factors mitigate them in this inquiry. First, each of these texts is concerned with a set of abstract concepts: concepts such as law, rules (or rights or principles), authority, obligation, coercion, justice, sovereignty, validity. The sets are not identical but there is overlap between them. The concepts are given different content in the different theories but they have, at least, the same linguistic form. Formal and abstract as each concept undoubtedly is, and incomplete as is the overlap, a discursive terrain is constituted by them.

It is not that there are, pie in the sky, objective forms of law, authority, justice, etc. No Platonist version of realism is espoused here. Nor should it be imagined that these abstract, formal concepts are sufficient as maps of and for the social realities of legal relations and practices. No social or legal theorist who is familiar with contemporary critical theory could be unaware of the chorus of disapproval of monolithic concepts (Hindess and Hirst 1977; Phillips 1982). It is well founded disapproval insofar as there are problems of reductionism, of concealing discontinuities and of eliding differences in general theory. They are problems insofar as they disempower intervention at specific sites in both theoretical work and political action and organisation. The discovery of deconstruction, discontinuity and difference, however, should not blind us to the possibility of understanding thought other than our own by using these very abstract, empty and one-sided but unitary concepts. Rather than pie in the sky, these are constructs of human thought which have uses and misuses. They are mis-used when they pretend to describe reality and social reality. They are useful as toe-holds in the inscrutable face of ways of seeing.[1] As we move comparatively from concept to conception (that is from the most abstract to more determined ideas (cp. Dworkin 1986: 70–72) in different theories we can learn something of other ways of thinking.

The second factor which mitigates the difficulties of giving an accurate account of these theories of law is that each theory has, in embryonic or developed form, a particular view of the nature of legal reasoning and so a particular conception of legal rationality. Each text claims moreover to participate in some degree in that same form of rationality. Familiarity with legal doctrine gives an understanding of legal reasoning independent of the understandings put forward in the texts. Without again denying differences in conceptions of legal rationality, that understanding yields a point of view internal to the texts. It is, so to speak, a pathway into the strange world of Jurisprudence.

The difficulties remain. I attempt to avoid some of them by liberal use of quotations and by adjusting the language of my accounts to the language of the text. Giving an account, as against constructing a model, is a chameleon task. By undertaking it, I hope to avoid some of the man-of-straw arguments by which Jurisprudence moves from one theory to another without ever engaging with its own character as a form of ideology.

THE CONCEPT OF LAW: LAW AS A SYSTEM OF RULES

Method and traditions

> There are therefore two minimum conditions necessary and sufficient for the existence of a legal system. On the one hand those rules of behaviour which are valid according to the system's ultimate criteria of validity must be generally obeyed, and, on the other hand, its rules of recognition specifying the criteria of legal validity and its rules of change and adjudication must be effectively accepted as common public standards of official behaviour by its officials.
>
> (Hart 1961: 113)

This passage can be taken as a core of Hart's concept of law. It answers the question which dominates the text – what is the distinctive structure of a legal system? It answers it moreover, in a way which shows Hart's method of answering such questions, namely, by description of the conditions under which statements making characteristic use of the term 'law' are true. It is followed almost immediately by another revealing passage.

> The assertion that a legal system exists is therefore a Janus-faced statement looking both towards obedience by ordinary citizens and to the acceptance by officials of secondary rules as critical common standards of official behaviour.
>
> (Hart 1961: 113)

Herbert Hart, Professor of Jurisprudence at Oxford University from 1953 to 1968, is an ordinary language philosopher (Austin 1956; Ryle 1963; cp. Edgley 1985; Eagleton 1986: 99–130). He takes the line that puzzling and persistent questions about law – philosophical questions – are best answered by explanation of the core meaning of the term 'law'. 'Words', Hart's philosopher colleague J. L. Austin said, 'are our tools, and as a minimum, we should use clean tools; we should know what we mean and what we do not and we must forearm ourselves against the traps that language sets us' (Austin 1956: 7). The idea here is that ordinary language, as a conventional and rule-guided social practice, is our window on the world. To quote Austin again, 'our common stock of words embodies all the distinctions men have found worth drawing, and the connections they have found worth making, in the lifetime of many generations' (Ibid.). The world, it would seem, is a fairly straightforward kind of place in which this or that is the case. If it matters to people how the world is on a particular matter, then this concern will be reflected in language. Puzzles that arise, then, are not fruitfully considered as puzzles about how the world is, but as products of inadequacies and ambiguities in linguistic expression. Tidy them up and the puzzles disappear.

It would seem that the fashion of ordinary language philosophy was shorter lived than the appeal of Hart's application of it in Jurisprudence. *The Concept of Law* is an influential text. It is extensively studied in Law Schools in the United Kingdom and Australia (Barrett and Yach 1986) and has drawn a significant amount of Jurisprudential debate in the United States into its ambit (Summers 1970). However much the paradigm for thinking about law which Hart proposes in it has been criticised by opponents and modified by disciples (MacCormick 1978, 1981; Raz 1970), it has been the dominant one in Anglo-Australian Jurisprudence and an important one in American Jurisprudence.

To understand this success we need to look beyond ordinary language philosophy to three other traditions which Hart draws into his work. First, and perhaps most significantly, Hart is a legal positivist and his work is firmly located within this tradition (J. Austin 1954; Bentham 1970; Kelsen 1970). Second, he is utilitarian. The figure who looms largest in his background is Jeremy Bentham, but he has debts too to Hobbes, Hume and J. S. Mill. Third, he brings into Jurisprudence an awareness of debates on method in the philosophy of science and social science, which, if not quite an introduction of hermeneutic (interpretive) method to the discipline, was sufficient to open doors in that direction. Here, Winch's *The Idea of a Social Science* and some of Wittgenstein's remarks on rules in *The Philosophical Investigations* are either followed or parallelled. In all four directions, this is a thoroughly British line-up. Such foreign products as are woven in to Hart's cloth, the thought of Hans Kelsen (on the systematics of legal norms) and of the American Legal Realists (on rule scepticism), are thoroughly domesticated.

The positivist enterprise

Leaving aside questions of any other phenomenal form which it might take, there is an undeniable sense in which law exists as a body of doctrine. For academic and practising lawyers – perhaps more clearly for the former than the latter – this doctrine is the stuff of legal discourse. The doctrine is what is taught in most courses in law schools, is the subject-matter of text books and is, together with the facts of a case, what is argued about in court. Questions like 'Is it the law that proof of provocation reduces a charge of unlawful killing from murder to manslaughter?' or 'Is it the law that parties taking a benefit under a contract who are not themselves party to the contract, cannot sue for performance of the contract?' will be understood by lawyers as questions about the substance of legal doctrine.

It is an over-simplification to say that arguments in Jurisprudence are about how that body of doctrine should be represented – as rules, as rights or as a form of practical reasonableness – but not, I think, an unhelpful one. For in drawing attention to the centrality accorded to legal doctrine in answering the question 'What is law?', it begins to explain why Jurisprudence is such a closed book to non-lawyers. Its arguments are about a thing (legal doctrine) which is itself largely unknown to non-lawyers. Trying to follow those arguments, is like trying to follow arguments about how snarks ought to be represented without having any clear notion of what snarks are. Nonetheless it is not hard to imagine that the protagonists in such arguments might believe that the point of their enterprise is precisely to remedy such lacunae in conceptual clarity. For, so it might be thought, the best representational form will be the one which tells most about law (legal doctrine) or snarks. Certainly Hart's claim for philosophical Jurisprudence is that it seeks an admittedly abstract but otherwise undistorted understanding of law, which will enable lawyers to follow their doctrinal discipline into its highest reaches of generality and give the non-lawyer the idea of what law is.

Hart identifies three persistent questions within Jurisprudence and undertakes to answer them within his text. How is law related to coercion? How is law related to morality? What are rules and to what extent is law a system of rules? (Hart 1961: 13). The aim of the text, as I have mentioned, is an 'improved analysis of the distinctive structure of a legal system' (Hart 1961: 17). As part of that improved analysis, Hart seeks to clarify what for him are fundamental legal concepts – law itself, rules, obligation, public and private powers, authority, validity and systematics.

We should be cautious of Hart's claim that this agenda of issues 'has been the chief aim of most speculation about the nature of law' (Hart 1961: 13). Though the issues are sufficiently broadly formulated to make the claim defensible, the claim conceals the existence of differing traditions of thought within Jurisprudence. Hart's agenda of persistent questions is an agenda of and for the legal positivist tradition. The positivist concern is to show law as a distinctively human product, with well defined sources in deliberate acts of law making which mark it off from other phenomena of social life. Since there can be little doubt that the regulation and control of human behaviour is part of the legal enterprise, other ways in which that is done, specifically the use of force and the designation of behaviour as moral or immoral, come to the fore as needing to be distinguished from law.

Hart agrees with earlier legal positivists, specifically with the nineteenth century jurist John Austin, on two points. First, that the right place to start an analysis of law is with 'the fact that where there is law, there human conduct is made in some sense non-optional or obligatory' (Hart 1961: 80). Second, 'that there is no necessary connexion between law and morals, or law as it is and law as it ought to be' (Hart 1961: 253). Thereafter he makes a substantial revision of the tradition, by opposition to the idea that all laws are essentially commands or imperatives which are either backed by (Austin, Bentham), or conditions for the exercise of (Kelsen), coercive state power.

Contrary to Bentham, Austin and Kelsen, Hart argues that the relation between law and coercion is contingent and factual, rather than necessary and logical. Ostensibly this does not deny the significance of the relation. It merely asserts that we do not need to make reference to the use of coercive force to understand what law is. Sanctions are used to back up legal prohibitions and prescriptions. That is a fact and Hart does not deny it. But, he argues, we can understand an act as legally obligatory by reference to the intention of the law even if no sanction is attached to it. Sanctions are in fact attached because human nature is such that some people, some of the time will break the law. If they were allowed to get away with it, there would be no reason for other, potentially law-abiding citizens to comply. Thus

> ... at least in a municipal system it may well be true that, unless *in general* sanctions were likely to be exacted from offenders, there would be little or no point in making particular statements about a person's obligations. In this sense, such statements may be said to presuppose belief in the continued normal operation of the system of sanctions ... Nonetheless, it is crucial for the understanding of the idea of obligation to see that in individual cases the statement that a person has an obligation under some rule and the prediction that he is likely to suffer for disobedience may diverge.
>
> (Hart 1961: 82)

The relation between law and morality for which Hart argues is, with some qualification, of the same kind as the relation between law and coercion. It is contingent and factual not necessary and logical. From five truisms about human nature – human vulnerability, approximate equality, limited altruism, limited resources and limited understanding and strength of will – and given only the general aim of survival, Hart argues that there are certain rules of conduct which any social organisation must contain if it is to be viable. Law and morals must both contain this 'minimum content

49

of natural law' for without it the aim of survival could not be achieved.

> ... men, as they are, would have no reason for obeying voluntarily any rules; and without a minimum of co-operation given voluntarily by those who find that it is in their interest to submit to and maintain the rules, coercion of others who would not voluntarily conform would be impossible.
>
> (Hart 1961: 189)

Although Hart disagrees with the idea that law can have any content (Hart 1961: 203), his line is to suggest that we are talking here about human beings and the world in which they live rather than about law or, for that matter, morals. That is, we are talking about conditions of existence of society, and about law and morality only insofar as social life is presupposed by them.

Minimalist as it is, this is a qualification on the claim that there is no necessary connexion between law and morality. Another qualification, though equally thin, goes more directly to the concept of law. Justice as fairness, Hart argues, is referred to when we are concerned with distribution of the benefits and burdens of social life between classes of individuals, and when compensation or redress for an injury is claimed. Formally, demands for justice in such cases are demands that like cases be treated alike. Lacking criteria of what cases are like cases, this remains an empty form. But so far as the *application* of the law to particular cases is concerned, such criteria are found within the doctrinal rule itself. That is, rules prescribing sanctions for murder are justly applied when they are applied to persons defined as murderers by them. Hart argues that this gives us, in addition to the notion of formal justice, the notion of procedural justice. From this notion of procedural justice as the application of a rule according to its terms, we can derive certain maxims, such as giving both parties to a dispute a right to be heard, and letting no person judge in their own cause. In other words, Hart argues that, in form and in process, acting justly and acting according to law are the same. Furthermore, he argues that because a structure of reciprocal rights and obligations proscribing the grosser sorts of harm is the basis of the morality of any social group, and because this moral structure treats peoples as equals in this limited respect, compensatory justice, like distributive justice is linked to the idea of treating like cases alike.

Now from this point, Hart argues that to have said this is to have said very little of substantive moral significance. So far as distributive justice is concerned there remains the standing possibility that a law, though justly applied, is itself unjust. So far as constituting people as equals through a system of reciprocal rights is concerned, this can be done merely within and for a very restricted segment of a population. Justice and law are alike through their conceptual connexions with the notion of rules, but the minimum content necessary for society aside, they may be widely divergent on the content of those rules. Even so, the legitimative content of Hart's account of the relationships between law, coercion and morality is, as we shall see in subsequent chapters, considerable.

A classification and model of rules

In dealing with Hart's account of the relation between law and coercion and law and morality before elaborating on his conceptual analysis of a legal system, I have reversed the order of his text. This is mainly an exegetical strategy, though it is faithful to the text insofar as Hart's argument for his concept of law begins with a critique of a model of John Austin's command theory of law. We can now say that whatever Hart's concept of law is, it has substantial autonomy from coercive force and morality. It remains to fill in the blank 'whatever'.

Hart's model of Austin's theory represents the theory as reliant on the persona of sovereign and subject. This, I think, is a defensible reduction, though his use of a gunman–bank-teller model of command is properly controversial (Moles 1987; Edgeworth 1989). By critique of the model, Hart argues for the idea which he considers to be at the centre of the concept of law: the idea that law involves a union of two different kinds of rule – primary rules which lay down standards of behaviour for citizens, and secondary rules of recognition, adjudication and change which are rules about rules. Primary rules, it would seem,[2] are paradigmatically of an obligation-imposing type. Secondary rules confer powers, both public and private, on officials and on citizens. Secondary rules conferring public powers enable officials to identify, decide disputes according to, and alter, legal rules. Secondary rules conferring private powers augment the individual citizen's capacity to expand the sphere of his or her individual autonomy by making contracts and wills, declaring trusts, getting married, etc., and so choosing to

51

participate in a range of social practices which plan and regulate life out of court.

If the union of primary and secondary rules is at the core of the concept of law, there remains the question of its outer boundaries, for clearly enough, the construction of law as a domain of human endeavour substantially autonomous from morality and politics, requires boundaries. Hart's idea here is that there is one complex rule, the ultimate rule of recognition which, existing as a matter of official practice, authorises the deliberate creation of legal rules and establishes a hierarchy of criteria for the identification of rules as legal rules. In his own words

> One of the central theses of this book is that the foundations of a legal system consist not in a general habit of obedience to a legally unlimited sovereign, but in an ultimate rule of recognition providing authoritative criteria for the identification of valid rules of the system.
>
> (Hart 1961: 245)

The modalities of the ultimate rule of recognition are different from those of all other legal rules. In the first place, its mode of being is factual. It is what it is by virtue of being what officials do. The mode of being of all other legal rules, by contrast, is to be valid or invalid by reference to the ultimate rule. Thus in the second place, the ultimate rule of recognition is related to all other rules within the system, their validity being nothing other than a function of this relationship. An example may help to clarify this. Suppose a local council decides that all rate-payers must contribute to an additional levy imposed by the council for upgrading the parks. A rate-payer is under a legal obligation to pay the levy if the decision creates a valid legal rule. This depends, in Hart's account, on whether the local council is given the power to impose such a levy by another, higher order, rule – for example, an act of Parliament setting up local councils as public bodies, defining their offices, and vesting in them certain powers of government and administration. If there is a higher order rule conferring this power, the same pattern of questions is directed at this higher order rule. Is its source, here the Parliament, a body given power by the Constitution to set up local councils? If it is, its rule is valid, that is legal, so long, again, as this Constitution is valid. Ultimately, however, we reach a point at which there is no higher order authorising rule to which reference can be made. There is just what the officials in fact do.

Hart's notion of a legal system as a hierarchy of rules has similarities with Kelsen's 'pure theory' of law as a hierarchy of norms. Whereas Kelsen, at least in his early writing, is neo-Kantian, and rests his basic norm on an *a priori* concept of 'ought', Hart's practice conception of the ultimate rule of recognition seems to owe much to Wittgenstein.

> 'How am I able to obey a rule?' – if this is not a question about causes, then it is about the justification for my following the rule in the way I do.
> If I have exhausted the justifications I have reached bed-rock, and my spade is turned. Then I am inclined to say: 'This is simply what I do.'
>
> (Wittgenstein 1958: 85e)

Much debate in positivist and analytic Jurisprudence centres on these ideas of the grounds of law. We shall engage with these controversies only as they become relevant to the argument of this book. For present purposes it is sufficient to note that what Hart has done here is replace an idea of law as the command of a superior in might (the sovereign) to habitually obedient inferiors (the subject) with an idea of law as a system of rules. He has thus moved away from a personification (sovereign–subject) on which the older positivist model relied to tie its doctrine-centred representation of law to social life. Not the least significant aspect of Hart's work is the way he replaces that tie – his social practice theory of rules.

Social rules, normativity and the internal point of view

Hart's most general idea of rules is that they are standards by reference to which particular actions can be criticised or assessed as right or wrong (Hart 1961: 32). His social practice theory of rules is an empiricist explanation of the constitution and function of these standards in social life. The key to this explanation is a depiction of rules as practices of action and reason. They are behavioural insofar as the existence of a social rule involves patterns of convergent behaviour. But convergent behaviour may, he thinks, be merely habitual (that is, unreflective) or be the result of coercion, and in neither case can such behaviour be said to be rule governed. Rules, Hart argues, have an internal aspect. That is to say, they function in social discourse as justificatory reasons for the behaviour within their scope and as grounds for the criticism of divergent behaviour.

This internal aspect of rules comes from the attitude of (at least some) members of a group who 'look upon the behaviour in question as a general standard to be followed by the group as a whole' (Hart 1961: 55). Such group members have an internal point of view. This, for Hart, is an amoral, epistemological perspective ('... a critical reflective attitude to certain patterns of behaviour as a common standard ...' (Hart 1961: 56)) which displays itself in characteristically normative terminology – 'ought', 'must', 'should', 'right' and 'wrong'. Such rules impose obligations, where they are supported by an insistent general demand for conformity. They are believed to be necessary to social life and may conflict with individual desire (Hart 1961: 84–5).

This account of social rules of obligation constructs obligation as an objective, conventional notion. But it is not yet, in Hart's theory, an account of legal obligation. The explanation of legal obligation uses a typology of social forms which envisages two kinds of society. The first, which Hart characterises as pre-legal, has only social practice rules of obligation. Such a group, which is perhaps intended to correspond to a customary society as an ideal social type, must be small, close knit and reliant for its viability on a widely diffused internal attitude of its members to its rules. It suffers, Hart suggests, from three 'defects' – stasis, uncertainty and inefficiency in its mechanisms for changing, identifying and resolving disputes concerning its rules. The remedy for each of these defects is the introduction of secondary rules of change, recognition and adjudication, and with the introduction of such rules we step from the 'pre-legal into the legal world' (Hart 1961: 91).

This remarkably simplistic characterisation of social forms is fundamental to Hart's ideas of how the union of primary and secondary rules can explain legal obligation as conceptually distinct from moral obligation. The idea of rules as social practices is carried over from one social form to the other, but the *kind* of legal rule resting in social practice is no longer the primary, obligation-imposing type. Nor is the group whose behaviour and attitude constitute the rule, the whole, or at least a substantial number, of the society. The social practice rule of legal society is the ultimate rule of recognition and its supporting group is the group of officials. All other rules can now be deliberately made in accordance with it. If the officials are sufficiently powerful or manipulative, and so long only as they retain their group identity as officials by an internal attitude to all secondary rules as correct standards of legal behaviour, legal obligations can be imposed by normative rules and coercively enforced. We come then to the two necessary and sufficient conditions for the existence of a legal system with which we began, and its Janus-face. Sovereign and subject has been replaced, through the notions of rules, with officials and citizens.

There are two further matters for mention. First, by incorporating into his notion of legal meaning, the idea that communication through language involves 'open texture', that is a penumbra of indeterminate application of words or rules (Hart 1961: 124ff), Hart gives a sketch of legal reasoning which allows for cases in which judges have discretion, that is, a legally undetermined choice of conclusion. This idea, by no means new at the time (Edgeworth 1989), becomes a focus for Dworkin's rights-based argument that there is one right answer to (most) hard cases.

The second point concerns the internal point of view. Point of view is an epistemological notion. Where, within a philosophical framework or interpretive schema, individuals are constructed as knowing subjects, a question of the point of view most adequate to knowledge and central to meaning arises. Hart's theory employs such a framework. Within the theory, the internal point of view is a point of view relevant to normative discourse. If we ask the question 'What does it mean to say that X ought to do A?' then, so the theory goes, we must consider the central case as being the meaning of the proposition to X where X is fully committed to the belief that A ought to be done – that is where X has an internal point of view. As a positivist, however, Hart separates normative and descriptive discourse. He sees himself as describing a normative social phenomenon – law. So now, within his framework, a question of the adequacy of the description arises. Is general theory of law to be written from the point of view of those committed to the norms or not?

Hart takes the view that it should not; that descriptive social and legal theory must be written *with reference to* the internal point of view but *from* an external point of view – that is, the point of view of the disinterested, non-committed observer of the phenomenon in question, who understands the internal aspect of rules and so takes account of the meaning of the rules for those committed to them. This point of view, rightly or wrongly, has been celebrated as introducing hermeneutic (interpretive) method into Jurisprudence (Hacker 1977).

But questions of internality and externality in Hart's theory do not quite end here. There is a theory of a social group at least implicit within Hart's concept of law. His social practice theory of rules, in tandem with an individualist social philosophy, entails the idea that it is the social practice of rule following and rule application which constitutes social groups. That is to say, individuals whose state of nature is atomistic but rational meet minimal conditions for social life by mutual forbearance from acts of unrestrained aggression, theft and promise breaking. Actual social groups will have a more complex series of obligation-imposing rules. The aggregate of individuals to whose behaviour the rules extend form the social group. Individuals therefore are internal or external to social groups.

This internal–external classification is not the one which Hart intends, but is nonetheless implicated in the account. In referring to the internal aspect of rules and the internal point of view, he refers to the reasoning of those *within* the group who accept and enforce the rules. This, as Hart is well aware, need not involve all members of the group because, so far as obligation-imposing rules are concerned, some may conform their behaviour to the rule without having an internal attitude to it. The meaning of law is thus tied to the justificatory practices of one section of a group. Yet Hart represents his own point of view, as a legal theorist, as that of the non-committed, disinterested observer who understands the internal point of view without necessarily sharing it.

This is certainly confusing. Its practical consequences are matter for subsequent discussion.

NATURAL LAW AND NATURAL RIGHTS: LAW AS A REQUIREMENT OF PRACTICAL REASONABLENESS

Tradition and method

There are human goods that can be secured only through the institutions of human law, and requirements of practical reasonableness that only those institutions can satisfy.

(Finnis 1980: 1)

This opening sentence of John Finnis' *Natural Law and Natural Rights* locates his Jurisprudence within the sphere of practical reasoning and states the position for which he argues: law is a necessary condition for the achievement of human well-being and legal obligation is a form of moral obligation.

Now if we consider 'law' in a pre-classical sense, say in the way in which Australian Aborigines regard the law of their culture as part of the Dreaming – part of a *logos* or principle of order; part of an imaginative act whereby human beings make themselves and their universe objects of contemplation and seek, within these objects, principles for living – then Finnis' claim is understandable. But then, as Stanner reports an old Aborigine as saying:

> White man got no dreaming
> Him go 'nother way.
>   (Stanner 1987: 225)

Finnis is perfectly well aware of that other way; perfectly well aware of human law as an artificed, institutionalised, professionalised and coercive ordering of human behaviour. His project, however, is to relate human law back to a notion of natural law; that is, to a transcendent set of principles of practical reasonableness in ordering human life and human community. His theory continues the Aquinian tradition of neo-Aristotelian thought referred to as classical natural law theory.

The central jurisprudential problematic of this tradition is the relationship between human law and natural law. We should not therefore expect an extensive analysis of the distinctive structure of a legal system which is radically at odds with professional orthodoxy on that issue. What Finnis has to say about the structural and institutional aspects of a municipal legal system is clearly informed by the work of jurists such as Hart, Kelsen and Raz. He accepts human law as, formally, a system of rules or norms. Similarly, at a functional level, he incorporates the thesis of the American jurist, Lon Fuller, that law has an 'internal morality', that is, a set of principles of legal process which are operative when a legal system is working well (Fuller 1969). But for Finnis these are subsidiary theses of his project. To justify his idea of law as a necessary condition of human well-being, he has to say what that well-being consists in, and how and why the institutions of human law are necessary to it.

The issue with legal positivism is the assertion of a conceptually necessary relation between law and morality, and beyond that, a meta-theoretical difference on the appropriate boundaries of Jurisprudence. These issues arise because of framework or philosophical differences between natural law theory and legal positivism, differences first made apparent in Finnis' preliminary methodological and epistemological argument. Descriptive social science, Finnis argues, cannot escape the evaluations of the theorist in the selection of what is important and significant in the field of familiar data and experience. Selection of a central case and focal meaning of a term such as 'law' must itself be justified. It must be made from the viewpoint of those whose activities constitute the phenomenon to which the term refers, because understanding the purposes and intentions of their actions is necessary to an accurate description of the actions. That is, a justified selection of a central case must consider the practical point of view – the point of view which asks what ought to be done.

Thus far, Finnis' approach, though differently worded, is similar to Hart's use of the internal point of view. Finnis, however, finds a hierarchy within the internal point of view. He points out that the practical point of having law will not be the same for all constitutive actors. So again, we must select between them. Those who understand best the data and experience that are most important and significant to the central case of law, are, he says, those for whom it is of 'over-riding importance that law as distinct from other forms of social order should come into being' (Finnis 1980: 15). This is the viewpoint of those committed in the strongest sense to the legal mode of social ordering; those who see legal obligation as a form of moral obligation. This, however, is not yet quite the tip of the hierarchy. Within the group of those who understand legal obligation as a form of moral obligation, there will again be differences; some will be more practically reasonable than others in the sense that their reasons for understanding legal obligation as moral obligation will be more consistent, attentive, aware and concerned. This is the viewpoint necessary to understanding law.

This does not mean, Finnis says, that an objectively defensible social science is not possible. It does not mean that it is 'inevitably subject to every theorist's conceptions and prejudices about what is good and practically reasonable' (Finnis 1980: 17). On the contrary, it is the guarantee of social science – where 'science' means knowledge and understanding. For there is, he argues, a universal viewpoint, a point of reflective equilibrium achieved by moving to and fro between one's assessments of the good and one's descriptive knowledge of the human context. It is from this universal viewpoint that what is and what is not practically reasonable is determinable. One must suppose Finnis has achieved it.

Closed theories invite closed responses. Finnis is arguing that there is an objective form of practical reasonableness which is knowable to human beings and is described by classical natural law theory. We should not indulge any inclination to immediately dismiss his claim as negatively ideological. Our task at this point is to understand his theory and to do that we must suspend our own ideas about what there is and whether and how it is knowable. Paradoxically, we must open our minds to the possibility that it is right to close them if we are to follow what Finnis has to say.

The natural law and the common good

The natural law, in Finnis' theory, is a set of moral principles knowable to humans through reason but existing time out of mind as reason. It is derived from a list of basic goods (life, knowledge, play, friendship, aesthetic experience, practical reasonableness and religion) and a list of basic principles of practical reasoning (such as, formulating a rational plan of life, having no arbitrary preferences between persons, and never choosing to act directly against a basic good). For Finnis, these basic goods and the basic principles of practical reason are self-evident. That is not to say that they are obviously true to all, rather that they are a bottom line; a discovery of reason beyond which reason itself recognises that it is neither necessary nor possible to go. This natural law is morality and Finnis argues that his approach to it outlines the deep structure of moral thought. It is, he considers, a critical reflective grasp on principles of morality which hold good for all places and at all times.

What Finnis has done here is outline the structural principles and basic values of moral reasoning within the classical natural law tradition. In understanding his Jurisprudence, we must grasp this as an approach to the question 'what is law and why do we have it?' – the 'why' in the question being premised on the assumption that human law is a morally justified institution. Moreover, for Finnis, the 'what' and 'why' of the question are logically inseparable; we do not understand what law is unless we know how, and that, it is justified. Further development of the theory proceeds through a theory of community or social life, followed by conceptions of justice, rights and authority. Human law is then considered as an instantiation of these notions in nation states; an instantiation which is related to the natural law by (Aristotelian) logical relations of derivation and by practical determinations. This yields a framework within which Finnis elaborates conceptions of moral and legal obligation and, using these conceptions, deals with the question of the moral obligation to obey an unjust law.

Finnis' theory of community is neo-Aristotelian. He considers that friendship is the central case of different ways in which individuals associate. Now friendship, conceived as an ideal reciprocity in which each individual constitutes his or her own good by acting for the sake of the other, is one of the basic goods. Friendship is also, for Finnis, the form of association of the family. The family's material, intellectual and cultural needs form the basis of a network of other forms of association (work, play) which ultimately form a complete political community. Thus while the individual and not, as in Aristotle's ethics and politics, the *polis* (complete political community) is the subject of moral and political thought, the individual–society dualism which structures post-seventeenth century liberal thought is avoided.

This associative account of society has two significant consequences. The first is a derived political principle, known as the principle of subsidiarity. It states that the proper function of association is to help individuals constitute themselves through individual initiatives of choosing and fulfilling commitments in work, play and friendship. This principle functions within the theory as a basic principle of political justice. Secondly, Finnis argues that friendship constitutes a third point of view (the two others being the individual points of view of friends) – 'the unique perspective from which one's own good and one's friend's good are equally "in view" and "in play"' (Finnis 1980: 143). The heuristic device of the impartially benevolent ideal observer is thus, for Finnis, a simple extension of 'what comes naturally to friends'.

All properly constituted objects within Finnis' approach have a purpose or *telos*, an end or aim. The aim of the community is the common good. It is the shared objective, point or purpose for which associated individuals have co-ordinated their activities. In the case of the complete political community it is that set of conditions which enables the members to attain their reasonable objectives. The content of this conception of the common good is explicable in terms of ideas of justice, authority and law.

Justice, Finnis argues, is a quality of individuals in their dealings with others and, in its general form, is a practical willingness to favour and foster the common good of the community. Since the common good is fundamentally the good of individuals and is the object of justice, it is a requirement of justice that common enterprises serve individual ends. These require the exercise of private initiative and enterprise and the opportunity for private ownership of property, including private ownership of the means of production.[3] General justice has two particular forms in Finnis' theory. Distributive justice is concerned with the distribution of resources. Commutative justice is concerned with all problems of social relations, its basic question being: what dealings are proper between persons? Finnis regards private property and enterprise as required by both forms of justice – commutative justice is involved in constituting individual autonomy; opportunity to use and control resources is a good which must, *prima facie*, be distributed to each individually.

A consequence of this analysis is that the right to private ownership given under Finnis' concept of justice is closer to feudal notions of property than to liberal capitalist notions, because it is a right already qualified by an obligation of *noblesse oblige* (privilege entails responsibility): it must be deployed toward the common good. It is not, in other words, an absolute claim right vested in individuals, which is defeasible only to obligations to redistribute placed on the state by liberal conceptions of justice. The individual's entitlement, in Finnis' theory, bears obligations of productivity, conservation and maintenance of competition and also to redistribute a balance of the fruits of use and enjoyment after satisfaction of the owner's needs in 'reasonable measure and degree'. Only where individuals fail to recognise and act upon their duties as private owners, can the public authority rightfully undertake them via taxation and welfare.

Here again it is evident that the relationship between the individual and the state that Finnis has in mind is not the antithetical relation which structures liberal theories of justice. The requirements of justice are *always*, according to Finnis, requirements placed on individuals. The obligation of redistribution of wealth is the obligation of the private owner of property and may be exercised by the state only in the event of recalcitrance by individuals.

Thus the move from talk of justice to talk of rights is, for Finnis, merely the employment of an alternative vocabulary. Modern rights talk, he considers, can give expression to almost all the requirements of practical reasonableness. The conceptual framework of those requirements is the one which he has already elaborated in his discussion of community, the common good and justice. Thus

> ... the modern vocabulary and grammar of rights is a many-faceted instrument for reporting and asserting the requirements or other implications of a relationship of justice *from the point of view of the person(s) who benefit(s) from* that relationship. It provides a way of talking about 'what is just' from a special angle: the viewpoint of the 'other(s)' to whom something (including, *inter alia*, freedom of choice) is owed or due, and who would be wronged if denied that something.
>
> (Finnis 1980: 205)

Finnis' discussion of rights constructs an historical narrative on the development of rights talk in Western Europe and presents and comments on classifications and debates of and about rights in Jurisprudence.[4] Two points, though both could be inferred from other sections of the text, may be brought out here in order to bring Finnis' natural law theory of rights into relation with liberal rights theories of law. First, he claims, that given the modern idiom of rights talk, the concept of duty or obligation has a more strategic explanatory role *vis à vis* the requirements of justice than does the concept of rights. In contrast, liberal rights theorist, Ronald Dworkin, gives rights strategic explanatory priority in his discussion of justice.

The second point is not unrelated. It is a claim that there are absolute human rights, that is, entitlements which cannot be defeated by other considerations – even other considerations of justice or, to put that another way, other competing rights. These absolute human rights are derived from one of Finnis' basic principles of practical reasonableness – the principle that a person should never choose to act in a way which goes directly against a basic good. They are

> ... most obviously the right not to have one's life taken directly as a means to a further end; but also the right not to be positively lied to in any situation ... in which factual communication ... is reasonably expected; and the related right not to be condemned on knowingly false charges; and the right not to be deprived, or required to deprive oneself, of one's procreative capacity; and the right to be taken into

respectful consideration in any assessment of what the common good requires.

(Finnis 1980: 225)

Other rights, as within liberal theory, are to be balanced against each other in determining the specific entitlements and obligations of individuals living in a complex society.

Authority and human law

The acceptance or exercise of authority is, according to Finnis, a condition of the common good. For, he argues, co-ordination of activities can be achieved only through unanimity or acceptance of authority. In a large and complex society unanimity is impossible, so authority is necessary. Since authority is necessary, then those individuals who can exercise co-ordinating power ought to do so. But this co-ordinating power must be exercised for the common good and so in accordance with the requirements of justice. On the other hand, power struggles, where different people can and want to exercise this co-ordinating power, will arise. They must be avoided by having rules of succession and these rules must be established by virtual unanimity – people's practical judgment on the question of who is to be ruler must be 'brought into line' (Finnis 1980: 249). Such unanimity, however, is difficult to attain.

> The effort to bring everyone to at least an acquiescence in this judgment is usually very taxing and exhausting for all concerned, and makes clear to all what is indeed the case: that those general needs of the common good which justify authority, certainly also justify and urgently demand that questions about the location of authority be answered, wherever possible, by authority.

(Finnis 1980: 249)

This is not, of course, an historical argument. The ideal justifying concept is 'virtual unanimity' and if, in fact, some of the ruled are so practically unreasonable as to make the wrong judgment, and some wicked people aspire to rulership for motives other than furthering and fostering the common good, the only solution is to seek a more widespread exercise of practical reasonableness.

So, according to Finnis, justice, in its general form, requires individuals to favour and foster the common good. Rights are what

63

they get in return through acceptance and exercise of authority as a condition of the common good. The next short step is to human law as a coercive and directive co-ordination of activity within a complete political community, that is, the community which is sufficiently large and complex for the attainment of individual human flourishing. In practice, in the contemporary world, it is the nation state, and though Finnis finds a place in ideal theory for international community, this qualification has no practical significance in this theory. Practically, formally, and functionally Finnis considers that there are institutions and characteristics of national legal orders which make them indispensable to human well-being.

At the practical level Finnis argues that law is necessarily coercive. In other words, the institutions of punishment are justified. They are pragmatically justified, because a system directing the behaviour of individuals in a complete political community must cope with the problem of human recalcitrance. They are also morally justified because, in justice, criminals both deserve to be punished and need, for their own good, to be punished.

At the formal level (law as a 'pure type' of authoritative co-ordination), Finnis conceives law as a system of rules and institutions. A specific method of determining the validity of these rules makes reference only to intra-systemic criteria. The rules regulate their own creation, administration and adjudication (compare Hart's secondary rules of recognition, adjudication and change), the existence and function of interrelated institutions, and the creation of legal relations by private individuals (compare Hart's public and private power-conferring rules). At this analytic level then, law has a degree of autonomy from other methods of social ordering. Formal legal discourse, Finnis considers, has the specific virtue of bringing precision and predictability into human affairs by various techniques which construe human life as a stylised and manageable drama. Thus we need a legal profession – a group having expert knowledge of technical legal doctrine and the capacity to think in an artificial and stylised, but precise and predictable way.

At the functional level, Finnis says that a legal system exemplifies the rule of law or 'is working well' when its rules are prospective, able to be complied with, clear, promulgated, coherent, stable, self-referencing and are actually administered by accountable officials. Where these conditions are met, citizens are assured maximum self-direction and freedom from manipulation. They are requirements of justice in the legal process – norms of method, or to put that another way, correct ways in normal circumstances of realising the values instantiated in law. So while, pro Fuller and contra Hart (Hart 1958; Fuller 1958) they are not morally neutral, they are not applicable in all circumstances. A Constitution, Finnis tells us, is not a suicide pact and if some members of the community ('conspirators against the common good' (Finnis 1980: 274)) are using the law to legitimate their own unprincipled accession to power, then the natural law may require the temporary suspension of the rule of law. In less euphemistic terms: declarations of a state of emergency, and the revocation of civil liberties which accompanies such declarations, may be justified.

This brings us to Finnis' fourth analytic level, the structural level, and to what is, for him, the most significant dimension of human law – its being as a derivation and concretisation of the natural law. Following Aquinas, Finnis argues that human law consists of rules 'derived from natural law like conclusions deduced from general principles' (Finnis 1980: 284) and in determinations or concretisations of those rules. The derivation of human law from natural law gives general principles of what to do (such as, for example, the principle that no one may kill an innocent person) which extend to general principles of how to make human law. So, for example, a principle of conservatism, that 'those human goods which are the fragile and cumulative achievements of past effort ... are not to be treated lightly in the pursuit of further goods' (Finnis 1980: 287) is, in Finnis' view, a principle of good law-making which is derived from the natural law. The notion of determination or concretisation of such derived principles involves the thesis that

> ... in positive law we can find a mode of derivation of specific norms of action (that is of practical reasonableness) by an intellectual process which is not deductive and does involve free choice (human will) and yet is intelligent and directed by reason. This process Aquinas labelled *determinatio*.
>
> (Finnis 1980: 146)

Finnis uses an analogy between a builder interpreting and determining an architect's plans to explain this notion. The legislator/judge fills in the details of rules and regulations and has freedom of choice in so doing so long as he or she stays within the principles of the natural law.

Since the natural law (morality) is instantiated in some degree in a human legal system there is a *prima facie* (moral) obligation to obey the law. But legal systems like other natural organisms can be healthy or corrupted, and human laws, given human fallibility, can be just or unjust. Whereas the discursive specificity of legal obligation (in the sense of obligations prescribed by formally valid laws) is that they are absolute, the moral obligation to obey the law is one of practical (not formal legal) reasonableness. In a particular case it may therefore be outweighed by other requirements of practical reasonableness.

It is not too much of an over-simplification to say that just as Hart's concept of law includes a minimum content of natural law, Finnis' includes a minimum content of legal positivism. There is a difference of priorities here on just the question with which Finnis begins his text – the evaluation of the significance and importance of relevant data, given that some agreement on what is relevant comes from the character of Jurisprudence as an internalist philosophy of law. Different philosophical frameworks fracture the supposedly singular notion of legal thought. They bring with them differences on fundamental questions about law and society which go to characterisation of the relations between law and morality and law and coercion as internal or external to the concept of law. At the meta-discursive level, these differences emerge in arguments about the proper boundaries of the domain of Jurisprudence. With Dworkin's text we move to a delimitation of that domain by political principles of United States, New Deal liberalism.

LAW'S EMPIRE: LAW AS INTEGRITY

Method and politics

The courts are the capitals of law's empire, and the judges are its princes, but not its seers and prophets. It falls to philosophers, if they are willing, to work out law's ambitions for itself, the purer form of law within and beyond the law we have.

(Dworkin 1986: 407)

Dworkin is willing. *Law's Empire* proposes a general concept of law as integrity and argues that this conception of law is the one which must be adopted if the law in the United States and the United Kingdom is to continue on the trajectory of working toward its Utopian goals.

Ronald Dworkin, presently Professor of Jurisprudence at Oxford University and Professor of Law at New York University, is a liberal rights theorist. For over two decades now he has argued three interrelated theses. Against legal positivism in general and Herbert Hart in particular, he has argued that law is not an autonomous system of rules but a matter of politico-moral principles. Against liberal utilitarians and pragmatists he has argued a theory of rights as individuals' trumps against collective goals. Third, and as a foundation for those rights, he has argued that when appellate court judges decide cases there is, in principle, one right answer. These theses were argued, from 1963, in journal and newspaper articles and essays, thematically edited into two anthologies *Taking Rights Seriously* (1978) and *A Matter of Principle* (1985).

Law's Empire is his first presentation of a sustained argument for a general theory of law. In it he adopts philosophical and methodological foundations for his themes. In an extension of the hermeneutic method of understanding the meaning of normative discourses (which, as we have seen, finds an origin in common law Jurisprudence in Hart's notion of the internal point of view) into a theory of constructive interpretation, Dworkin claims in this text to have travelled a great distance from all previous Jurisprudence. He draws selectively but heavily on the work of Hans-Georg Gadamer (1975) and Jürgen Habermas (1984) – writers apparently outside the Anglo-American common law tradition.

Yet *Law's Empire*, unlike Finnis' text, is no stoic assertion of the truth and goodness of a tradition which, if classical, is somewhat beside the point of contemporary mainstream professional culture. On the contrary it is a vigourous assault on the high ground taken up by legal positivism in the United Kingdom and legal pragmatism in the United States. Hart may be taken as exemplifying the former. Legal pragmatism is a label affixed by Dworkin to American Legal Realism. As mentioned above, this tendency in Jurisprudence emerged in the early decades of the century in the United States and made a wide-ranging critique of the then dominant version of legal formalism.[5] In part, this critique took the form of advocacy of a sceptical attitude toward rules as determinants of judicial decision-making. Karl Llewellyn, for example, distinguished between paper rules ('the law in books') and real rules (descriptions of what judges actually do when they decide cases), and argued that legal scholarship should have as its central focus official behaviour rather than 'prescripts' – principles, normative rules, rights-based entitlements, etc. (Llewellyn 1930 1931). The Realists also insisted that policy preferences formed the bottom line of many appellate court decisions so that when, in such cases, the courts assigned rights and duties to the parties, they were in fact engaging in a form of retrospective legislation (Holmes 1897). Dworkin characterises legal positivism as backward looking (to established legal rules) and legal pragmatism as forward looking (to desirable policies). Both approaches, he argues, are incomplete. Law must provide for the future while keeping 'the right faith with the past'. His idea of law as integrity takes in this temporal dimension: law has integrity or coherence over time.

The politics of these theoretical battles deserve much fuller attention than they can be given here. There are politics, of course, in all the texts, but in this one they are on the surface. At least prior to the publication of *Law's Empire*, Dworkin found a certain amount of acceptance amongst leftish legal theorists because of his acknowledgement of the political nature of judicial reasoning (O'Hagen 1984). The insistence on one right answer is a puzzle only if it is located outside politics. Against the rise of New Right ideology and action by moral majoritarians to circumvent the sphere of individual freedom in matters of sexual behaviour and preference (Levitas 1986), Dworkin's welfarist and permissive liberal answers were welcome. Against positivist denial of the political nature of legal institutions and thought, Dworkin's approach seemed, if not to flow in the same stream as the sociological movement in law, at least to converge toward it.

It was perhaps always clear that the one right answer was never embedded in the *in general* political nature of the legal process, but on particular principles of New Deal liberalism (Dworkin 1985: 181ff). Adapted to Euro-British thinking, this could be commitment to a conception of the rule of law which gave clearer entitlements to human and civil rights, even to welfare rights. What becomes very clear in *Law's Empire*, if it was not clear before then, is that the one right answer derivable from liberal politico-moral principles is not proposed as the one right answer for *liberal* Britons and Americans but as the one right answer for *all normal* Britons and Americans.

> What is law? ... Law's empire is defined by attitude, not territory or power or process ... It is an interpretive self-reflective attitude addressed to politics in the broadest

sense. It is a protestant attitude that makes each citizen responsible for imagining what his society's public commitments to principle are, and what these commitments require in new circumstances ... Law's attitude is constructive: it aims, in the interpretive spirit to lay principle over practice to show the best route to a better future, keeping the right faith with the past. It is finally a fraternal attitude, an expression of how we are united in community though divided in project, interest, and conviction. That is, anyway, what law is for us: for the people we want to be and the community we aim to have.

(Dworkin 1986: 413)

The 'we' in question here can hardly be those of us who do not locate our personal and political identity in nationality, whose attitude to law involves questioning its innocence, and who are neither male nor prepared to accept honorary status as males under a sexist canon of interpretation. Here again, however, it is necessary to resist being turned away from our critical task by the provocations of a chauvinist narrative. We must understand, in that sense of understanding which is explanatory and not justificatory, that Dworkin's tradition is the tradition of United States liberalism. Those who are not either voluntarily participant or committed to this tradition, are bound to perceive law's empire with cultural and political distaste. Common lawyers are not yet, not quite, US marines or executives for Coca Cola. That said, the point is to see how Dworkin's beliefs hold together.

As with Finnis and Hart, method matters a lot. In *Law's Empire* it is tied to philosophical hermeneutics. This involves an interpretive theory of meaning which like artistic interpretation

aim[s] to interpret something created by people as an entity distinct from them, rather than what people say, as in conversational interpretation, or events not created by people, as in scientific interpretation.

(Dworkin 1986: 50)

Dworkin terms this *creative* or *constructive* interpretation and considers it to be essentially concerned with purposes rather than causes. Moreover, the purposes in question are not, as in conversational interpretation, the actual purposes or intentions of speakers. They are the purposes or intentions of the practice itself;

69

that is, purposes which fit the intentions (in Gadamer's (1975) expanded sense) of participants in the practice and which show the practice in its best possible light (Dworkin 1986: 52–65).

Dworkin claims, consistently with this theory of interpretation, that a social theory of law must be written from the point of view of participants in legal practices – that is, the internal point of view. It must take account of the point of view of sociologists and historians of law (the external point of view) and reflexively adjust its understandings to such external knowledges, but the internal point of view has priority over the external point of view.

Participants in legal practices, most generally, are those who have a practical interest in knowing which legal claims are sound and why. They are first introduced as people 'who make claims about what law permits and forbids' (Dworkin 1986:13). However, the focus is then shifted to the judges' viewpoint as the paradigm case of the internal point of view because 'the structure of judicial argument is typically more explicit, and judicial reasoning has an influence over other forms of legal discourse that is not fully reciprocal' (Dworkin 1986:15). The claim for the internal point of view then, though differently made than in Hart and Finnis, still comes down to the claim that there are some who know better what 'law' means than others. And as with Finnis, but against Hart, there is a claim that legal theory must be written from the internal point of view.

Yet if Dworkin reverses Hart on this point, the final salient feature of Dworkin's method in *Law's Empire* shows a continuity with Hart. Dworkin places his text within the mainstream of both British and American Jurisprudence by constructing models of the most widely accepted schools of legal thought in those countries and arguing for his views by critique of them. Legal positivism is modelled first as the 'plain fact view' then as 'conventionalism'. American Legal Realism is modelled first as 'the cynics' view' and then as 'pragmatism'. The first set of models are used to argue that all jurists have, prior to Dworkin, been so affected by 'semantic sting' (that is to say, they have worked with theories of meaning based on a particular epistemology, rather than with a theory of interpretation) as to misunderstand the nature of judicial disagreement. The second set is used to argue for his concept of law as integrity. This gives an expository structure for this account, and I shall deal with the substance of his arguments within it.

The nature of judicial disagreement

When judges disagree on the law which governs a particular case, Dworkin argues, their disagreement is theoretical. That is to say, they disagree because they have different conceptions of what law is or different theories of law. They are not disagreeing about the fact of whether or not a particular rule is on the books. This kind of disagreement Dworkin terms 'empirical disagreement' and he suggests that it is a simplistic 'hard fact view' of law which promotes the view that this is the form of judicial disagreement. They are not disagreeing because there is no law governing the case and they have therefore to make a policy decision. This idea of judicial disagreement comes from the 'cynics' view' that there is no law, only policies and politics. Nor, as Hart and others would have it, are they making a discretionary judgment in a penumbral area of the meaning of a rule. Judges, according to Dworkin, have different ideas as to the grounds and the force of law. For that reason they select different propositions of law to govern the case or they differ on the weight to be given to competing propositions.

We shall come back to the grounds and force of law, but before that we should look at Dworkin's idea of the essence of law. If, as Dworkin tells us, there are right answers and wrong answers to questions of law, what are we to make of the fact that judges disagree? Simply, Dworkin argues, that law is essentially an argumentative practice.

> [Law's] complexity, function and consequence all depend on one special feature of its structure. Legal practice, unlike many other social phenomena, is *argumentative*. Every actor in the practice understands that what it permits or requires depends on the truth of certain propositions that are given a sense only by and within the practice; the practice consists in large part in deploying and arguing about these propositions.
>
> (Dworkin 1986: 13)

This, according to Dworkin, is no bad thing. It is not that some judges are incompetent and get the wrong answer. It merely attests a protestant, pluralistic society to which individuals contribute their differing views as to the requirements of the public good. Law is the social practice which, more than any other social practice, is expressive of this way of life.

71

We should note a shift in the passage just quoted – it brings us back to the grounds and force of law. Hart and Finnis would say that when lawyers argue, they are arguing about the applicability and interpretation of *rules* or *norms*, and that norms are not true or false but valid or invalid. Propositions of law, for them, are statements describing the norms, and are therefore secondary objects of legal knowledge. Certainly, they would say, propositions of law are asserted and denied in legal argument. But they are propositions *about* norms, and whether or not they are true, false or neither (being propositions about what the law ought to be in a penumbral or discretionary domain of legal meaning), depends on whether there are, already in existence, valid norms which clearly apply to the case in hand.

Dworkin moves away from the distinction between the legal norm and the legal proposition but replaces it with a distinction between the grounds of law and the force of law. The grounds of law are propositions of law. The force of law is the reasons which support propositions of law. This enables Dworkin to make his case for rights and for the one right answer. Legal principles are propositions of law which describe rights. Rights exist as a matter of politico-moral fact. And when a judge decides a case he or she gives the one right answer if the propositions of law affirmed in the judgment correctly state the rights in issue. Judges in this view of things neither find nor make the law (rights). They say it.

The tricky thing here is the notion of politico-moral facts. They are not, in Dworkin's discourse, considered to be facts in consequence of the existence of natural laws of the universe. They are facts of normative consistency within a cultural tradition (Dworkin 1985: 119). They are statements of what is the case within a narrative account of the Anglo-American liberal common law tradition which portrays that tradition in its best possible light. They are facts within the vision of society given by a liberal reading of the Constitution of the United States of America. But for Dworkin, they are fact, not fiction because, progressively though incompletely, they have been instantiated in the way of life of the United States and the United Kingdom.

Critics of *Law's Empire* have claimed that Dworkin's theory of interpretation amounts to advocacy of a rose-coloured view of these ways of life (Hutchinson 1987). Such claims, however, miss the strength of Dworkin's theory – the recognition (in Dworkin's case, the celebration) of the power of the legal profession and the appellate court judiciary, especially in the United States, in the construction of social reality. How extensive that power is, is a contentious issue and may well tend to be over-estimated by many legal practitioners and academics. But in questioning this over-estimation, we should not imagine that the courts are powerless. They have some power and Dworkin's point is to expand it discursively. He is, to use an idiom popular in the media, 'talking up' the power of the courts and, in particular, of the appellate court judiciary. More seriously, he is deploying discursive power in an attempt to *make it the case* that individuals get what they are entitled to within his theory, and that society is structured and institutionalised in accordance with his liberal vision.

Dworkin argues that in order to achieve these goals, legal interpretation should follow a three stage process. At the first 'pre-interpretive' stage, rules and standards constitutive of the social practice of law are identified as given with a culture. The necessary condition for this stage, is the existence of an interpretive community of persons sharing roughly the same assumptions about the practice. He considers that there is such an interpretive community within the societies of which he writes and that it encompasses most people. At the second 'interpretive' stage, the interpreter settles on a general justification of the practice identified in the first stage, by reference to its point or purpose. This general justification must fit in with pre-interpretive identification of the practice according, it would seem, to empirical criteria of 'fit'. Third, there is a 'post-interpretive' stage where the interpreter adjusts the idea of what the practice *really* requires, that is, what would make the practice best serve the justificatory purpose which has been identified in the second stage. In short the third stage revises understandings of the practice so as to show it in its best possible light (Dworkin 1986: 65ff).

Applying this process to 'law', Dworkin argues that at the pre-interpretive stage '[o]ur discussions about law by and large assume' that

> ... the most abstract and fundamental point of legal practice is to guide and constrain power of government in the following way. Law insists that force not be used or withheld, no matter how useful that would be to ends in view, no matter how beneficial or noble those ends, except as licensed or required by individual rights and responsibilities flowing

from past political decisions about when collective force is justified.

(Dworkin 1986: 93)

This concept, Dworkin says, poses three questions which must be answered at the crucial, interpretive stage where a general justification of legal practices is settled upon.

> First, is the supposed link between law and coercion justified at all? Is there any point to requiring public force to be used only in ways conforming to rights and responsibilities that 'flow from' past political decisions? Second, if there is such a point what is it? Third, what reading of 'flow from' – what notion of consistency with past decisions – best serves it?
>
> (Dworkin 1986: 94)

His three models, law as conventionalism, law as pragmatism and law as integrity, answer these three questions in different ways. For Dworkin, law as integrity is the best answer.

Law as integrity

Integrity

> ... requires government to speak with one voice, to act in a principled and coherent manner towards all its citizens, to extend to everyone the substantive standards of justice or fairness it uses for some.
>
> (Dworkin 1986: 165)

Here, Dworkin is using the notion of integrity as an ideal of a liberal political regime. He formulates what integrity requires into two principles. Legislative integrity requires legislators to make new law coherent with existing law. Adjudicative integrity requires those deciding what the law is to view the system as a whole as coherent and thus allow the past 'a special power of its own' (Dworkin 1986: 167).

We might observe that Dworkin's three questions are variations of Hart's 'persistent questions' of general legal theory: what is the relation between law and coercion? what is the relation between law and morality? is law a system of rules and what is a rule? The mode of variation, however, is quite as significant as the shared theme. For unlike Hart, who purports to answer his questions in a descrip-

74

tive and explanatory way, Dworkin's questions and answers are openly justificatory. In his theory, law is empirically linked with coercion. So Hart's first question becomes: is this linkage justified? The link is assumed to be a tie with past political acts. Law, to put that another way, is already within the domain of politics. Given a pluralistic political culture, there will be different justificatory ideas about the tie. Thus Hart's second question becomes: which is the best justification? The third question then becomes: what is the right way for judges to go about maintaining this justified link with the past? In other words, what is the best theory of legal reasoning?

In summary, Dworkin considers that the linkage between law and coercion is justified when coercion is used by the state to maintain individual rights. Individual rights exist in a society which satisfies certain conditions. Given such a society, the notion of consistency with past political acts which best serves it, is one which interprets the past so as to progress in the present towards the ideal of law – perfect substantive justice between the individual and the state. This shows law as integrity.

We should note again that law as integrity is no universal form of law. It is the form of law only in a society which satisfies the conditions for individuals' having rights. So we must consider what kind of society Dworkin thinks that is. For Dworkin, society in general is a metaphor. Its constitutively real source is an aggregate of flesh-and-blood individuals who are, by nature, associative. Their association takes the form of social practices, and one such practice is the practice of thought and language whereby the state or the society is personified for the purpose of having moral responsibility ascribed to it. Society is real (in the sense of being a distinct entity) not in the way that flesh-and-blood individuals are real, but because it is treated *as if it were* real by these practices of thought and language (Hunt and Kerruish 1988).

There are, of course, conditions of the emergence of this discursive practice. They are, in Dworkin's theory, the existence of a true community. The history of social practices defines the community to which we actually belong. A bare community meets genetic or geographical or other practice conditions capable of constituting community. A true community, in addition, will be characterised by interpretive practices which meet four reciprocity conditions. Obligations are considered as *special* to members of the community and as *personal*. They must flow from a general attitude of *concern for others* within the group. And members of the group must

75

suppose that the community's practices show an *equal* concern for all its members. Such a community, in Dworkin's language, exhibits the virtue of being 'fraternal'.

Where these conditions are met, a community may, and in Dworkin's book, the communities of the United States and Britain do, ascribe the moral obligation of acting with integrity to the state. Thus the two principles of integrity are, for Dworkin, ordinary principles of American and British political life. They impose on state officials obligations to act in different ways than in their private life. In private life, citizens are entitled to pursue their rational self-interest; to prefer their family and friends to strangers and to expect reciprocal preference in return. In public life, they must treat like cases alike. Within such a community individuals have rights.

This argument at once gives an account of political community and of political obligation. There is a *prima facie* obligation to obey the law of a true community for the law is organic to it, is that set of principles which describes its members' rights. The law, however, may be unjust, either internally in a failure of equal concern and respect, or externally in relations with non-members of the community. If the injustice is great then individuals may regard the obligation to obey the law as suspended. However, given a liberal concept of justice as a general goal of true community, and so as a feature of the interpretive approach to its law, we can very often rely on such injustices' being progressively interpreted out of the law. On the other hand, fairness may require adherence to past practices. In that case, rights must be balanced and apportioned.

Law as integrity can now be seen to mean that understanding of law which best serves a political community committed to liberal notions of justice, fairness and fraternity. It is a theory of law which considers law as a set of politico-moral principles and as a method of reasoning which, by use of precedents and statutes, and with due regard to the role of government in policy making, can, in principle, lead judges to the one right answer in most cases.

Law, in this sense, is no derivation and determination of a universal natural law. It is law contained within the liberal and common law culture of the nation states of the United States of America and Great Britain. The common law, of course, dates back to feudal England or even beyond. Dworkin acknowledges but makes small mention of this component. Law's empire is more profoundly grounded on the other side of the Atlantic in a New

Deal liberal interpretation of the basic value of equality, and a Supreme Court with power to interpret a written Constitution. Here, equality means abstract equality – the entitlement of individuals to equal concern and respect. But it is a basic value so that, within limits set by the need to maintain the family, the market and the nation state, individuals are free to pursue their own notions of the good and the state must be neutral as between these notions. Here too is the home of Judge Hercules – the ideal appellate court judge whose capacities (great patience, and omniscience *vis à vis* the relevant legal literature), and whose grasp of the method of legal reasoning entailed by conceiving law as integrity, give the sense in which the one right answer to hard cases is defensible. They are the answers at which Hercules would arrive if he existed.

The law beyond the law

The lengthy analyses of doctrinal issues in *Law's Empire* suggest that Hercules is Dworkin's *alter ego* (other self). But perhaps, consistent with the recourse Dworkin makes to literary interpretation, it is more appropriate to consider Hercules as Dworkin's muse. However that may be, in the final chapter of *Law's Empire*, Dworkin's Jurisprudence merges into Utopian political theory (Dworkin 1986: 408). Here Dworkin draws on a notion from legal mythology which historically has been significant in American jurisprudence: the notion of the law beyond the law (Dickinson 1929). As the purer form of the law we already have, the law beyond the law is the guide for

> the impure, present law gradually transforming itself into its own purer ambition, haltingly to be sure, with slides as well as gains, never worked finally pure, but better in each generation than the last.

> (Dworkin 1986: 400)

This notion of the law working itself pure is, Dworkin says, an old trope of sentimental lawyers. Yet he says: 'There is matter in this mysterious image, and it adds to both the complexity and power of law as integrity' (Dworkin 1986: 400).

No doubt it does, but the complexity borders onto obscurity. From what I can make of this section of the text, Dworkin intends to use his liberal conception of justice as a regulative principle, that is, as a goal which can never be achieved but toward which progress can be made. The law beyond the law, however, is not the pure form of this conception of justice, but is pure integrity. Or perhaps pure (liberal) justice and integrity are merged. It does therefore seem to be a genuinely utopian vision – '[a] ... purified interpretation [which] speaks, not to the distinct duties of judges or legislators or another political body or institution, but directly to the community personified' (Dworkin 1986: 407). Dworkin's idea is perhaps that writers of Jurisprudence must keep imagining what perfection in law's empire would be like, in order to maintain law as an institution for social justice.

> So utopian legal politics is ... law still. Its philosophers offer large programs that can, if they take hold in lawyer's imagination, make its progress more deliberate and reflective. They are chain novelists with epics in mind, imagining the work unfolding through volumes it may take generations to write.
>
> (Dworkin 1986: 409)

If this is the best possible light, then perhaps the owl of Minerva has indeed flown.[6] Still, through a glass darkly, and by reference to an increasingly commercially oriented legal profession which disappoints not only those who cannot get access to its services, but also those of its own members whose commitment is to the liberal ideology of the rule of law (Burt 1987), Dworkin's point here can be seen. Lawyers and legal academics with a commitment to justice and to the capacity of their profession and discipline to empower them in meeting that commitment, can be valuable allies for people with working-class, feminist and anti-racist standpoints. The limitations which the ideology of law places on such alliances, however, need careful exploration.

3

TRADITION, AGREEMENT AND ARGUMENT IN JURISPRUDENCE

The previous chapter gave accounts of three texts that may be taken as symptomatic of philosophical Jurisprudence. The purpose of this chapter is to bring them into relationship with each other by a consideration of, first, the tradition of the texts, and then by drawing out points of agreement and argument in and between them. To put this another way, in this chapter we consider the dialogic relations between the texts as a further step towards understanding Jurisprudence. The discussion and the relations considered remain broadly Jurisprudential because my aim here is to continue an account of the discipline. Analysis of it as a negative form of ideology is undertaken in Chapter 4.

It should not be thought that matters of agreement and argument will fall within neat and mutually exclusive analytic boxes, nor that they are similarly sealed off from the tradition of the texts. Dialogic relations are often constituted in agreement on the relevance of an area or topic for discussion, and disagreement on the specification of the topic. So, for example, the internal point of view is a significant notion in each text but there is argument about both the correct specification of the internal point of view and its role in theory construction. Tradition, agreements and arguments are dimensions of Jurisprudence to be mapped within the discursive context they combine to create.

TRADITION

There is an obvious and uncontroversial point of similarity between the texts examined. Hart, Dworkin and Finnis all proceed by elaboration and critique of selected ideas of law, revising those ideas but remaining within a general school of thought about law of which

79

the ideas are part. This is a matter of method in theory construction, but it is not only a matter of method. Implicitly or explicitly there is a claim within each text that the school selected is a proper and sufficient context within which to explain what, or what and why, law is. Such claims are basically competing claims about the concept of rationality which is embedded in law. The schools of thought operate within a broader Jurisprudential tradition.

As Williams notes, 'tradition' in its most general, modern sense is a difficult word (Williams 1976: 318). Among other things it encompasses the ideas of *handing down knowledge* and *passing on doctrine*. Both of these ideas are relevant here. The idea of handing down knowledge is involved, because a claim to be communicating or constituting knowledge and understanding of law is made by each text. Each author writes as if, by virtue of being privy to a privileged understanding of law, he is uniquely placed to tell others what and why law is. If we question this claim, then the sense of tradition which involves the passing on of doctrine becomes apparent. For doctrine is that which is taught. What is taught may or may not be true, but within a tradition, the intention is that it will be accepted as true (or perhaps as valid) by virtue of the authority of the teacher. The distinction between knowledge and doctrine now becomes blurred and if, within a particular tradition, doctrine is thought to be truth, the distinction may not be recognised at all.

To understand the tradition of these texts, however, we need a more concrete idea of tradition than this. So we will look at three considerations relevant to each text – the site of its production, its doctrinal background and the school of thought about law which each text continues.

Sites of production

Institutionally the site of production of each text is a university – Oxford University in the case of Hart and Finnis; Oxford and New York Universities in Dworkin's case. Any university, elite or not, is a site for the reproduction of ideology in both its neutral and negative senses: the neutral sense insofar as part of the business of a university is to deal in ideas, the negative sense insofar as much of that dealing is with ideas which accept and justify existing, materially unequal social relations. The latter are the ideas of and for dominant standpoints. Within the university, the site is the law school or faculty where aspirants to the legal profession are encultured, trained and tested for that job.

It may be doubted by some that the site of production of a text has significant relevance to its content. It may also be urged that the experience of academic authors is not necessarily limited to university life; that any of the texts under consideration could be considered as products of their authors' political or theological or professional engagements. The first point is not tenable, though some weaker claim, perhaps that the relevance of the site will be variable, makes sense. The place of the academy in the reproduction of hierarchical relations in education, culture and society has been too powerfully argued (Bourdieu and Passeron 1977) to be denied relevance as a site of production. Until Bourdieu's case is answered, denials of that relevance can fairly be seen to be merely participant in the processes Bourdieu describes. The second point is well made. Stereotyping academics or lawyers, no less than stereotyping women or blacks or working-class people, misses the point that the standpoint of any individual is not to be read off from their job, gender, race or class. However, it is not the individual experience of authors which is at issue here. Rather we are looking at law schools and practices within law schools. One such practice, that of legal pedagogy, is very significantly a practice involving the passing on of doctrine. Even if writers on Jurisprudence were not also teachers in law schools; even if, being teachers in law schools, they were to teach Jurisprudence in a way entirely differently to the way in which they teach doctrine units, Jurisprudence would still be being taught to law students and read by lawyers who are being, or have been, trained to accept a doctrinal discourse.

Doctrinal background

A condition of production of any text in philosophical Jurisprudence is the jurisprudence of a developed system of legal doctrine. Doctrine is learned within the context of national legal systems. English, United States, and Australian national law are relevant in this way to our texts. They are all called common law systems.

The classification of the world's 'legal families', that is larger groupings of national legal systems, is debated by comparative lawyers (Zweigert and Kotz 1987: 63ff). It is, however, common to recognise the Anglo-American or the Common Law family as distinct from the families of other Western European legal systems, however the latter may be grouped (Zweigert and Kotz 1987; David and Brierly 1985; Van Caenegem 1987). Thus 'common law Jurisprudence' gives a conventionally accepted, broader context within which the texts may be placed.

The imposition of the common law system on indigenous people throughout the world was differentially accomplished by British imperialism. Differentially, because the British gave different degrees of recognition to the legal systems of the indigenous peoples of the countries of which they took control. Where, as in Australia and the United States, colonisation involved the confiscation of the land to white use and ownership, the slaughter of its indigenous owners and the disruption of their culture, the common law system was made supreme. The doctrine of *terra nullius* in Australian law is the lowest point of this aspect of imperialism.

It seems unlikely that the fact that Britain worked with a common law rather than a Romanist or Germanic system significantly contributed to the extent of its imperialist depredations. Western Europeans – Belgian, Dutch, French and Germans as well as British, took their law with them on their colonising missions (David and Brierly 1985: 22–5). It is argued by Malstrom that, on the basis of multiple features common and exclusive to them, legal systems which are European in origin are properly classified together, in contrast to socialist, Asian and African systems (Zweigert and Kotz 1987: 65). The point here is certainly not to dismiss the comparative lawyer's or legal historian's project in its applications to Western European law, but rather to indicate the uncertain signification of 'the common law tradition'. One thing that is clear, however, is that instruction in the doctrine of the national legal system dominates legal education in the common law countries of England, the United States of America and Australia. The first point of reference in common law jurisprudence is thus the national identity of a system. This point finds an unambiguous expression in the celebration of national traditions in *Law's Empire* (Dworkin 1986: 195ff, esp. 206).

Nonetheless, legal professional discourse in English-speaking common law countries celebrates 'the common law tradition'. It is a self-celebration since what is thought to be distinctive about the tradition is the enhanced role of judges and lawyers in the formulation of law through adversarial litigious process. Again, this comes through most clearly in *Law's Empire* where Dworkin's theory

82

explicitly ties the concept of law to a theory of adjudication. In my view, beyond the celebratory rhetoric, however, there is little substance in the idea of a unified tradition. The common law has been differently developed in different places. In the result, the combination of a chauvinist preference for national legal traditions and reference to a unitary common law tradition gives rise, in Jurisprudence, to a competition about who understands the latter best.

Hart, Finnis and Dworkin each have a stake in this competition which can find support in different historical periods.[1] Hart and Dworkin play a 'Who's best on either side of the Atlantic' game which for all its tedium seems to be taken very seriously by some supporters (Lee 1988). Hart characterises American jurisprudence in terms of 'The Nightmare and the Noble Dream' (Hart 1983: 123) while Dworkin makes less ambiguous shots:

> If the rights conception of the rule of law were to become more popular in this country [England] than it has been, legal education would almost certainly become broader and more interesting than it is now, and men and women who would never think of a legal career, because they want a career that will make a difference to social justice, will begin to think differently. The profession would change, as it did dramatically in the United States earlier this century, and the lawyers whom that profession values and sends to the bench would be different.
>
> (Dworkin 1985: 31)

Finnis' position in this game is significantly different to that of Hart and Dworkin. As noted, his theory is linked to pre-modern periods in the common law literature. Further there is a supra-national flavour to a text which is elaborating a universal form of practical reasonableness. Finnis' first allegiance is to the classical natural law tradition of which not the institutions of modern common law systems but the Roman Catholic church is the 'principal bearer' (Finnis 1980: 124). The common law in England, America and Australia is but an instance of human law. Equally, however, it is clear that Finnis considers a common law system as par for the course as a derivation and determination of the natural law, giving an extended analysis of English bankruptcy law as an example of justice (Finnis 1980: 188–93). Looking at that same point from the human law side, Finnis engages in debates in common law jurisprudence, specifically debates in contract (Finnis 1980: 181–2,

320–5) and tort (Finnis 1980: 180–1), to show how natural law thinking can contribute to them. To some (for example, a debate popularly initiated by the American Legal Realist hero, Oliver Wendell Holmes, on whether contractual obligations are obligations to perform the contract or to pay an assessed price for non-performance) natural law theory offers definitive answers (Holmes was wrong!). To others (for example, debates on principles of compensation in tort and contract) natural law theory offers a view from above which shows either view to be defensible.

A further question which arises here is the extent to which each theorist acknowledges the particularity of the doctrinal systems which inform their general theories of law. Dworkin quite explicitly acknowledges that the doctrinal systems which are conditions of his theory of law are those of the United States and the United Kingdom. He makes no claim for his concept of law as integrity which extends beyond the Anglo-American tradition. In contrast, Hart and Finnis neither acknowledge the doctrinal system which conditions their theory, nor place any limitation on the universality of their concepts of law. With Finnis this can be explained in the same terms as his apparent distance from the nationalist rivalry between Hart and Dworkin. Since the emphasis lies on a timeless, placeless natural law of which systems of human law are derivations and determinations, the conditioning effect of particular doctrinal systems is apparently weak. If, contrary to the philosophy Finnis espouses, it is the case that his ideas about law are generalisations from doctrinal jurisprudence, that is concealed by the level of abstraction at which most of the text is set. Hart on the other hand, according to his own empiricist and ordinary language philosophy, is generalising his account of 'the distinctive structure of a municipal legal system' from the British legal system and the English language. Rather than guarding his theory from accusations of ethnocentrism by limiting its reach (as does Dworkin) or by justificatory argument for the universality of his point of view (as does Finnis), it would seem that Hart remains sublimely unaware of there being a problem of ethnocentrism in the construction of general theories of law! This is in no way an endearing innocence. It is precisely what made the British see Australia as *terra nullius*.

Schools of thought

'Legal positivism', 'classical natural law theory' and 'rights theory' are general terms which accommodate a range of particular theories each with its own specificity. These terms are taken, *within* Jurisprudence, as complete descriptions of Jurisprudential traditions. We need not accept this internalist perspective as providing a helpful map of the terrain. But we do need to consider it. The different schools have their different traditions within their ideas of tradition. In constructing an idea of a Jurisprudential tradition, I do not wish to elide this.

It brings us back to our starting point in this section – the ways in which each author argues for his concept of law by locating himself within a school of Jurisprudential thought and revising earlier theories within that same school. Hart works securely within legal positivism and Finnis is just as uncompromisingly within the classical natural law tradition. Dworkin, whose concern is with law's *empire* rather than one of its municipalities, constructs for himself a context of Anglo-American politico-legal culture and argues his case against two dominant theories within this culture – legal positivism and legal pragmatism. His school is nonetheless that of liberal rights theory. The claim to synthetic transcendence of all that has gone before is merely characteristic of it.

Selection of a theoretical context for revision by an author is not arbitrary. Where what is being written is a general theory of law it bespeaks a claim by the author for that context: a claim that a *general* theory of law can be formulated from within this *particular* theoretical context.

The texts in question take different ways with this profoundly philosophical problem. Hart and Finnis support (different) theories of knowledge which involve the idea that philosophy can provide certain foundations for knowledge. They each have foundationalist frameworks (Hunt 1988). The claim they make for, on the one hand, empiricism and, on the other, neo-Aristotelian rationalism is that these do provide such foundations. Dworkin, on the other hand, imports into Jurisprudence a modified version of the hermeneutic idea that philosophy involves conversations between persons working within different frameworks (Rorty 1980, Ch.8). At the end of the day this is where he leaves us – swapping large narratives of law's Utopian dreams. But in between, the day's work is highly competitive. The job in hand is to impose meaning on legal texts and since other jurists are misleading popular opinion by claims about 'law' already having this meaning or that, he is 'entitled – indeed obliged' (Dworkin 1985: 350) to claim truth for his political theory.

We may well question the distance which lies between Dworkin's framework and those of theorists infected with 'semantic sting' when, on the bottom line of each theory there is an exclusive truth claim. That is a point to be pursued later. The point I want to make here, is that the truth claims made by the texts together with their claims to be written from or with reference to *the* point of view which is internal to law, amount to the claim made by each text that the way of reasoning and concept of rationality endorsed in it is that of the law.

Thus we arrive back at Williams' idea of a tradition as involving a handing down of knowledge and a passing on of doctrine. To come down to earth on it we might ask: what are we looking at? what are we talking about? We are looking at and talking about law schools in two common law countries within which students are inducted to a discourse in which knowledge is knowledge of doctrine, and doctrine, credentialed by 'authorities' (the cases, statutes or scholarly opinions which must be cited in support of any proposition of law), is said to provide rational means of knowing who is to be punished, who is to have the advantage in legal relationships, who is to rule us and how they should do so for our own good. That is another way of understanding the Jurisprudential tradition.

POINTS OF AGREEMENT

Points of agreement between the texts can be shortly stated as follows. Each of the texts examined elaborates a concept of law within a particular theory of society. Each is made from a point of view which is internal to legal practices and so to the social formation of which those practices are part, and each is made for the purpose of showing law's legitimacy. Each text assumes that the object of knowledge of law is the norm, develops a form of individualist social theory and constructs authority and obligation as central categories of legality.

There are four separable though interactive claims within this characterisation of the texts and the discipline of which they are part and I shall deal with them seriatim.

Concepts of law elaborated within a theory of society

Though the Jurisprudence exemplified by the three texts examined is concerned with general theory of law, the different concepts of law are proposed and defended within background theories of society. The theories of society may be thin, background contours painted with a broad brush and with only so much attention to detail and controversy as is dictated by the idea of law propounded. They are no less an integral part of the texts for that. Though this is very often lost sight of in Jurisprudential debates which continue the practice of de-contextualised doctrinal argument, it is not controversial. It holds even for Kelsen's 'pure theory' of law (Tur and Twining 1986: 22).

Being about concepts or ideas of law rather than about social relations, practices and institutions which are characteristically and identifiably legal, is what distinguishes philosophical from sociological Jurisprudence. Hart, for example, writes:

> Just as there could be no crimes or offences and so no murders or thefts if there were no criminal laws of the mandatory kind ..., so there could be no buying, selling, gifts, wills or marriages if there were no power-conferring rules; for these latter things, like the orders of courts and the enactments of law making bodies, *just* consist in the valid exercise of legal powers (my emphasis).
>
> (Hart 1961: 32)

The most charitable interpretation of this passage is to say that Hart is talking here about the *legal meaning* of the *concepts* of buying, selling, etc., not about practices of the exchange and distribution of goods or commodities or of human cohabitation. But a social scientist might certainly be excused for finding Hart's assertion very odd and not the less so were she or he to trace the thing back to a world of rules.

Although the ideas of law are the ideas of the schools and differ in content and detail, they share the assumption that it is the idea of law embedded in doctrinal legal discourse on which philosophical Jurisprudence must go to work. Finnis, it is true, uses 'law' in the context of natural law in a different sense which, he says is 'only analogically law in relation to my present focal use of the term' (Finnis 1980: 280). The focal use referred to is the meaning of the term 'law' within professional legal discourse. Jurisprudence may be concerned to rationalise the idea of law in question by showing its derivation from, and coherence with, a broader natural or cultural tradition. If so, as with Finnis and Dworkin, the Jurisprudence is rationalist. The alternative, exemplified by Hart, is empiricist. The meaning of 'law' is grounded in the lawyer's experience and needs no further metaphysical derivation to attest its authenticity.

Differences between these approaches are discussed later in this chapter. However, there is an important sense in which they are all in opposition to the realist framework of this essay. None of these theories of law acknowledges the necessity of 'tracing the way in which reality appears'. The Jurisprudential project may be to refine, revise or rationalise the idea of 'law' in professional legal discourse but it simply does not ask how that idea was formed. Of course it is to be expected that lawyers' ideas of law will be basic in this way to philosophical Jurisprudence. This form of Jurisprudence is a legal discipline in the sense that it is part of the professional legal culture. The realist, however, will consider these ideas as phenomenal forms of social relations and social practices; as being themselves in need of explanation – not just of a refined representation, revision or justification. If that possibility is contemplated then the task in hand will not be just to tidy up fuzzy understandings, nor to decide between various competitive rather than contradictory conceptions of law. A serious task of ideological analysis will have to be contemplated.

From an internal point of view

It is the centrality of lawyers' understandings of law to these texts that supports the characterisation of Jurisprudence as an internalist philosophy of law. This again is uncontentious. But the internal point of view is a narrower notion than that of lawyers' understandings. The different specifications of the internal point of view need to be set down here in order to grasp the notion.

As we have seen, Hart describes the internal point of view as a critical reflective attitude to certain patterns of behaviour as a common standard, evidenced by demands for conformity and expressed in the normative language of 'should', 'ought', 'right' and 'wrong'. Finnis conceives it as the point of view of the person for whom legal obligation is essentially moral obligation – a requirement of the natural law of individual self-realisation. For Dworkin, it is the point of view of participants in legal practices who want arguments about the soundness of their claims about the truth of propositions of law and it is paradigmatically exemplified by the attitude of the appellate court judge.

The question of what agreement underlies use of the phrase 'internal point of view' is not an easy one. It is further complicated by the fact that the texts differ on the point of view appropriate to theory construction. Whereas Hart argues that a theory of law must take account of the internal point of view of officials but be written by the disinterested philosopher of ordinary language, Dworkin argues that a social theory of law must be written from an internal point of view, taking account of the sociologists' or historians' external point of view, and Finnis' ideal observer has an internal point of view.

Moreover, Dworkin might say that we should not assume that any point of agreement *at all* underlies common use of the phrase 'internal point of view'. It could be 'an essentially contested concept' (Gallie 1955–6). That is, there may be disagreement on the *kind* of use appropriate to the concept. Indeed, given that Dworkin argues that disagreements about the term 'law' are of this type (Dworkin 1986: 42),[2] and argues the radical difference of his theory from all previous 'semantically stung' theories, it seems quite likely that this is what he would say.

Certainly, telling a story from a particular point of view (Dworkin) and viewing an object from a particular point of view (Hart and Finnis) are different kinds of activity. In each case, however, the purpose of specifying a point of view is to draw attention to the fact that the narrative or view will vary according to points of view. So this is one point on which they agree. It poses a problem: what kind of claims can be made for this narrative or for this account of the object viewed? Hart, Finnis and Dworkin are all telling us what law is and telling us somewhat different things. They do agree, however, unsurprisingly, that human actors are participant in law making and that their participation is intentional. So these intentions (what participants think they are doing) come into the story or picture of what law is. Thereafter a difference arises. Finnis and Dworkin think it appropriate to bring in another thing – the purposes of participants or of the practice. They want to talk not only about what participants think they are doing but why they are doing it. Hart uses a different method of generalising his theory – an assertion about the function of law and a classification of participants according to role as officials or private citizens. So for him the internal point of view is just a matter of official functionality, or to put that another way, a matter of conditions for the existence of certain kinds of rules basic to law.

Noticing this, however, brings us to another point of agreement between the texts as regards point of view. As a point of view of (all or some) participants in legal practices, the internal point of view concerns reasons for action and decision – not necessarily in the sense of reasons as motives for action but rather in the sense of justificatory reasons or reasons which support the rationality or soundness of an act or decision. In this sense the internal point of view is concerned with understanding the structuring assumptions and conventions of a discourse and with some form of commitment to them. That is, the internal point of view requires that some thought be given to *how* to participate within the discourse; it must be critical in the sense that the participant would know how to carry it on in a case or situation which has not previously arisen. Again, however, that may or may not be thought to necessitate a convergence between the actor's values and those of the discourse.

For the purpose of showing law's legitimacy

While this characterising claim would certainly be contested by a legal positivist such as Hart, it is openly acknowledged in natural law and rights based theories. It is therefore controversial to say that each of our text writers agrees on the purpose of their theoretical endeavours. Nonetheless, I think the sense in which it is true that each text has the purpose of showing law's legitimacy can be explained without distortion of the positivist position.

The notion of legitimacy is a vague and confused one. It is a normative notion, insofar as it makes implicit reference to a standard against which some thing is characterised as legitimate or not. One point at which confusion arises is that the standard in question varies in different uses of the term. Commonly enough the standard is a rule or principle of law, so that 'legitimate' is interchangeable with 'lawful'. Although this, obviously enough, is not the sense in which it is used here, it does help to clarify the term, because the question of *law's* legitimacy is a question of the conformity of its institutions and practices to *political* principles. Which and whose political principles is the often-enough unasked question which makes the notion so vague.

This is why Hart might be expected to argue that his text is not written for the purpose of showing law's legitimacy. A theory of law written for the purpose of showing law's legitimacy in this sense would be a political theory. Indeed, this is precisely the sense in which Dworkin claims that Jurisprudence is continuous with Utopian political philosophy.

Neither the minimum content of natural law which Hart includes in his concept of law, nor insistence that the internal point of view (as Hart uses it) is a moral or political point of view, gives a sufficient basis for arguing that the purpose of Hart's theory is to show law's legitimacy. The minimum content of natural law argument is intended to refute the Kelsenian claim that positive law can have any content. But the content for which Hart argues is so minimal that a legal system may have this content and yet be opposed in its substantive values to the welfare liberal (or perhaps, more accurately, labourist (Edgeworth 1989)) and utilitarian principles which Hart espouses. So far as his internal point of view is concerned, even if Hart were to acknowledge a moral or political commitment as part of it, he does not claim that his concept of law is formulated from the internal point of view; it merely takes account of that point of view but is otherwise written from the point of view of the philosopher who is merely concerned to describe what is the case.

So argument that legal positivism has the purpose of showing law's legitimacy must begin with the observation that this purpose is pursued by a different strategy in empiricist versions of that theory than in rationalist ones. It must also acknowledge that the notion of purpose being employed relies on an interpretation of the texts rather than on authorial statements of purpose.

Positivist strategy is to show that the structure of advanced legal systems is politically neutral. Legal positivists such as Hart acknowledge that law has a capacity to be misused which inheres in the centralisation of coercive power (Hart 1961: 197ff). This capacity is the accompaniment of institutionalised norm creation, identification and change, which in Hart's theory, can cure the 'defects' of stasis, uncertainty and inefficiency inherent in 'pre-legal' society. It is, Hart argues, a matter of achieving 'solid gains' at a certain cost. Furthermore, sanctions are not logically part of Hart's concept of law. He considers that the effectiveness of domestic legal systems is guaranteed by sanctions, but represents this as a function of human nature, not of law. So like a machine, law may be used for good or ill. The moral or political point of positivist Jurisprudence is to draw attention to this, so that those on the side of the angels will be vigilant and clear headed in ensuring that their moral and political will prevails because it is politics and morality, not law which determine, the content of legal norms (Hart 1958; 1961, Ch.8, 9).

Hart's argument works on two fronts. On the one hand, in the context of political philosophy, the neutrality of legal forms of social ordering and control makes it at least consistent with liberal utilitarian principles. On the other hand, in the context of a Jurisprudence which Hart places in the genre of descriptive sociology, law is legitimated by its inherent capacity to be (relatively) flexible, certain and efficient. Dworkin might call this fairness, but I hope it is unnecessary to make this further abstraction of Hart's theory to see its status as a legitimising theory. Certainty, flexibility and efficiency are, perhaps in general, but clearly in Hart's view, desired qualities of a social order.

Ascribing a legitimating purpose to Hart's positivist Jurisprudence, then, finds support within his text. His claim would be, however, that the purpose of his text is descriptive; and that if it turns out, on an accurate description of a legal system, that all other things being equal, legal ordering is beneficial, then that is a discovery. This claim must be dealt with later.

Norms, individuals, authority and obligation

My claim here is that basic shared assumptions of these three texts are that norms and individuals are the objects of knowledge of law and of society, and that the concepts central to law are authority and obligation. As with other points of agreement discussed, this holds, on the face of the texts, in two cases (this time, Hart and Finnis) but needs some explanation for the third (Dworkin).

The idea of an object of knowledge is not an easy one and is differently understood in different theories. I am using it here to mean what a particular kind of knowledge is ultimately about. Another way of putting that is to say that an object of knowledge is an idea about what is real in and for a form of knowledge – here legal and social knowledge. If inquiry is being made into, say, child abuse, a researcher will have to decide what data to collect – the testimony of children and/or parents, statistics on incidence, type, socio-economic context, data on family structures, psychological types, parenting practices, behaviour, etc. Such decisions are theory dependent. They will be made, and the research programme structured, according to what it is thought an explanation should be given in terms of: according, in other words, to ideas of objects of knowledge.

Nor, I think, can it be assumed that the idea of norms is a familiar one outside, particularly, Kelsenian Jurisprudence. My dictionary gives 'standard', 'pattern' and 'type' as synonyms for 'norm'. The entry continues: 'standard quantity to be produced or work to be done; customary behaviour etc' (Concise Oxford Dictionary 1964: 703). There is no entry for 'norm' in my philosophy dictionary but it does give: '**normative**. Tending to establish a standard of correctness by prescription of rules; evaluative rather than descriptive' (Flew 1984: 251). Kelsen says: 'By "norm" we mean that something *ought* to be or *ought* to happen, especially that a human being ought to behave in a specific way'; and a little later '"Norm" is the meaning of an act by which certain behaviour is commanded, permitted or authorised' (Kelsen 1970: 4).

I use the term here, despite difficulties with it, in the very broad sense of a norm being an action guiding construct of thought – a rule, or principle, or standard, or idea of right. In this sense, the idea that norms are the object of knowledge of law is so deeply embedded in legal doctrine, that to lawyers it must seem self-evident. Dworkin, it is true makes propositions of law his 'grounds' of legal knowledge, but the propositional form merely clothes their normative content. Lawyers' knowledge is, in large part, doctrinal knowledge, and where arguments in Jurisprudence as to how this body of doctrine should be represented do seek some more fundamental explanatory level, that search is for higher order norms such as principles of natural law or political principles or, in Hart's case, for a general theory of rules.

Similarly, although each of these texts puts forward or relies upon a different theory of society, each theory incorporates some form of individualism. For Hart, societies are aggregates of rule-following individuals and social facts are explained in terms of facts about individuals, the kinds of rules they follow and the reasons they have for following them. In Finnis' and Dworkin's texts individuals are associative, rather than rule-following, egoists. Finnis' individuals participate in different degrees in ordering their lives according to the requirements of his conception of practical reasonableness. So they associate in families and, by extension through relations of work and play, in nation states. Dworkin notes the necessity of 'giv[ing] up *methodological* individualism' (my emphasis) (Dworkin 1986: 63) in interpreting social practices and so of explaining social facts in terms of facts about individuals. He moves to giving social explanations in terms of the intentions and purposes of the practices themselves. Yet he hangs on to 'flesh-and-blood' individuals at the ontological level, asserting that social practices are 'composed, of course, by individual acts' (Dworkin 1986: 63), and that 'the community has no independent metaphysical existence, ... [but] is itself a creature of the practices of thought and language in which it figures' (Dworkin 1986: 171). These are all variations on a theme which constitutes individuals, rather than or with priority over social relations or collectivities, as objects of knowledge of societies.[3]

To question the assertions that norms are *the* objects of knowledge of law, and that individuals are *the* objects of knowledge of society, involves no questioning of the existence of legal norms or of individuals. There are rules and principles of law and there are 'real flesh-and-blood' people and in my view, it is pointless or confused to argue otherwise. To argue that they are not *the* objects of knowledge of law and society is to claim that explanations of law and society which take norms and individuals as fundamental, are deficient as explanations. They do not go far enough; do not penetrate the surface level of appearances in search of causes and conditions of individual action. They are like explaining the phenomenon of fire in terms of the paper and wood and matches with which the fire was lit.

Objects of knowledge are always and inevitably constructions within a discourse. They are not given either *a priori* to the mind or empirically to the senses. They are products of a theory or a prevailing common sense. And they are always questionable – whether they are the objects of knowledge within one's own theory or other theories. For this reason, my preference is to speak of social relations, which, in my framework are what, ultimately, social theory is about, as objects of inquiry rather than of knowledge. The terminological change does not resolve the problems of explanation that this topic touches on (Keat and Urry 1982), but the absence of the questioning that prompts it in these Jurisprudence texts is salutary. It indicates agreement on appropriate objects of knowledge and so indicates a level of shared discourse despite quite different philosophical positions.

The centrality of obligation and of authority in Jurisprudence is consequential on this agreement. 'Legality' in each theory is a quality of a particular form of social life. It involves the idea that certain classes of act are removed from the overall set of acts which individuals are at liberty to do (obligation). Who may decide which classes of actions are so removed and are to be so removed, and how such decisions are justified, are questions answered in terms of some notion of authority.

For Hart, legal obligation and legal authority are elaborated by reference to secondary, power-conferring rules. Ultimately these rules exist as a matter of fact in the social practices of a group. Their normativity derives from their internal aspect and exists in the attitude of those individuals who are responsible for the cohesion of the group. Hart says almost nothing about how groups, constituted by the acceptance of certain kinds of practices, come into being or about how individuals get to be officials of those groups. However, as I have argued above, it is not correct to say that Hart's concept of law lacks a theory of society. Hart uses an idea of natural necessity – the natural necessity of association for individuals, who have a particular nature, and who are rational in the sense of being able to perceive what they need to do in order to survive. Obligation in general, which is, for Hart, the rational acceptance of a number of very broad norms of mutual forbearance, binds atomistic individuals into a pre-legal society. Authority is similarly grounded in rational acceptance of the need for general rules (Hart 1961: 121). In complex society, requirements of certainty, flexibility and efficiency explain the vesting of powers to make, change and adjudicate on the rules, in a determinate group. These rules give preemptory reasons for action. Legality comes with the emergence of this group of officials.

Finnis' and Dworkin's individuals are already associative. Obligation and authority are purposive concepts which are necessary not, as in Hart, to the fact of that association but to its justice. But the fact and the justice of association are not disjoint because goals more complex than bare survival are put forward. Finnis' goal is the common good and this is put forward as being desired by practically reasonable individuals. Dworkin proposes his four reciprocity conditions of a 'true' community. Neither Finnis nor Dworkin need to reason from a conception of human nature, because they characterise their individuals as associative. It is therefore the ideals of that association, described by the natural law in Finnis' version, and by the rights individuals have in a true community in Dworkin's, which ground obligation and authority in their theories.

Again, I do not wish to cover over differences between the three theorists here. My point, however, is that they are differences about the correct or best answers to the same questions, namely, 'Why do laws bind?' and 'How is law's restriction on individual liberty justified?'. Here then is another level at which the field of Jurisprudence is constituted by agreement. Neither Hart, Finnis nor Dworkin doubt that laws, in some sense, ought to be obeyed. On the other hand, they also agree that individuals ought to be free from coercion to a variable point, perhaps just prior to the awful transformation of liberty to licence and anarchy or, in Finnis' case, some way back from that.

ADVERSARIAL RELATIONS: DISAGREEMENTS WITHIN JURISPRUDENCE

It goes without saying that Hart, Finnis and Dworkin propound different concepts of law and have different social theories. Hart thinks of law as a system of rules, Finnis considers it an embodiment of a universal notion of practical reasonableness, and Dworkin's idea of law as integrity expounds a conception of law in Anglo-American culture as a coherent expression of that culture's aspirations to justice and fairness. The boundaries of Jurisprudence as an intellectual discipline are implicated in these differences. One way of putting that, keeping in mind the law school site of production, is to suppose each theorist to be asking how the doctrinal legal training of law students ought to be philosophically supplemented. At the risk of over-simplifying a complex question, I suggest three fairly clear – and clearly different – answers to this question are implicit in the texts examined. Hart, I think, wants a supplement which will aid clarity of thought and expression about law; Finnis wishes to give moral guidance to judges, legislators and citizens; Dworkin seeks to persuade judges, lawyers and legislators that judges ought to decide cases in a way which will further liberal political ideals.

Dworkin is right in saying that these are competitive rather than contradictory aspirations for Jurisprudence (Dworkin 1986: 90ff). Insofar as there is argument here, it is argument about priorities (which questions ought to be treated most seriously), about point (what philosophical Jurisprudence can accomplish), and about method (how it should accomplish it). But, overall, the question of defining the province of Jurisprudence is more a power play than a nicely engaged argument – a power play which we shall examine in the next chapter. The boundaries are drawn where they need to be drawn in order to defend the views espoused.

Three better defined disagreements arise in the course of this game. First, there is argument about the specification and function of the internal point of view. Second, there is argument about whether law is, significantly, autonomous or not. Third, there is argument about the nature of legal norms and their use in legal reasoning and argument – or to put that in Dworkin's simpler way, about the grounds and force of law. More technical questions, such as the individuation of laws, the modalities and logic of norms, or analyses of legal reasoning, are pursued by some and denounced as spurious by others. I believe, however, that the broader contours within which these issues are pursued are sufficiently mapped in terms of the three disagreements first mentioned.

Specification and function of the internal point of view

I have argued that Hart, Finnis and Dworkin are agreed on the relevance of the understandings of participants in legal practices to the meaning or interpretation of those practices because of the intentional nature of that participation. Further that in each case the internal point of view is tied to reasons for action and decision. Differences, I have suggested, concern specification of the internal point of view and whether or not a theory of law should be written from the internal point of view. Whether or not these two differences are treated separately or merged, depends on the extent to which an interpretive (or hermeneutic) method is being used. Where, as in Dworkin's theory, it takes the place of theory of knowledge and meaning (epistemology) they are merged. For Hart and Finnis, they are separated, though, again, in different ways.

I do not believe that the epistemological and hermeneutic approaches are as opposed as current debates in philosophy and Jurisprudence would have us believe. Real theoretical differences in the understanding of this study are related to different standpoints. We find similar philosophical debates within feminism and within Marxism as we find within mainstream philosophy and Jurisprudence. So this preliminary point on whether differences concerning the internal point of view are on two fronts or one need not hinder our understanding of them. They can be considered separately and their interrelatedness shown.

Differences in specification of the internal point of view have already been stated but, for convenience, can be summarily repeated here. For Hart the internal point of view is a critical reflective attitude to a standard or rule as establishing a correct standard of legal conduct. For Finnis it is the point of view of the person who regards legal obligation as *prima facie* moral obligation. And for Dworkin it is the point of view of those who have a practical interest in making claims about the truth or falsity of propositions of law.

Hart's insistence that the point of view internal to legal discourse is non-moral (Hart 1961: 198) and Finnis' insistence that it is a moral point of view (Finnis 1980: 14ff) appears as a well-defined issue of difference. It is, however, a mess of issues – including, significantly, various questions and approaches to semantical and logical relations between statements involving an 'is' and statements involving 'ought', debates concerning the relation between reason and desire, and the autonomy of law from morals and politics. What qualifies as 'a moral point of view' is never clear, so argument about whether or not the legal point of view is a moral point of view becomes entangled in argument about what a moral point of view is. It is more revealing, I think, to pursue the difference in specification by asking who each theorist has in mind as participants within legal practices, and what it is that is being referred to as 'internal' – motives, reasons, desires, attitudes or what. Hart's internal point of view is that of officials. It is explicitly said not to involve feelings or behavioural motives (Hart 1961: 56, 198–9). Noting, without endorsing, a distinction between reason and desire which is basic to Hart's framework, we can say that for him, the internal point of view is an attitude of 'the official mind'. This attitude involves (a) an understanding of the internal aspect of rules (their behaviour-guiding function) and (b) an acceptance of them as setting standards of correct (official) behaviour such that reference to the rule is seen as a sufficient explanation for action done in accordance with it. So if it is asked 'why did you fail that student?' it is for Hart a sufficient explanation to say 'Because there is a rule in this Law School that students who do not attend 80 per cent of classes shall fail'. It is also, for officials as officials, a sufficient justification of the action, though he insists that whether or not the action is also morally or politically justified is a different question.

Finnis makes no initial distinction between classes of participants in legal practices in terms of a social role. His internal point of view is that of all those participants – official or citizen, plaintiff, defendant, lawyer, judge, etc., who regard legal obligation as *prima facie* moral obligation. The person with this point of view is 'the good man' not 'the official'. An epistemological hierarchy is then built up within this class, by reference to knowledge and understanding of natural law and human law and to the quality of being in fact practically reasonable. The community relevant to his internal point of view is a community of people who share an understanding of moral obligation. At its centre are people whose worldly passions have been subdued by intellect operating in the mode Finnis prescribes, so that what is desired by them is consistent with the basic goods. Finnis distinguishes between feelings (of pleasure, of hatred), desires (for experiences) and reasons for action (Finnis 1983: 30ff). His point of view is epistemological. But what it understands *and* desires for itself and others, is (his conception of) human flourishing. Since, according to his notion of practical reasonableness, it would be practically unreasonable to pretend understanding of legal doctrine without professional knowledge of it, Finnis' internal point of view sums as that of the legal expert who understands the natural law and desires the goods basic to it.

Dworkin's account of the internal point of view involves the reader in an intended ambiguity. It progresses from people who have a practical interest in making claims about what the law permits and forbids, to participants in doctrinal legal argument to its paradigm case – the appellate court judge. It is opposed to the sociologist's or historian's point of view which is external. If we ask who Dworkin is talking about, the text gives us two answers. On its wording – pretty much everyone who will take legal permissions and prohibitions into account in deciding what to do – 'citizens, politicians and law teachers' (Dworkin 1986: 14) as well as judges and lawyers. The progression, however, through people making claims about law, to participants in legal argument, to judges, connotes people in court: plaintiffs and, reactively, defendants, their lawyers and judges. 'Practical' in the context seems only to mean action-guiding and encompasses Holmes' 'bad man' who washes everything in cynical acid and wishes only to avoid the axe of the law (Holmes 1897: 210; Twining 1973a: 280).

The second reading, together with the reference to sociologists and historians, suggests the community of legal professionals and puts Dworkin closer to Hart with his officials than to Finnis. Yet Dworkin's literal wording is in no way there merely to avoid his sounding like an apologist for the legal profession. Dworkin's theory of interpretation relies on a notion of an interpretive community and this interpretive community is, like Finnis', constituted by those sharing a moral and political ideology. As a community of those having a practical interest in knowing the truth of propositions of law, it shares a pre-interpretive conception of law as guiding and constraining the use of State coercion by reference to past political acts (Dworkin 1986: 92ff). These past political acts may have been guided by popular morality or tradition or by what 'true justice requires of any state' (Dworkin 1986: 96). But they must have been guided by one of them. Those who do not agree on this pre-interpretive meaning of law are outside Dworkin's interpretive community. But it contains, he thinks, 'most people' who discuss the nature of law. So just as Finnis would argue that those who do not accept the existence of a natural law are mistaken about the nature of reality, so Dworkin's internal point of view is contextualised by the ideology which constitutes an interpretive community.

The internality of Dworkin's point of view is a matter of interpretive attitude to law. At this point we cross over to the second point of difference – the role of the internal point of view in theory construction – because in Dworkin's theory the specification and function questions are merged. Dworkin, on this point like Finnis and unlike Hart, does not merely make reference to his internal point of view. Both Dworkin and Finnis claim that an adequate social theory of law must be written from the internal point of view.

Very generally the difference is that Finnis and Dworkin support their point of view by argument which justifies the understanding or interpretation of a subject who is admittedly within a social practice. Hart on the other hand, having taken on board the idea of objective knowledge as the value-free observations of the disinterested and independent knowing subject, speaks as if he were outside the practice which he observes. His methodological problem is not to justify this position. He is quite secure in the common-sense realism which the empiricist understanding of objective knowledge represents. His problem is to adapt it to social inquiry – to rules as human practices with an unobservable internal aspect. Yet to 'see' the problem is to solve it. We become aware of the internal aspect of rules as participants in a broader rule governed social practice – language use. The internal aspect of rules of official practice can be drawn into the picture by extension.

That said, there is a further difference here between Finnis and Dworkin which should be noted. Finnis believes that there is a viewpoint from which all may be known – the viewpoint of the ideal observer. Like Hart he is no anti-epistemologist and like Hart he works with a conception of objective knowledge. Indeed his epistemology extends to objective knowledge of basic goods and the one true mode of practical reasoning. Dworkin, by contrast, extends his hermeneutics into the terrain of theory of knowledge and meaning. Commitment to a liberal ideology and a theory of interpretation aimed at imposing meaning on texts and practices, entitles and obliges him to assert the truth of his theory for the purpose of exempting it from its own sceptical claims (Dworkin 1985: 350). This is still a justification of his point of view, but it does not pretend to be grounded in objective knowledge of what is true and good. Rather he drops the very notion of objective knowledge (in Hart and Finnis' sense). Again, however, the reality of the disagreement between them needs to be questioned.

The autonomy of law

No one claims that law is actually independent of other social practices. That is not what the autonomy debate is about. The question is one of knowledge and politics. It is a question about whether law is and/or ought to be conceived as a form of politics or morality or economics, or as a social phenomenon which is so distinctive as to justify thinking of it as an independent category of social life.

Hart argues that law is and ought to be conceived as an autonomous domain. Dworkin and Finnis argue that it neither is nor ought to be so conceived. Yet here again, they do not deny that human law is a distinctive domain of thought and practice. As I have commented, Finnis incorporates a 'minimum content of legal positivism' into his theory in his account of the formal features of human law. Dworkin narrates a tale of law as a politics of principle distinct from 'the battle ground of power politics' (Dworkin 1985: 71).

The lack of a sociological dimension on this most sociological question – the relation between legal and other social practices – makes it tempting to dismiss differences concerning the autonomy thesis. Each theorist can accurately enough be said to acknowledge a *relative* autonomy of law from other social practices, so why not leave it at that? Why bother about the minutiae of their disagreement? The reason for resisting this temptation is that positions on the autonomy thesis are tied in to the way in which law is legitimated in Jurisprudence. Ideologically, it is not only Dworkin who endeavours to show law in its best possible light. He just brings to the surface a premise that is constitutive of Jurisprudence.

If the obligation to obey the law is presented as a form of moral obligation, then law is being assumed to be, in general, morally legitimate. Legal positivism, ostensibly, makes no such assumption, but that is because the consideration of moral or political legitimacy is defined as lying outside the domain of Jurisprudence. If we ask why, and also, what criteria of domains are being used in positivist thought, we come up against the idea that questions about what some thing is are logically different from questions about what it ought to be and that the relation between them is the concern of moral philosophy. If, stubbornly, we query that, then the positivist will assert that the relation between is and ought statements in legal thought has its own specificity and it is this that is relevant to Jurisprudence. He or she will say that the fact that a certain act is required by law *means* that there is a legal obligation to do it because that is axiomatic in formal legal thought. How and where the axiom comes in, is a further question that divides an empiricist positivist such as Hart from neo-Kantian positivists such as Kelsen.

Now, clearly enough, this response assumes the autonomy thesis and avoids the point of the questioning. But it begins to explain how this debate can go on without sociological inquiry. It is a debate about ways of thinking and reasoning. In the context of the site of production of Jurisprudence, it has a powerful consequence. In the absence of a focused sociological dimension to the autonomy debate, law students and teachers who are not familiar with the history of philosophical thought map it on to what they know about law. If that is, principally, a knowledge of legal doctrine, the autonomy question is translated into an approach to legal reasoning. The relevant activity becomes forensic argument and decision making. This is an activity from which non-lawyers are by and large excluded but, paradoxically perhaps, the sociological exclusivity of the domain of legal reasoning makes it fine grist for the non-autonomist's mill. For if it can be shown that in this paradigm of legal practice, decisions about what the law is are grounded in considerations which are drawn from outside a formal system of legal rules, then surely at other levels of legal discourse or in legal practices where non-lawyers are more active participants, law must be all the more non-autonomous. On the other hand the distinctiveness of law, the calm of its deliberations as against the rough and tumble of politics, and its public and objective image in contrast to the private perplexities of moral dilemmas, is affirmed by locating it in court.

If this is 'progress' in Jurisprudence then it is progress of a curious kind. The obvious truths that a legal system is part of a social system, that in the systems in question there is an exclusive legal profession whose technical expertise involves knowledge of legal doctrine, and that doctrinal legal discourse involves rules and the use of axiomatic assumptions (dogmas and fictions), are obscured by the autonomy debate. Given that a legal system is part of a social system, what we need to know are the details of interaction at various loci. Given the existence of an exclusive legal profession with a particular expertise, we need to understand what political power that profession has, how and where it exercises it and the extent to which that power is constituted by and constitutive of its expertise. Given the use of rules and axioms in doctrinal legal discourse, we need to understand reasoning within formalist systems, as well as the principles and politics of their construction. But the autonomy debate has not gone beyond arguments for giving priority to the interactive or to the self-contained and self-referential aspects of legal practices.

I have suggested that this is because it is a political debate, which is about the nature of law and its relation to economics, morality or politics, only insofar as it is concerned to establish a guide for understanding 'law' which will further the actual legitimacy of law as that is perceived by protagonists to the debate. Differences between Hart, Finnis and Dworkin here, lie in a conjunction of time-, place- and framework-specific perceptions which, taking place as they do between theorists with shared standpoints of class, race and sex–gender, become enmeshed in competing strategies for maintaining dominance.

More specifically, Hart affirms law's autonomy because it is observably the case that officials of a state with centralised and institutionalised monopoly of coercive power, may or may not be integrated into the wider political community. This is a perception which clearly reflects the experience of the imposition of the English common law by British officials on peoples whose cultural and political practices were inconsistent with it. Hart's idea of law's actual legitimacy is that it makes a form of life navigable; it guides life out of court. For this it is necessary that legal rules are balanced between certainty and flexibility, and that they are applied in a way representable as fair. He argues the autonomy thesis because he thinks it is true. His political concern is to ensure that law is clearly distinguished from morality and politics, so that law appears as neutral to subjective and partisan concerns. This constructs an appearance of legitimacy which is part of a strategy of power.

Finnis and Dworkin reject the autonomy thesis by placing legal reasoning centre stage, or to put that another way, by making the form of rationality which they see embedded in law their focal point. Their ideal of legal reasoning supposes a singular and male subject (the practically reasonable man; Hercules) who is at one with the natural or cultural law of the political community whose human law is in question. These perceptions are more attuned to strategies of maintaining power which require the dissemination of an ideology beyond the loci of official action. Two decades separate Hart's *Concept of Law* from Finnis' and Dworkin's texts. They are decades in which national liberation struggles have challenged British and American complacency about the civilising effects of the imposition of their law on culturally different people. Making the centre hold requires more than management of an achieved constitutional and institutional structure.[4] It requires incorporation of professionals, trade unionists and members of dissident movements into a more diffused exercise of State power. Ideology that will persuade those outside traditional coteries of political, economic and legal power that they are linked in to those coteries is required too.

Finnis and Dworkin genuinely understand law as non-autonomous. They have rather different perceptions of its specificity. For Finnis law's actual legitimacy comes from its being a form of practical reasonableness. For Dworkin it comes from its being as a coherent expression of principles observed in the social practices of a true community. Their political concern in arguing the non-autonomy thesis is to show, against Hart, that human law's true legitimacy is not a function of its formal and procedural qualities; of its being disjoint from the moral and political practices of individuals in community. On the contrary, law's legitimacy resides in law's necessity for that community as a true community.

Legal norms and normativity: the grounds and force of law

I have argued earlier that a significant point of agreement in Jurisprudence is that the basic object of knowledge of law is the norm. There is a difference in terminology here between Dworkin on the one hand and Hart and Finnis on the other. Dworkin talks of the grounds and force of law. Hart and Finnis talk of rules or principles and of reasons for following and applying them. I have suggested that there is little substance in this difference. Similarly, while Dworkin treats propositions of law (that is descriptive statements of what the law is) as his grounds of law, I have suggested that this is not more than a representation of normative content in propositional form. More significant differences, I think, arise in answer to the questions: which norms is legal knowledge about? why these? and how do they function to render certain actions permissible, obligatory or prohibited.

For Hart the kind of norm in issue is the legal rule, that is, a standard, identified by having a particular pedigree and properly classified, in the first instance, as obligation-imposing or power-conferring. Finnis takes legal rules, identified by pedigree *and* first and second order principles of their derivation and determination from the natural law, as his objects of knowledge of human law. Between these two texts, the important difference lies in Finnis' adoption of the contention that '[i]n every law positive well made is somewhat of the law of reason' (Finnis 1980: 281). This does not entail a denial, on Finnis' part, of the legal status of unjust rules. It does entail a denial that they are 'well made'. Unjust rules are thus not the central case of a legal norm. Rather the central case legal norm will be a positive rule, satisfying the formal tests of pedigree, and made in conformity with first and second order principles of its derivation from the natural law.

Dworkin considers legal norms to be, most significantly, principles. Principles are propositions describing rights. In his earlier work, Dworkin made much of distinguishing principles, policies and rules (Dworkin 1978: 14–45). Less weight is placed on these distinctions in *Law's Empire*. Rules appear as conventionally agreed upon standards which have the limited role, in law's empire, of providing settled bases for action and so enabling expectations to be formed on how others will act. Policies are goal-oriented strategies for furthering the general interest, as that is conceived by the policy-making body. Both rules and policies are part of the social order which Dworkin supports, but his main point is that the requirements of both rules and policies are defeasible to the requirements of principles. Principles describe abstract rights and obligations which are made concrete in the process of deciding cases. This process involves taking account of rules and policies, particularly where, as will often be the case, there are competing principles in play. The very idea of law as integrity is that it finds, through interpretive judgment on what principle requires, a coherent expression to what may and may not be done.

This leaves open the possibility of a conflict between justice and integrity because, in a particular human and therefore imperfect culture, the norm required by the coherence test may conflict with a requirement of justice. In such cases, according to Dworkin, Hercules will compromise, weighing the extent of the injustice against the obligation to obey the law (that is, requirements of integrity) of a true community, and assign rights and duties so as to acknowledge both justice and integrity. Dworkin's illustration of how this can be done uses gender discrimination as an example of injustice. From both socialist and feminist standpoints, it succeeds only to bring the chauvinism of his text to the surface (Hunt and Kerruish 1991). We shall consider this further in the context of rights fetishism. Here we will stay within the chosen contexts of the texts.

In philosophy the debate on the nature of the legal norm is related to different views on the relation between fact and value and the construction of independent standards of right and wrong. Conventions or pedigreed rules, universal principles of justice, and rights as moral facts or facts of normative consistency within a narrative account of a culture, all claim some form of independence from individual judgment on what to do, though Hart, of course, confines his right or wrong to legal right or wrong.

Rather than enter these labyrinthine ways of moral and Utopian political philosophy, in order to understand differences between the texts in terms common for them all, consider the following answers to the questions raised above: which norms? why these? and how do they function to make certain acts obligatory?

Briefly and bluntly, Hart might say: rules, normative rules identified by a practice rule; because if we understand what law is in these terms we get a theory with great explanatory power and because, by keeping legal and moral norms quite distinct, we can be more clear-minded in resolving their conflicts. They function to make certain acts obligatory, others permitted and so forth, simply through being in place, for that is what it means to say that an act is obligatory, etc. How they function is to give people reasons for acting in conformity with them. Finnis might say: rules, normative rules of a particular formal kind, which are derived from, and are concretisations of, a perfectly coherent set of principles which guide all human beings in thinking and acting so as to achieve their own individual self-realisation. Why these? Because that is how it is and can be known to be if, by being intelligent, informed, concerned and reasonable, we place ourselves in the position of the ideal observer. They function to oblige, permit and so forth, through reason which, being practically reasonable, desires individual well-being. And Dworkin would say: principles; because principles are propositions which tell us what we should say is right and is wrong if we want to maintain the normal way of life in England and America and make it even fairer and more just than it already is. They are expressions of rights individuals have by virtue of being members of a true political community and they function in arguments between members of such communities about how best to interpret its flourishing legal practices. Obligations exist correlative to these rights.

These answers, I suggest, show again that differences between Hart and Dworkin are in large part strategic. Finnis' belief in an absolute and universal standard of value, the natural law, sets him apart. Yet if his desire for a community in which responsibility attaches to privilege indicates the carrying through of feudal notions, his acceptance of the formal and institutional arrangements of modern legal systems indicates the standpoints he shares with Hart and Dworkin within the social relations of contemporary social formations. These shared standpoints account for the possibility of finding a basic, normative, postulate for all Jurisprudence: *reason so as to maintain existing social relations*. Differences, I suggest come from different beliefs as to how this norm can be made most effective.

The most useful conceptual relations within which to understand these differences are the relations of general and particular, subject and object, and internal and external and their cognates. But this moves us on from an analysis of relations between the texts to a consideration of the discourse in which they participate – the Jurisprudence Game.

4

THE JURISPRUDENCE GAME: THE LEGAL CONSTRUCTION OF OBJECTIVITY

Law is part of our social reality and Jurisprudence makes certain representations of lawyers' ideas of it. In the last two chapters we have considered three of its texts, substantially in their own terms. This chapter presents Jurisprudence in different terms – terms which seek solidarity with those who are put down by law. There is no notion of standpoint in Jurisprudence. It is a discourse which is blind to its own standpoint relativity. It presses understandings of law on us that would extend that blindness. Dworkin claims that if we understand the nature of legal argument better 'we know better what kind of people we are' (Dworkin 1986: 11). I doubt that. We may gain from Jurisprudence some understanding of who Dworkin would like us to think 'we' are, but we must seek standpoints that are of and for subordinated people if we are to take control of our own being in law. From such standpoints we can view Jurisprudence as a game constituted by its agreements and played by its arguments. But like law itself the game is not mindless. Its purpose is the justification of the legal construction of objectivity or, to put that another way, the construction of law's truth. And it is only subjects of a special kind which can know that truth.

SETTING GOALS AND DRAWING BOUNDARIES

Debates in Jurisprudence are said to be about the nature, grounds and value of law. Phrases like 'the nature of law', 'the value of law' and 'the grounds of law', make a verbal appeal to some more fundamental aspect of law's being, yet go no way to returning us to the complex diversity of actual legal practices and institutions. Where they do take us, however, is in one sense fundamental to

Jurisprudence, and indirectly to law. It is to the preoccupations of jurists. The doubt and the fear is of and for law's objectivity.

In its contemporary Jurisprudential form this preoccupation is most evident in debate on judicial discretion (in relation to the nature and grounds of law) and in discussions of scepticism in and about law (in relation to its grounds and value). I have said little of these debates for this is old wine being poured into new bottles. The problem which gives rise to the preoccupation is an old one. The law is general but the circumstances of cases are particular. How then can it be right to decide different, particular cases by applica- tion of the same general rule? Aristotle's formulation of it will do:

> ... the law can do no more than generalize, and there are cases which cannot be settled by a general statement. So in matters where it is necessary to make a general statement, and yet that statement cannot exclude the possibility of error, the law takes no account of particular cases, though well aware that this is not a strictly correct proceeding.
>
> (Aristotle 1955: 167)

Aristotle's solution to this problem is to find a place for equity as a higher form of justice; to allow that the law cannot regulate every- thing and to construct the 'equitable man' who will, on occasions, desist from claiming his strict legal entitlements. In general, though Aristotle has no doubt that the law should rule and that its universals are 'reason unaffected by desire' (Aristotle 1938, III 16 1287a), it is not systems of positive or humanly made law that he is considering, but rather the ideal of natural law or justice. But the problem remains the same for those who would justify human law.

It would seem from the way in which this fundamental philo- sophical problem of the general and the particular is all but ignored in our texts, that its solution has been found. In contemporary thought, the simple answer to the problem of the generality of laws and the particularity of acts and cases, is that particular cases can be relevantly the same. Of necessity this involves abstraction. That is, cases are treated as if they were the same by disregarding certain of their aspects, or to put that around the other way, by equating them according to selected criteria. This, on one way of seeing things, is already interwoven with the notion of a rule (Wittgenstein 1958: 86e; Hart 1961: 156). In another way, more consistent with Dworkin's approach, as a matter of consistency in judgment guided by the desirability of having, at one time, overall coherence between the judgments. Either way, the 'solutions', as our jurists admit, are formal. The criteria of cases being 'relevantly the same' could be skin colour or sexual preference. Judgments may consistently discriminate against women or people of colour and cohere in the construction of an overall sexist or racist world view. The difficulty then is to guarantee that the process of constructing sameness from difference is not one which systematically strips people of valued identities and ignores their wants and needs.

This difficulty becomes acute within forms of life which construct 'the individual' as the basic component of society and as the economic, political and ethical subject. Jurisprudence, then, really does have an uphill struggle. On the one hand, economic policy is to encourage people, by the promise of personalised material benefits, to break with tradition and eschew socialist ways of life, and act according to the dictates of economic self-interest. Political theory finds in the notion of civil society the realm of private, personalised right. Ethics celebrates free will and individual choice. And against all this, Jurisprudence has to persuade us that in all those situations and circumstances in which our lives are regulated by law, we are, in relevant respects, the same.

However, being in relevant respects the same can be conceived as equality. Equality avoids the insult to individualist egos which sameness as identity implies. It also carries with it a link to freedom. Between master and slave or lord and serf, equality can be imagined only from the standpoint of the subordinate or through the idea of a being whose difference from humans enables them to be thought of as a unified class. Equality between the free runs into no such conceptual problems. Moreover where people are bonded or enslaved, freedom, in the negative sense of freedom from coercion and constraint, will lie in the dissolution of such social relationships. Here then is the solution to the problem. If to be equal is to be, in relevant respects, the same, the question becomes one of saying what those relevant respects are. The task for Jurisprudence is to persuade us that law has the capacity to give an objective or objectively right or the one right answer to that question. That is its goal.

With so much in the balance, however, difficulties and differences are bound to emerge. On closer inspection we find that objectivity is a difficult notion. Within one way of seeing things, objectivity is a function of reason which is opposed to the feelings, emotions or passions of the thinking subject – subjectivity. Where the notion of objectivity is contextualised by a framework which deploys a knowing-subject–known-object dualism (such as Hart's), it is a quality of knowledge (of objects) as distinct from beliefs (of subjects). Objectivity in this context connotes independence and impartiality in judgment as distinct from interested and partisan judgment. In contemporary, neo-Aristotelian frameworks which recognise interaction between subject and object in processes of inquiry, objectivity is correct judgment. According to Finnis '[a] judgment or belief is objective if it is correct' and a 'proposition is correct if one is warranted in asserting it' on, amongst other bases, its self-evidence (Finnis 1980: 75). Subjectivity in this context has the meaning of 'arbitrary opining' but also of being 'merely relative to us (where "us" has an uncertain but restricted reference)' (Finnis 1980: 373).

Both of these notions, however, are wearing a little thin. Dualistic frameworks, certainly, are alive and well. But denial of or oblivion to inter-action between subject and object, at least in the social sciences, has not survived the anti-positivist thrust of Marxist, feminist, hermeneutical and critical theory (Outhwaite 1987). Nor, for those unconvinced by a particular proposition, is an assertion of its self-evidence much to the point. The conclusion, drawn by some hermeneutic and critical theorists is that objectivity is just a mirage. Their aspiration is to go beyond objectivism and relativism through subjectivity (Bernstein 1983). This, for Dworkin, offers the possibility of relocating the game and leaving the objectivists and their sceptical critics to carry on in a minor league. So, he argues, '... the whole issue of objectivity, which so dominates contemporary theory in these [interpretive, legal, moral] areas is a kind of fake' (Dworkin 1985: 172). But it is just a *kind* of fake, because Dworkin does want to persuade us that there is, at least within a tradition, one right answer to legal questions (Dworkin 1986: 76–8).

Differences and difficulties aside, however, it is clear that if law is seen as giving an objective or right answer to questions of how different individuals are the same, then its generalities are legitimated. They can be viewed as stating truths about its human subjects. These legal truths may be empirical truths or politico-moral truths or metaphysical truths. Their reference may be to plain facts or moral facts or brute facts. More to the point is that if that sameness or equality is formulated in terms of entitlements and obligations, then we have, within all three frameworks, a justificatory reason

111

for forcing deviant subjects to conform or pay a price for not conforming.

This formulation is not difficult to achieve. Even if, as Hart would have it, laws are empirically factual kinds of things, such as conventions, they have an intentional aspect. If, on the other hand, laws are principles of practical reason or statements of politico-moral fact discoverable through reason, then, of course, they are already matters of obligation and entitlement. What we should notice here, though, is that to have an objective or objectively right or singularly right answer to questions about what the law is on any particular issue, it is necessary to have, depending on the notion of objectivity being used, either a well-defined object of which questions are asked, or belief in universal standards of right and wrong which exist independent of human activity, or an identifiable context (a narrative, a tradition, a way of life) within which normative consistency is possible.

If Jurisprudence is to accomplish its goal, these conditions for claiming objective or right answers must be established. This is done by drawing boundaries around an area of inquiry and then justifying them. That the first text in philosophical Jurisprudence in England to be widely studied was called *The Province of Jurisprudence Determined* (Austin 1955) is in no sense accidental to the discipline. Construction of and argument about boundaries is constitutive of the game. Such justification, however, is not openly made in terms of what is necessary to show law's objectivity. The arguments take the form of argument concerning the autonomy of law. I have outlined positions taken up in this debate, and suggested that it should be understood in terms of competing strategies for legitimating law rather than as a serious inquiry into the relationships between legal, moral and political practices (above: 101ff). We are now in a position to see that the legitimating idea at work here is an idea of objectivity or rightness. Hart seeks to construct a well-defined object, 'law', by isolating legal from moral and political practices. Finnis' construction of the natural law is the construction of an independent standard of right. Dworkin supposes a context of principles – those of Anglo-American liberal legalism – with which and within which, judgments about entitlement and obligation can be more or less coherent and consistent. Once we accept his idea that law is an interpretive concept of and for a particular culture, then we accept that propositions of and about law are propositions about what law is thought to be.

No doubt they are, but by whom? According to Dworkin, by 'us' – an interpretive community comprising 'most people'. Some, not quite normal people, are outside this community. But those within it share Dworkin's abstract concept of law or, if not that, then at least his conviction that law is, like justice or integrity or fairness, a thing of value. Since law's empire is ultimately defined by attitude, Dworkin can celebrate the moral and political beliefs, of that attitude by reference to his own beliefs and commitments. Any sceptical question concerning these values and beliefs, then, merely shows us to be outside the normal interpretive community.

NAMING THE PLAYERS: THE INDIVIDUAL AND THE STATE

What, then, are we to make of an argument which is pursued as an argument about the domain of considerations relevant to knowledge and understanding of what law is, but which can be interpreted as an argument about where disciplinary boundaries should be drawn in order to show that law gives objective or right answers to questions about how different things or people are the same?

Finnis gives an important clue. A lawyer, he argues,

> ... sees the desired future social order from a professionally structured viewpoint, as a stylised manageable drama. In this drama, many characters, situations, and actions known to common sense, sociology and ethics are missing, while many other characters, relationships, and transactions known only or originally only to the lawyer are introduced.
>
> (Finnis 1980: 282–3)

We have seen in the previous chapter that one of the points of agreement between the texts is that they construct individuals as objects of knowledge of society. This point of agreement is in no way an accidental coincidence of thought. In general, in the framework of thought supposed by the common law, society is seen in terms of 'the individual' and 'the state' (or 'society' or 'community'). To go back to Finnis, the professionally structured viewpoint creates its own *dramatis personae* – legal 'persons' who are bearers of rights and duties. In doctrinal discourse legal personality is 'natural' where it is ascribed to individual human beings or 'artificial' where it is ascribed to a non-human entity or to a construction of legal thought such as a corporation. It is a peculiarity of doctrinal legal systems based wholly or partly on the common law of England, not to have a developed concept of the state as a corporate legal person. But the doctrinal maze surrounding notions of 'the Crown' and its relation to public and semi-public corporations need not concern us here. What is significant is that the legal person is an individualised bearer of rights which has general characteristics of legal personality, freedom and reason. Beyond that the legal person has the identity of the rights it holds. So we have landlords and tenants, licensors and licensees, promisors and promisees, husbands and wives, etc. As Salmond puts it:

> So far as legal theory is concerned, a person is any being whom the law regards as capable of rights and duties. Any being that is so capable is a person, whether a human being or not, and no being that is not so capable is a person, even though he be a man. Persons are the substances of which rights and duties are the attributes. It is only in this respect that persons possess juridical [i.e. legal] significance, and this is the *exclusive point of view* from which personality receives legal recognition (my emphasis).
>
> (Fitzgerald 1966: 299)

The exclusiveness of the legal point of view in the construction of the subjects of rights and obligations points to an important difference between Jurisprudence and sociology of law. Jurisprudence, though it concerns ideas of law elaborated within a background theory of society, is not seriously concerned with social theory. There are three clear and clearly different classical social theories. We have, and have had for decades, Weber and individualist theory, Durkheim and collectivist theory and Marx and relational theory. Discussion of society in philosophical Jurisprudence, however, all but ignores these theories. This kind of Jurisprudence is a representation of lawyers' ideas of law and of a correlative concept of the social. Rather than beginning from an understanding of the society of which the law is a product, Jurisprudence begins from the legal person of doctrinal legal discourse. The most it offers is a caricature of collectivist theory against the possibility that some may question the common-sense assumption that the real components of society are 'individuals' (see e.g. Dworkin 1986: 168–9; Finnis 1980: 144–50). As Salmond points out, 'all legal personality involves personification' (Fitzgerald 1966: 306) and the point of that personification is the construction of an appropriate subject for the law's ascriptions of guilt, responsibility and right, including the right to punish. Dworkin locates the personification in cultural practices having the purpose of ascribing moral agency to the state, rather than in doctrines of legal personality, but this difference between a positivist and a rights-based approach is relevant to the justification to be proposed. The personification functions similarly in both approaches.

What we have then in doctrinal legal discourse is an admittedly artificial or fictitious construction of social life – a script for a 'stylised manageable drama' within which we find legal persons as 'arbitrary creations of the law' (Fitzgerald 1966: 306). What we have in philosophical Jurisprudence is presentation of different interpretations of this drama which, however, never admit (or possibly even contemplate), the constructedness or artificiality of the person – society antinomy. Nor, it would seem, could such an admission be made. For this antinomy is essential to the story about our selves and our society which law tells. The tension between them is a structuring structure of the drama. Law, in Dworkin's words, 'holds out the promise that the deepest, most fundamental conflicts between individual and society will once, someplace, finally, become questions of justice' (Dworkin 1985: 71). If, without denying the conflicts with which Dworkin is concerned, we take the view that a very large part of the problem is just this construction of the legal, moral and political subject as the antithesis of the social, we can only say that law is promising to give up its agency in this construction: not, I think, what Dworkin intends.

The justificatory dimension of doctrinal legal argument is mainly directed to achieving consistency and coherence within doctrinal discourse. Concern for the articulation of judicial reasoning to prevalent common senses is certainly not absent but tends to come a poor second. The exclusivity of the legal point of view ensures that. Nor is that exclusivity purely epistemological. Lawyers tend to enjoy the intellectual challenge of their peculiar form of argument and to protect it from the debasement of lay understandings. Its artifices, moreover, are the stock in hand of their expert knowledge. In this, doctrinal legal knowledge is not different from other professional knowledges. But the constructions of the law are backed up by the open use of coercive force. 'Prisons are built with the stones of Law ...' (Blake 1966: 151). So it falls to Jurisprudence to undertake a justification of law in general terms: to 'position' law in relation to other normative discourses, particularly, in philosophical Jurisprudence, to moral and political philosophy, and to the prevailing common senses. It is in this light that we should view Finnis' and Dworkin's associational accounts of community. Just as the positivist notion of subject–object, as already given and mutually independent categories, has been modified to take account of developments in sociology and social theory, so an atomistic model of society no longer holds much water. By dubbing individuals as associative, the complete political community, which remains, in Jurisprudence, the nation state, can be envisaged as an extension of associational modes of everyday life – namely of family, friendship, work, and play. The difficulty that political, as distinct from personal, relations are relations between strangers (Ignatieff 1984) is not met by this move. But perhaps there is no real concern that it should be. For the law's stylised representation of social life as a dualism or interaction of 'persons' presided over by the state, just is the model within which law is thought. That it involves a misrepresentation of social life is not an available option within Jurisprudence.

It is from this closure that a negatively ideological moment of Jurisprudence takes off into fantastic arguments aimed at persuading us that society really is an aggregate of atomistic or associative individuals, and that the state really is a good idea. The embodiment and specific institutional structure of the state is not of great concern. It can be designated as comprising 'officials'. How they get to be 'officials' way back when, might be acknowledged as a matter of power, but in legal society, that power is 'authority'. For the rest it is just a matter of these atomistic or associative individuals choosing, for good reasons or bad, to undertake the benefits and burdens of public life.

I say these arguments are fantastic not, primarily, because they do not engage with serious psychological and sociological work on who we are and how we live. Lawyer philosophers are free to create an intellectual game for their own and their students' edification. It may be thought to develop skills of ever more abstract justificatory argument. Through its articulation to philosophy, it provides some insurance against the trade school idea of law schools. Further, one of the skills a lawyer needs is to be a 'quick learner'. They have to understand a wide range of specialised human activity and thought in order to be able to participate in regulation of and conflict resolution within these spheres. A subject that encourages them to bring philosophical arguments and ideas into their ambit of operational competence serves a useful purpose in this respect. I say they are fantastic because what I would see as the real value of critical reflection on one's own discipline – namely the discovery and transcendence of its limits – is ruled out by the purpose of justifying these limits. This, as we shall see in subsequent chapters, has a great deal to do with rights fetishism.

If we do not think in terms of the person–society antithesis; if we think that materially unequal social relations are generative of both our selves and our way of life; and if we take a standpoint of or for those on the down-side of these relations, then Jurisprudence becomes a discipline aimed at persuading us that our way of thinking, our conception of our selves and our society is quite erroneous. This is a point at which people who do not experience themselves as conforming to stereotypes of race, gender and class will find, in Jurisprudence, a paradigmatic instance of the discursive repression of their own senses of identity. And where added to that, we are told that we ought to accept and dignify the idea of law's being urged on us by this discipline, then its claims really do appear as fantastic. We are being asked to value that which denies the very point of our own struggle to speak and to find political community with those who share that struggle!

If we can get through the confusion, the feelings of stupidity and incompetence that being an object of this attack brings, it becomes clear that the closure in question is made precisely against the idea that social relations are generative of selves and societies; so against analysis of English, Australian and American society as constituted by materially unequal social relations; so against a theoretically useful conception of ideology; and so ultimately against the very idea of standpoint and the standpoint relativity of knowledge. Clearly it is a significant move and we must look at it more closely in order to discover its power.

The *dramatis persona*, Individual, may be represented, as by Hart, as an atomistic being which connects itself with others via norms of reason or voluntary contracts, or as by Finnis and Dworkin, as an associative being whose good is dependent on its finding its way into, or helping to construct, a 'true community'. Like the debate about autonomy, however, this debate has no sociological or psychological significance. It is a debate about what characteristics should be ascribed to the abstract idea of the individual in order to legitimise the state. We should be quite clear about the questions that can be asked regarding the legitimacy of the state. One can question *whether* the state is legitimate. Alternatively one can assume that it is legitimate and ask *why* it is legitimate. It is the latter question with which Jurisprudence is concerned. The difference between these two kinds of inquiry is obscured, though in different ways, by both positivist and natural law and rights based theories. There is nothing wrong with making an assumption that the state is legitimate for the purpose of constructing a theory of its legitimacy in competition with others who make the same assumption. All theoretical arguments make assumptions and Jurisprudence, of course, is no exception. The trouble is a subtle shift whereby theories of legitimacy get to be articulated to truth claims about society and self.

The polarised view of what is the case on which adversarial modes of argument rely, is an important mechanism of this shift. Polarisation divides things into two exclusive and exhaustive categories so that if something can be shown not to fall within one category it follows that it falls within the other (Taylor 1983: 106ff). It is a technique deeply embedded in metaphysics, in logic and in legal argument. An accused is guilty or not guilty; a claim is valid or invalid. The lawyer, by and large, argues one of these cases, from an assumption of its truth. The technique is effective for the argumentative resolution of a dispute. What is presupposed though, if the resolution is considered in terms of truth finding, is that the polarised classification of possibilities is adequate to the actualities of the case.

In the context of legal argument, after judgment is given, the situation changes and it is from this change that Jurisprudence can draw most. Whether or not the presupposition was initially, descriptively adequate, after judgment there is a more concrete sense in which the accused is guilty or not guilty, the plaintiff's claim is valid or invalid. The coercive enforcement of a judgment realises these abstract notions. It articulates legal meaning to the practical activity of daily life. People go to gaol, are fined, lose their jobs, businesses and farms. Coercive enforcement is absent from Jurisprudence but Dworkin's idea of constructive interpretation is compatible with it. Jurisprudence has the task of imposing meaning on legal practices; of making the liberal lawyer's conviction that the rule of law legitimises the coercive exercise of power by the state, 'truth'. Discursive, as distinct from coercive, power is relied on to accomplish this. It is deployed along multiple lines of culture and

practice. On the one hand the competitive, as distinct from contradictory, character of arguments in Jurisprudence ensures engaged
argument only with those who share the assumption of legitimacy.
Given the nature of theoretical argument this might be inevitable.
But it is articulated to the hierarchical organisation of and within
tertiary institutions, which, while necessarily part of such institutions within societies structured by unequal social relations, is in no
way inevitable. The consequence is an elite fraternity of jurists,
competing with each other, but combining to marginalise those
who do not share their assumption of legitimacy.[1] On the other
hand, and quite independent of Jurisprudence, it is the case that
compliance with the rule of law does place constraints on the
arbitrary exercise of political power (Thompson 1975). Separate
again, there is the never-ending bombardment of right-wing law-
and-order ideology (Belsey 1986). These factors give plausibility to
theories of the legitimacy of the state and we lose sight of the
presupposition from which the whole debate takes off: the person–
society antithesis as a polarity adequate to our social reality.

Jurisprudence adds another characteristic to the freedom and
reason of the legal person – self-interest. The individual of Jurisprudence 'naturally' prefers itself and its own to others. What must
be kept in mind is that the individual is a category of thought. If
one works with this category it can be invested with whatever
characteristics one likes. It is disembodied and de-contextualised
and has virtually nothing to do with flesh-and-blood people living
within particular social relations and having historically and psy-
chologically concrete identities. It is thus no counter to this mode
of thought to invest the individual with the characteristic of altruism. That is merely a continuation of the same kind of argument.
The ideological significance of self-interest is that the idea of the
state or society which is talked about in Jurisprudence is formed by
the idea of the individual. It is its antithesis or other. The ways in
which historically and geographically specific social relations of
economic production and political power constitute and distribute
authority, the institutions of social regulation and control which
arise, the configuration and articulation of these institutions to
social practices of seemingly different kinds – health, education,
social welfare and entertainment – are all absent. As the counterpart
of the individual, the state's assumed artificiality, against the assumed reality of 'individual human beings', has the consequence
that it lacks the 'natural' characteristic of self-interest. So it has the

capacity for neutrality. It holds a monopoly on the use of coercive force and so has the capacity to be hostile to freedom. Yet as the community of self-interested individuals it is their moral *alter ego*.

There are three things which link this representation of society or the state to actuality. The first is the undeniable fact that physically unique, flesh-and-blood bodies are observable and that society, as a unitary thing, is not. The second is the equally undeniable fact that law licenses and requires coercion and that police and prison officers and bailiffs and executioners have official status to use physical force. The third is that legal practices seek to make their presuppositions true, to constitute people and the social order in their own images, and they are not without effectivity. To some extent, they succeed. Where social science has taken account of ideological frameworks, it has given the simple fact of the separateness and observability of human bodies no greater weight than a physicist or chemist, in analysis of the physical and chemical structure of an iron bar, will give to the observed solidity of a physical object. But Jurisprudence is not social science. Its point is not to find things out about our selves and our way of life. It is to supplement the coercive and discursive imposition of doctrinal representations. In this endeavour it is assisted by the inevitable coherence between mainstream theories of the economic, political and moral aspects of our social reality and their popular dissemination in media, advertising and education. We are so used to, so imbued with, the person or individual–society couple, that bodies are transformed into 'individuals' on sight.

It is no more sensible to deny the reality of flesh-and-blood bodies than it is to deny the licensed use of physical force on them. The important point is that there is no way in which notions of the self, the person, the individual are any less complex than those of society. The characterisation of individuals as self-interested is not morally or politically reprehensible. It is simply vacuous – an intellectual space to be filled by a whole gambit of techniques aimed at getting people to conform their practical activity and their thought to the reproduction of existing social relations. As Naomi Scheman puts it:

> [The] largely unquestioned assumption, that the objects of psychology – emotions, beliefs, intentions, virtues and vices – attach to us singly (no matter how socially we may acquire them) is ... a piece of ideology. It is not a natural fact, and

the ways in which it permeates our social institutions, our lives and our senses of ourselves are not unalterable. It is deeply useful in the maintenance of capitalist and patriarchal society and deeply embedded in our notions of liberation, freedom and equality.

(Scheman 1983: 226)

There will always be a gap when, through thought and language, we refer to ourselves and our world. My references to physical environment and practical activity, to social relations and concrete individual identities, are not *as ideas* any less abstract than ideas of the individual and the social to be found in Jurisprudence. This is not the point. The telling point against the constructions of Jurisprudence is that there is nothing in the observable actuality of flesh-and-blood human bodies which grounds the claim that free and equal individuals constitute a bottom line for knowledge of what society is.

FINDING AN UMPIRE: RULES OR PRINCIPLES AS OBJECTS OF LEGAL KNOWLEDGE AND AS OBJECTS OF KNOWLEDGE OF LAW

Arguments are never conclusive of an issue. Jurisprudence has an answer to the point just raised and it is predictably urbane. What has been missed out of course is law – or rather the idea of law as rules or principles or the reason of rights. The assumption that law is a matter, ultimately, of norms is complementary to the assumption that society is a matter, ultimately, of atomistic or associative individuals. In that sense, the legal equation is Individual + Norm = Society.

In its own terms this equation makes sense. Something has to bind our atomistic or associative individuals together to form that unified, homogeneous, but secondary object called 'society'. If these individuals are all essentially self-interested in what seems to be the intended sense, they are bound to come into conflict. An umpire has to be found and that umpire has to have knowledge of something that is other than self-interest – some 'higher form' of rationality which can be recognised by the good and enforced against the recalcitrant. That is legal, moral or political principle.

The problem here is not one of incoherence. It is one of value.

121

This way of looking at ourselves and our society makes sense to Hart and Finnis and Dworkin and there is a perfectly good reason for that. Capitalist society is individualistic in every way – from its economic mode of production to its moral and political philosophy. Furthermore it is not very hard to see that the 'higher form' of rationality being urged on us is the rationality of empowered white men who do see themselves as superior to others and who like to explain that superiority in terms of the power of their intellects. Outsiders to this interpretive community, however, if they are not content to bear with its devaluation of them, are bound to question its explanations and constructions. The encouraging thing here is the extent to which such questioning is taking place, the diversity of questions being asked and of ways of asking them. There are questions about whether and how we should draw this all together. For the moment, however, I want just to contribute to these challenges by concentrating on the very specific question of how, in Jurisprudence, the norm is constructed as the object of knowledge of law, and then to look at the consequences of this construction.

I should first, however, explain the general point of this questioning in order to avoid misunderstanding. I do not suggest that law is not normative and I do not suggest that it does not involve norms. The argument is rather that norms are not non-reducible entities – expressions of some natural law or natural necessity – that together with another non-reducible entity, the individual, make up society. Law is normative and it involves rules, principles and modes of practical reasoning. Furthermore, doctrinal legal knowledge is about norms or normative propositions. But these norms, like other phenomena of social practices and relations, can be explained in terms of social practices and relations.

What seems to happen, roughly, is this. Doctrinal legal discourse is a dogmatic discourse – not in the pejorative sense of dogmatic, but in a more technical sense. That is to say, it is a discourse based on premises that are known *a priori* or laid down by authority. In either case the discourse rests on stipulated, unquestionable premises. Doctrinal legal knowledge is knowledge of rules or principles derived from these premises and of the ways in which they can be used in argument. In philosophical Jurisprudence, these objects of doctrinal legal knowledge are turned into objects of knowledge of law, that is, of a very abstract, unitary idea of law. The shift is subtle but important.

Doctrinal legal questioning asks what is *the* law on this or that issue, and answers these questions by the formulation of propositions of law which are propositions about rules or principles, that is, propositions about norms. Jurisprudence, as general theory of law, asks 'What is law?', but asks it from within an assumption that answers, ultimately, have to be about norms. To put that around another way, the assumption is that the normative form of answers to particular doctrinal legal questions stems, as a matter of logical necessity, from the normative form of the concept of law. Or the inference may be made in the other direction: the normative form of the concept of law may be abstracted from the doctrinal rules and principles. Or perhaps the logic goes both ways. Such questions are significant within the schools but they need not concern us here.

The normative form of a concept of law is a construct of thought; an historical and cultural variable. I suggest that norms become objects of knowledge of law as a consequence of individuals' being constituted as objects of knowledge of society. Both objects of knowledge are discursive products and in both cases they are active constituents in a way of understanding ourselves and our society that is pressed on us in law and in Jurisprudence. My argument against this understanding has two dimensions: first, that accepting norms as the object of knowledge of law gives privilege to lawyers' ideas of law: second, that justificatory arguments in Jurisprudence for this privileging are negatively ideological. In tandem with the construction of the individual as the object of knowledge of the social they are close to the heart of rights fetishism.

I have already explained that the idea of an object of knowledge which I am using (above: 92ff) is an idea of what a particular form of knowledge is about – of what we must know about in order to explain the structure and dynamics of a more complex phenomenon. I have also explained the notion of a norm as being an action-guiding thing – a rule, or principle, or standard or idea of right. A norm will always be a product of thought formulating an idea of what people *ought* to do from what is in actuality done or not done. Part of this notion of ought is an intention, held by whoever affirms the norm, to regulate their own or others' behaviour by discursive use of it. This intention is what is referred to by Hart and Finnis as the internal aspect of rules and what is taken by Dworkin to be the intention, in his expanded sense, of the practice of legal argument.

How any particular idea of what ought to be done is put together will depend on the method of reasoning being used. It may be supposed that all norms are instrumental in the sense that they are formulated as means of achieving a specified end. Within this approach, the specified end may be thought to be contingently or necessarily desired and, in the latter case, there will be differing accounts of the modality of necessity. It may be that the end in question is defined in terms of its being desired by subjects of the norm: classically, a definition of the good as that to which all things aim (Aristotle 1955: 25). Alternatively, it may be said that as a matter of observable but contingent fact, it is the case that all X desire Y; in Hart, for example, the observation that humans aim for survival (Hart 1961: 188). In other conceptions of practical reasoning, it may be supposed that some norms are categorical – that they give a form of thought which must be included in the conceptual apparatus of practical reason – 'the principle of a will which of itself conforms to reason' (Kant 1909: 31). The classical example of this idea is Kant's categorical imperative of practical reason: 'Act as if the maxim of thy action were to become by thy will a universal law of nature' (Kant 1909: 39).

Whether instrumentally or categorically conceived, a norm has qualities or characteristics of generality and bindingness. If formulated prescriptively its intentional content is to bind all those who are supposed to be subjects of it. If it is formulated propositionally, it states a reason for acting or not acting in a particular way which claims to hold good for everyone with the capacity for that action. They, it may be said, are subject to it. The quality of bindingness is similarly implicit in the notion. This quality, in the legal norm, gives it a capacity to replace fact with fiction, to close the door on further inquiry and so to be that which we cannot go beyond in our legal understanding. [2] Salmond again can be relied on for an unambiguous statement of this point.

> Even to [purely factual] questions the law will, on occasion supply predetermined and authoritative answers. The law does not scruple, if need be, to say that the fact must be deemed to be such and such, whether it be so in truth or not. The law is the theory of things, as received and acted upon within the courts of justice, and this may or may not conform to the reality of things outside. The eye of the law does not infallibly see things as they are. Partly by deliberate design and partly by the errors and accidents of historical

development, law and fact, legal theory and the truth of things may fail in complete coincidence. We have ever to distinguish that which exists in deed and in truth from that which exists in law.

(Fitzgerald 1966: 72–3)

The combination of generality and bindingness in the legal norm has the consequence of the exclusion of all relativity, or to put that another way, makes the legal norm into an absolute in the determination of legal meaning. Law's fictions become absolute truths for everyone who wishes to understand the legal point of view. An example best illustrates this point. It is not uncommon to find statutory provisions which deem something to be the case. Someone may refuse to sign conditions imposed by an official on his or her release on bail. Nonetheless, on completion by an official of specified formalities or procedures, that person can be deemed to have accepted them. The result is that quite different actions can have the same meaning in law. One person voluntarily signs the bail undertaking, fully understanding what he or she is doing. The other makes the most vigorous protest and refuses to sign. The result, mediated by the deeming provision, is the same. On breach of the bail condition, each person has committed the same offence. Legal norms, in the cognisance of courts of law, have the capacity to absolutely determine what is the case and so make all other considerations irrelevant. Kelsen's way of putting this is to say that the norm gives the *objective meaning* of the actions (Kelsen 1970: 2ff). That is another way of saying that the norm is, as a determinant of legal meaning, an absolute.

This does not deny the interpretability of legal norms or the significant latitude involved in their application to the facts of a particular case. But the interpretation of norms concerns their content – what action they require or permit, by whom, and in what conditions and circumstances – as distinct from their way of functioning in doctrinal legal discourse. Dworkin's extension of the interpretability of legal norms to the idea of law as an interpretive concept, relies on the interaction between what he calls the grounds and force of law. This recognises the fact that competing norms may be appealed to in legal argument and that resolution of this competition involves judgment as to the weight or force of different arguments. It allows a broader context of relevant considerations, but does not otherwise qualify the point being made: that once it has been spoken, law's truth is exclusive of all other truths. That makes it look as if the norm has some ontological primacy and conceals the fact that law's truths take precedence over others, in the end, by the use of physical coercion.

One of the main arguments in Jurisprudence, if not *the* main argument, is argument about the grounds of law. Are they rules of a particular pedigree, principles of a way of life, or reasons within a teleology? These arguments parallel the interpretive arguments about the content, and in Dworkin's case, the content and force of legal norms. They are again arguments between the schools, part of the play of the Jurisprudence game. What is significant about them, in this context, is that they take place within the assumption that the grounds of law are norms of some kind. As I have said, we need not doubt that the grounds of a legal judgment are norms or normative propositions. But there is a shift here from legal judgment to law; from assumptions appropriate to answering questions about what the law is, to those appropriate to answering the general question 'What is law?'. This shift takes place because argument in Jurisprudence, if not wholly continuous with doctrinal legal argument, is compatible with it. It is the discursive constitution of the norm as the object of doctrinal legal knowledge which, as Salmond notes, allows 'legal theory and the truth of things' to 'fail in complete coincidence'. The constitution of the norm as the object of knowledge of law in Jurisprudence has the same consequence. In both cases it carries arguments away from the understanding of those without legal training. For within these arguments truth acquires a new meaning, a legal meaning that may be radically different from its meaning for non-professionals.

I have been tracing this construction of meaning at the very abstract level of argumentative assumptions and the qualities of the legal norm. When we step into a court-room we find its embodiment and materiality. It is like stepping into another world – a world whose physical dimensions and psychological mechanisms support the displacement of non-professional perceptions and understandings. The judge or magistrate rules from an elevated roost; is addressed by professionals within an etiquette of mannered servility; is backed up with strategically placed, uniformed men and women – security and police; not so much open show of those trained for physical violence as to interrupt the mood of judicious calm; not so little as to let anyone doubt the steel fist within the velvet glove. And while, at one level, use of the vernacular language and admission of the public tells those outside the court-room fraternity that these courts are open to all, are courts of and for a democratic society, they are open only on strict terms of professional control.

It is a strategy of this control to insist that the non-professional cannot comprehend the argument; that norms as the objects of doctrinal legal knowledge are comprehensible only within a priesthood. Yet the technical and conceptual specificity of legal doctrine is not impenetrable without professional legal training. The stronger mechanism of exclusion is the profession's denial of that point – a denial which, against the non-lawyer who has taken the time and effort to understand legal argument, is a play of power. In terms of the kinds of argument used, legal argument depends heavily on the argument from authority. Who or what are 'authorities' is itself a doctrinal question. Sociologically, professional control over law's truth is much enhanced by making it into truth about the meaning and existence of norms over whose formulation and interpretation the profession has an institutionalised monopoly.

Doctrinal legal discourse may not be different from other discourses in constituting its own authoritative spokespersons. That is not the point being made. The point being made is that this exercise of self-legitimising power reveals the space between law and laws. The negatively ideological moment in Jurisprudence begins with the closure of that space. From a legal point of view, norms are the objects of knowledge of law *qua* legal doctrine. To infer from that, however, that norms are the object of knowledge of a social theory of what law is, supposes that what ought to be meant or understood by 'law' is what lawyers mean or understand by 'law'. Now this, precisely, is a constitutive assumption of Hart's and Finnis' Jurisprudence. It closes the gap between law and laws but it is vulnerable to several objections.

First, as the discipline itself attests, there is no such shared meaning. Different lawyers mean different things by 'law' and argue about these meanings in the discipline of Jurisprudence. We cannot even say that there is a shared meaning at the very abstract level of law as being a matter of norms. Some American Legal Realists argued that law should be understood in terms of the behaviour of officials (Llewellyn 1962). Dworkin makes a distinction between concept and conception which seems designed to patch this over. He argues for a shared concept (given in terms of 'the most abstract and fundamental point of legal practice' which 'our discussions ... by and large assume' (Dworkin 1986: 93)) and a plurality of competitive conceptions. But he goes to some pains to preface this move with a disclaimer. Neither jurisprudence nor his own arguments depend on there being such a shared concept. To think that it does is to fall prey to 'semantic sting' and to neglect the fact that law is an interpretive concept.

This objection can be met by reformulating the assumption to be that what ought to be meant by 'law' is what lawyers *ought* to mean by 'law'. This moves Jurisprudence to Dworkin's idea of it as constructive interpretation. It invests the discipline with a hortatory quality which is consistent with its claim to be a socially valuable one. But as it stands, it does not constitute norms as the object of knowledge of law. It is still open to say that law ought to be understood in terms other than doctrinal legal terms; for example in sociological or historical or behaviouristic terms. To exclude this possibility it must be argued that Jurisprudence, as social theory of law, must be written, not merely with reference to, but from, the internal point of view; that is, from the understanding of '*every* actor in the practice ... that what it permits or requires depends on the *truth* of certain propositions that are given sense only by and within the practice' (my emphasis) (Dworkin 1986: 13).

Such argument, however, though it answers the first objection to Hart's and Finnis' assumption, has more trouble with a second one. This is that whatever form the assumption takes, it unjustifiably privileges professional understandings of what law is. Hart and Finnis attempt to meet this objection by an objectivist epistemology which constructs an observational distance between the legal or internal point of view and the viewpoint of the philosopher theorist. Hart claims the perspective of the disinterested philosopher of ordinary language who simply describes what is the case. Finnis aspires, through reflective equilibrium, to the universal viewpoint – an Archimedean point which has the potential for completeness. They can, of course, *say* that they are not privileging lawyers' ideas of law; merely describing what law is or using a descriptively adequate framework for knowing what it is. Equally obviously we can be unmoved by such claims. On the other hand, Dworkin's approach, in giving up any pretension of a distanced objectivity, runs into scepticism about the propriety of writing a social theory of law from a dogmatic point of view.

Such scepticism has both philosophical and sociological warrant. Philosophically the argument returns us to scholasticism. Dworkin's devotion to the scholastic adage 'Where there is a contradiction, draw a distinction' is well attested (Hutchinson 1987), and the humanist critique of scholasticism for its excessively abstract subject matter, futile logic chopping and excessive reliance on authority (Flew 1984: 319) may also be thought appropriate. Without doubt, contemporary philosophy is revising the humanist judgment on scholasticism in light of the Enlightenment philosophers' own form of dogmatism – the belief that philosophy could provide certain foundations of knowledge (Rorty 1980), as well as the technical philosophical sophistication of medieval philosophy (Flew 1984: 315–19). That is to be welcomed. But if we are being offered a New Scholasticism by empowered, white men who claim truth in the sense of their own professional discipline for themselves, then the response can only be that this is nothing new.

Sociologically, lawyers are institutionally a well-defined social group and, in the countries of which I write, a visible one. The possibility that lawyers' understandings of law may be partial to their own interests is not one which, given the fact that lawyers draw significant benefits from the legal system, is remote. It is moreover a possibility that is reinforced for a private legal profession by construction of the individual as essentially and justifiably self-interested.

We shall return to Dworkin's response to scepticism in the final section of this chapter. The points made here are that Jurisprudential closure of the space between law and laws privileges lawyers' ideas of law and that there are reasons to be sceptical of this privilege. However this is regarded by non-legal professionals who take up a standpoint for empowered classes, it is unjustified from the point of view of subordinated groups and classes if their subordination is reproduced in legal relations by legal practices and institutions. Jurisprudence comes in here to assert law's innocence; to deny its complicity in racist and sexist attitudes and practices and to claim its detachment from the reproduction of exploitative class relations. This is a point at which Jurisprudence as ideology in both a neutral and a negative sense becomes evident. For the Jurisprudential defence of law's innocence requires more than the constitution of the norm as object of knowledge of law. We need also to be persuaded that these norms are values or are valuable. St Augustine's aphorism 'An unjust law is not a law' may be seen as an old lemon by Dworkin, an absurdity by Hart, and an embarrassment by Finnis. It gives, however, simple expression to this necessity of and for Jurisprudential thought. The threatening instance of the unjust law haunts the juristic project of showing law's objectivity or objective rightness or its capacity to deliver the one right answer. The contemporary way with it brings us to the internal point of view.

Discovery of the internal point of view, though trumpeted as a great advance in the sophistication of contemporary Jurisprudential method (Finnis 1980: 6ff; MacCormick 1981: 32), was a point of which the Soviet jurist, E. B. Pashukanis was aware in the 1920s (Pashukanis 1978: 64, 147; below: 182ff). Doctrinal legal discourse is a closed discourse that is part of our social reality. To understand it we must indeed take a point of view internal to it. To use my earlier example, the person who is told that she or he has 'accepted' bail conditions, having categorically refused to accept them, can make sense of this only by understanding the intention of the deeming provision and its acceptance as an absolute determinant of what is the case by magistrates and police.

Thus understanding law requires awareness of a point or points of view from which it is right that legal norms be enforced or accepted as determinants of what is the case. It does *not* require the justification of this point of view. Yet that is the further step taken in Jurisprudence and is, I suggest, a critical point at which the discipline becomes negatively ideological. The internal point of view is converted into comprehension of an absolute of reality or reason. One of the paths taken is to argue that the internal point of view is a moral point of view. Another is to say that its intentionality is not that of self-interested individuals but is the intentionality of the practice itself. Another is to say it is the point of view from which the real (conventional) existence of the internal aspect of rules (their intentionality) is observable. In each case, what is known from this point of view is the norm as an objective standard of right.

There is no recognition in these debates of there being a world of practical activity structured by unequal relations of wealth and power, which will at least assert its influence on the actual effect and concrete meaning of legal norms, and which can ground explanation of the very phenomenon of doctrinal legal discourse. That failure of recognition may be a consequence of blindness engendered by an epistemology which claims certain foundations for its knowledge, or it may be conscious participation in a discursive exercise of power. In either case, the claim in Jurisprudence is to know law's truth and to know that it is about norms in the first place and physical coercion, if at all, only as licensed or required by such norms.

If we accept the explanation and justification of coercion in terms of the disembodied intentionality of the norm and the convictions of the internal point of view, we lose sight of the symbiosis between ideological means and physical means of getting people to act in particular ways. And if we lose sight of that, I believe we lose sight of an aspect of our social reality which enables us to critically reflect on the value of law. If society is conceived as an aggregate of self-interested, individuated human beings (fact) then social being, as being *for others*, can only be conceived in terms of rule following or the inter-subjective sharing of principle (value). What follows from this overall misconception is an opposition of fact and value which, however it is rationalised, will re-appear as an opposition of objectivity and subjectivity or, putting old wine into a new bottle, of externality and internality.

We shall examine what we are encouraged to miss by this justificatory dimension of Jurisprudence in terms of rights fetishism later. However, it might help to articulate this analysis of the legal construction of objectivity to other understandings, to point out that there is a very close parallel between what I am doing in this chapter and the feminist and anti-racist projects of deconstructing gender and racial stereotypes. In considering the construction of the individual in Jurisprudence, we came upon a point at which the discursive repression of identity was evident. The stereotype is both a product and a producer of that repression. In the same way, the norm as the object of knowledge of law is part of an ideology that denies and distorts our relational being; reduces the materiality and liveliness of connectedness to a lifeless abstraction of oughtness. Projects of deconstructing gender and racial stereotypes emerge within a practice of reclaiming a suppressed personal and political identity. They involve rethinking questions of value and values within a social reality whose sex–gender relations devalue women and whose race relations devalue people of colour. They involve, if we are members of an oppressing race, struggling to come to terms with the gap between awareness and rejection of racism and experiencing it as a member of an oppressed race.[3] So here, theoretical deconstruction of the norm as the object of knowledge of law emerges within the practical context of resisting legal and moral obligations imposed on us by those with whom we do not share a standpoint. It is, indeed, a taking of the law into our own hands.

UNRESOLVED ISSUES: FUZZY RULES, GAPS AND THE ONE RIGHT ANSWER

The most sustained attempt in legal theory to deconstruct the norm as the object of knowledge of law was made by the Soviet jurist E. B. Pashukanis. Adhering very closely to Marx's occasional comments on law and to the method of analysis in the social sciences which Marx proposed in the Introduction to the *Grundrisse*, Pashukanis argued that the form of the legal norm was a derivation from the practice of commodity exchange. Its quality of universality, he argued, inhered in the reduction of its subjects to commodity owners – free and equal in their capacity and desire to exchange their goods. Its acceptance within legal thought as an absolute, as the ground of law and the source of legal personality, involved a pre-supposition of a norm-setting authority. Against this pre-supposition, Pashukanis argued that the political or norm-setting authority of the bourgeoisie is constituted by capitalist relations of production. The bourgeoisie, he argued, first acquired economic power within a transformation of feudal relations of production. Thereafter, law, the state and rationalist forms of morality emerged as political forms of their empowerment.

Pashukanis is, I think, greatly under-estimated as a legal theorist. If the use to which I put his text revises it in many ways, that should not occlude the debt this work owes to his – particularly on the very fundamental issues of grasping social relations as the grounds of law, and of making an analogy between commodity and rights fetishism. Here, I want to take up his more specific observation that consideration of the norm as the object of knowledge of law presupposes a norm-setting authority.

This presupposed norm-setting authority is God or practical reasonableness in Finnis, Anglo-American liberal legal culture in Dworkin, and the practices of empowered British men in Hart. Any of these notions is well enough articulated to other social practices to gain the acceptance of some. But equally, none is uncontentious. In Jurisprudence, the pre-supposition of a norm-setting authority involves slippage from the (relatively) uncontroversial proposition that norms of some kind are the objects of doctrinal legal knowledge, to the proposition that norms are the object of knowledge of law and justification of the consequent privilege given to lawyers' ideas of law. The institutional power of the profession to impose its understandings of law on other understandings is represented as the expert or scholarly authority of the lawyer–author to 'know' law. Here too there are factors militating for and against acceptance of this move. On the one hand the division of mental and manual labour, and the valorisation of mental labour that occurs within this division, supports the expert's claim to authority. Against this, the benefits which lawyers take from the legal system, when set against problems of access and alienation, engender scepticism.

If Dworkin becomes focal to our discussion of these unresolved issues in Jurisprudence, it is because his is the latest attempt to quell them and to do so in a climate increasingly sceptical of expert knowledges and of the separation of people from each other and their environment. Some change in the agenda of Jurisprudence is necessary because the task of justifying law and, as part of that, of constructing look-new theories of the legitimacy of the state and the general moral or political obligation to obey the law, has become more difficult.

Politically, these difficulties come in the form of strong feminist, anti-racist and environmentalist movements which, where they are not contained by liberal ideology, tend to favour a relational or process social theory. The power of relational social theory was weakened in its original Marxian form by a deficient sociology of basic social relations (below: 179). Today, there is an increased awareness of solidarity within groups on the down-side of sex–gender and race relations and between environmentalists, which has enabled feminist, anti-racist and environmentalist philosophy and social theory to invest relational theory with hitherto missing dimensions. This, together with the economic reality of class in a decade which, in England, Australia and America has seen a reversal in direction of wealth distribution, are the real forces of scepticism of law's objectivity and innocence with which Jurisprudence has to contend.

Law as the impartial arbiter between free and equal individuals and the guarantee of maximised individual liberty is the ideological message that has to be got across. The scepticism of this message that is most troubling is that which questions the impartiality. Perhaps this is because there is less truth in this claim than in the others. However that may be, scepticism of the impartiality of law can be focused either on the existence and effectivity of rules as reasonably certain determinants of legal consequences (judgments, transactional security, property entitlement, etc.) or it may be focused on the neutrality of any such standards. The 'rule-scepticism' of the American Legal Realists illustrates scepticism of the first focus (Llewellyn 1962). The critique of 'liberal legalism' in Critical Legal Theory illustrates the second (Kairys 1982; Fitzpatrick and Hunt 1987).

Jurisprudential strategies for coping with scepticism differ although, as we have seen, they all rely at bottom on constituting the norm as the object of knowledge of law. While classical natural law theory rules scepticism out by asserting it to be self-evidently untrue, positivist and rights-based theories try more subtle approaches. Thus having 'proved' his basic goods and basic principles of practical reasonableness Finnis does not bother too much more with scepticism. The pacification of the rule sceptic, however, forms a major part of Hart's enterprise. Dworkin's celebration of liberal legalism parallels Finnis' confidence in his own truths. He is culturalist rather than naturalist in his openly acknowledged affiliations. Additionally, however, he is dissatisfied with Hart's job on rule scepticism and has to transcend conventionalism and pragmatism to properly fortify law's empire. Nonetheless, what shows through these diverse strategies is that fuzzy rules and gaps (no-rules) are worrying chinks in juridical exclusion of social reality that have to be closed by strong argument for one right answer. In the terms of the debate in Jurisprudence, Hart's and Finnis' admissions of gaps in the law and that, on the margins, judges do have discretion in a strong sense to change or make the law, have to be denied.

Dworkin, whilst he ignores or is unaware of the political forces I have identified as necessitating this denial, acknowledges two arguments within his own political horizons as motivating his search for the one right answer. Ideological worlds cannot but be structured by reality. These arguments might be said to come respectively from the right and the left of liberal thought. The first is the conservative argument from democracy made, most commonly, in the context of debate on the United States Supreme Court's power of judicial review of legislation: judges are unelected and unaccountable officials who have, within a democratic society, no mandate to make or change the law. Judges, so this argument goes, derogate from the rule of law, if in their decision making they do other than adhere strictly to the law as it is (Dworkin 1986: 6ff; 1985: 33). The second argument, as made by J. A. G. Griffiths

(1985), debunks British rhetoric of the independence of the judiciary from political processes, by considering the class nature of the judiciary and claiming that unacknowledged policy judgements explain the outcome of cases with obvious political consequences (Dworkin 1985: 10).

Against both arguments Dworkin argues that judges, as princes of an empire which acknowledges the justice in minority claims to dissent from majoritarian rule, do and should decide cases on grounds of politico-moral principle (as distinct from policy). Justice, in this argument, comes in the form of individual rights to be treated as equals by government. This means, for Dworkin, that, within limits, government should be neutral as between conceptions of the good life and should sustain market allocation of material goods subject to intervention to correct 'various differences of initial advantage, luck and inherent capacity' (Dworkin 1985: 207).

Dworkin's strongest fire is aimed at rule-based theories of law for lending credence to these arguments. That view, he thinks, is ultimately responsible for both right and left deviations in liberalism: for the idea that judicial review is undemocratic *and* for the idea that there is no law, only policy-based decision making. It is responsible for the first error of thought because, if law is thought to be a matter of rules, then in hard cases, judges must be exercising discretion rather than saying what the parties' rights are. It is responsible for the second because, when people who have been taught to think of law as a matter of rules discover that in reality it is not, then they become cynics and declare there is no law, only policy. Law as integrity gives the answer to both heresies. Rights, as facts of normative consistency within a culture, are the true grounds of the law which judges neither find nor make but say. They are there within the politico-moral principles constitutive of a liberal conception of true community.

This loses some of its mystery if we take account of politico-moral principles as being reasons of a particular kind. They are reasons which justify action or decision, the justification taking the form of an assertion that the action or decision is consistent with, or required by, an ideal of a way of life. Dworkin's Jurisprudence of rights or principles is, in other words, a Jurisprudence of reasons (Schauer 1987). It is, I suggest, an attempt to avoid the problem of deciding particular cases by general rules with which we began this chapter. It is a return to equity which is parallelled in doctrinal developments (Waters 1988). Reasons of principle are abstract enough to allow interpretive flexibility and yet, in a complex and pluralistic society, numerous enough for the fabrication of an argumentative discourse. The argument takes place within a context of institutionalised practices of which rule-making is one. This context can and does give some certainty to law's essence. When and where it does depends on attitude.

Dworkin's strategy, then, is to give up the attempt to show the objectivity of legal norms from the position of the disinterested observer and to write a social theory of law which constructs an entire narrative of social life from a legal point of view. He writes, in that sense, not a social theory of law but a legal theory of society. Deciding which cases are alike and which cases are different is the principal activity of life in law's empire. The objectivity of criteria for these decisions then becomes the objective or purpose of this activity. Consequently, sceptical questions about the grounds or value (impartiality) of law, like sceptical questions about the general political obligation to obey the law, are re-located. Political obligation of all citizens of the true communities of the United States of America and Great Britain to obey the law is now seen as associative and not different in kind to personal obligations and friendship and family. It cannot then, Dworkin tells us, be denied without also denying these personal associative obligations (Dworkin 1986: 207; Hunt and Kerruish 1991). To put that another way, those who deny the existence of a general political obligation to obey the law are told by Dworkin that they carry a burden of proving that they are not also unreliable friends, irresponsible fathers and bad mothers! The relocated versions of scepticism are first scepticism as to the validity of his narrative as a representation of social life (external scepticism), and secondly scepticism as to there being, in principle, one right answer to hard cases (internal scepticism) (Dworkin 1986: 78–85, 266–7). The latter form is the more threatening, for if there is not one right answer, then life in law's empire loses its purpose.

Since Dworkin considers that any political theory is 'entitled – indeed obliged – to claim truth for itself, and so exempt itself from any scepticism it endorses' (Dworkin 1985: 350), one would hardly expect him to encounter great difficulties with either form of scepticism. Truth claims are easily made. The real problem will be powering them through; and why should Dworkin worry about that? He knows and lives the good life, does not seek to impose it on (extend it to)? others, but is ever willing to display his wares in the market of ideas and advertise their virtues in the nearby forum. Citizens are free to listen and buy if they choose. If they are too dumb or too deaf or too poor to do so, that is not Dworkin's problem. The level of mutual concern for fellow citizens, should not, in his view, reach 'unattractive levels' of caring as much for them as for himself, his family and his friends (Dworkin 1986: 215).

There is not, I think, much interest in refutations of scepticism as to law's objectivity and impartiality that rest on a claim to be entitled to believe that they are. Dworkin might think his relocation of these issues and the correlative issue of legitimacy and obligation leaves us no option but an illiberal and moralistic denial of this entitlement. Not at all. There are many attractive convictions within liberal ideology and not the least of these is the defence of freedom of belief. He is welcome to believe what he wants to believe. Moreover I would not argue that his convictions are irrational or held in bad faith. Rights and the ideal of the rule of law have brought significant benefits to people in the countries of which Dworkin writes.

But it is just those benefits and their limits that we must consider more closely. For it is, I believe, an odd thing when personal relations of love and caring get to be written in terms of rights and obligations. I wonder about passion and spontaneity. I wonder what emotions are to be put aside in order to calculate whether my friend or sister or colleague has responded sufficiently in the past to my requests for her attention for the purpose of deciding whether I should respond to hers. I wonder about babies and small children and the immense debts they must run up to their parents. I wonder if that is why their parents feel entitled and obliged to sustain the economy of nation states by budget deficits to be paid for by these future generations. And whether it has anything to do with the parent generation's continuing destruction of the environment. For Dworkin's derivation of political obligation from personal associative obligation works both ways.

It makes me think that while Dworkin's reason of rights may be seen as the Hegelian rose in the heart of the cross of the present,[4] it is also the rose of Blake's poem:

O Rose, thou art sick!
The invisible worm
That flies in the night
In the howling storm

Has found out thy bed
Of crimson joy
And his dark secret love
Does thy life destroy.
(Blake 1966: 212)

5

RIGHTS FETISHISM

THE RITES OF RIGHTS

The legal construction of objectivity rests on the assumption that
'law' is what lawyers think or ought to think it is. Understandings
of self and society that are sought in theory and practice resistant
to established social relations are systematically excluded. What is
so extraordinary about this sequence of thought is not its basic
assumption. If we are to think creatively and critically we cannot
but begin from our own ideas. We work with and through them.
What is extraordinary is the denial of the incompleteness of lawyers'
ideas of law.

The claim to exclusivity of a point of view authorises the use of
force against those who do not share it. Where such claims and their
enforcement are part of a political or religious ideology they are
characterised as viciously oppressive and strongly opposed by
liberal thought. Yet as part of legal ideology they are celebrated.
What religion and politics cannot do without being seen as repressive, law can. Somehow, law gets to be disconnected from the
partisan interests of dominant groups within the society and gets
widespread acceptance as a universal measure of what is owed or
due. Constructing notions of the objectivity or rightness of legal
norms is part of this process of disconnection. Jurisprudential
discourse on rights is the other side of this coin.

Within mainstream debates between jurists, two questions have
traditionally dominated discussion of rights. First, whether legal
rights are a species of the wider genus of moral or political rights.
This is another version of the autonomy debate. Second, whether
a choice or benefit theory of rights provides the best explanation
and justification of legal rights. The benefit theory of rights argues

that rights are benefits of various kinds (satisfied claims on others, choices, powers or immunities to change legal relationships) given as the reflex of a legal or moral rule or principle (MacCormick 1976: 305). The choice theory, finds a deeper purpose unifying at least all legal rules which confer rights, namely, respect for individual choices (Hart 1982, Ch.VI). Additionally, in recognition of the very wide range of meanings which the one word 'rights' has in the English language, writers such as Salmond and Hohfeld have produced analytic schemas of those meanings. Assuming that reference to rights involves a three term relation between two legal persons and a *res* or thing, they have drawn our attention to the difference between claim rights such as the right to exclusive possession of owned commodities; liberties or privileges, such as rights to freedom of speech and association; powers, such as a commodity owner's right to alienate his or her property; and immunities, such as a diplomat's right not to be sued in the courts of a receiving country (Fitzgerald 1966; Hohfeld 1913; see generally Finnis 1980: Ch.VIII).

Dworkin's mission of getting us to take rights seriously involves a relocation of these traditional debates. Assuming that legal rights are politico-moral rights and that their point is to give individuals trumps over collective goals, Dworkin's main concern is to persuade us of the reality and desirability (in his terms 'fit' and 'attractiveness') of his approach. To put that another way, he wants to persuade us that continued progress towards perfect substantive justice between the individual and the state is best assured by taking rights as facts of normative consistency within a defensible narrative of Anglo-American legal culture, as the grounds of law and the force of its reason. In the contemporary political climate of celebration of 'the West's' record on human rights and civil liberty against the old Stalinist regimes of Eastern and Central Europe and, in the West itself, concern for the erosion of civil liberties by neo-conservative regimes in the United States and the United Kingdom (Bartholomew and Hunt 1990), it is Dworkin's call to take rights seriously that has greatest claim on our attention.

We shall come back to a more detailed consideration of Dworkin and rights in the second section of this chapter. At this point, however, only half of the stage of contemporary debates on rights has been set and we must sketch in the other half. The debates, analyses and approaches already sketched are 'mainstream' in a cultural and political sense. Whatever the differences between writers on the issues being debated, they are agreed on two broad fronts. First, they take the view that individuals need protection against the state or government elected by the majority and that rights, legal or moral, are a necessary if not sufficient means of ensuring this protection. Second, rights are goods which individuals have. Choice and benefit theories, theories of rights as requirements of justice or liberty or equality or integrity debate the conceptualisation of the value of rights. But somewhere between the thirteenth and seventeenth centuries the meaning of the term 'right' (the Latin *jus*') shifted from *doing right* to *having or owning a right* (Finnis 1980, Ch.VIII). This remains the central case of the right and highlights its character as a possession of individualised legal persons.

Since, at latest, Marx's sceptical comments on the value of bourgeois conceptions of right and rights, comments best approached, in my view, through his mature reflections on rights in the *Critique of the Gotha Programme* (Marx 1974), socialist, feminist and critical theory has provided a less complacent context for their analysis. It is a context which reveals a very deep perplexity about rights and this perplexity has deepened in the contemporary political climate. Philosophically, the premise of mainstream debates which is *not* carried over, is the assumption that rights are unquestionably good. The parallel here is with the approaches to the legitimacy of the state noticed in the last chapter (above: 117–18). There are two different debates. We can, as in the mainstream debates, assume the value of rights and debate *why* they are valuable. Alternatively we can debate the question of *whether* and *when* rights are of value. This latter question is seriously asked in socialist, critical and feminist debates and it produces a range of answers which suggest that the deep perplexity to which I have referred is well grounded (Bartholomew and Hunt 1990; Campbell 1983; Hirst 1980; Hunt 1985; Klare 1981; Kennedy 1981; Olsen 1984; Smart 1990; Thompson 1975; Tushnet 1984). That ground, I contend, is rights fetishism.

It has given rise to extreme claims within the left debate which are less than helpful when it comes to evaluating law and rights from a standpoint for subordinated people. On the one hand there is E. P. Thompson's clarion call to the left to recognise, from English social history, the rule of law as an 'unqualified good' which, even as its rhetoric and celebration enabled the ruling class to restructure society to their own advantage, imposed actual limits on the arbitrary use of ruling power (Thompson 1975). In the Australian context, a similar claim has been made, again by an historian, in the context of an account of the Australian colonists' failure to extend the protections of the rule of law to Aboriginal people (Reynolds 1986). Reynolds' claim that 'the common law was corrupted in Australia by the nature of the relationship between settlers and Aborigines in the same way in which it was corrupted in Britain's slave colonies' (p.4), entails a notion of a pure, uncorrupted form of the common law; nothing other indeed, than a natural law or, within the rights theory idiom, a 'law beyond the law'. On the other hand, within the Critical Legal Studies Conference in the United States, it has been argued that rights are '[e]xactly what people don't need' (Gabel and Kennedy 1984: 33) and 'all lies and errors' (Kennedy 1981: 503).

The one-sidedness of both these positions is the work of rights fetishism. Rights, I contend, have contradictory forms of value which are concealed by their fetishisation. My project is to explore the substance of that contradiction. This, it seems to me, is inherent in the generality and exclusivity of legal judgment on the distribution of human goods and the ascription of social responsibility, and in the justification of such judgment. Juristic preoccupation with showing the objectivity or rightness of legal standards attempts to avoid it.

I have introduced the notion of rights fetishism in terms of its engendering in us a forgetting that rights are tokens for the lived experience of freedom, material equality and community. And I have indicated that the basic theoretical idea that fetishism can be a product of secular practices is taken from Marx's discussion of commodity fetishism (above: 18; see also Hope 1987). Throughout this chapter I shall fill out my understanding of rights fetishism, by tracing various lines of analogy between rights fetishism and commodity fetishism. Prior to that, we need a more general picture of rights fetishism which I include in this section, for it is indeed part of rites of rights. Further, since the notion of contradictory forms of value is as difficult and controversial a notion as any to be found in philosophy and social theory, I shall articulate it to everyday understandings of the benefits and burdens of rights, and then consider problems with Dworkin's demonstration example of how rights can resolve contradictory requirements of justice and integrity.

Rights fetishism is constituted by legal practices. Punishment, professional role play, and the verbal or practical formulation of rules as standards against which human acts are measured for the purpose of ascribing certain consequences to those acts – rights, obligations, powers or immunities, are all examples of such practices. Whether punishment, roles, rules or rights are involved, the practices involve the claim that A is right, or has a right to act (or refrain from acting) in a way which will harm or constrain Y. This claim can be understood as descriptive of social relations. For example, X's right as landowner to take money from Y who is tenant is an abstract description of a social relationship between them. The judge's right to order silence in the court and the imprisonment of anyone who disobeys, describes the empowered role of the judge in this setting. Yet in form the claim is justificatory. It imagines the existence of a general independent standard against which particulars are judged as right or rights.

We might, following the legal positivists, keep very steadily in mind, that the judgment is for the purpose of ascribing particular consequences to an act (such as the creation of a contract or a will or an act of parliament) and is not for the purpose of judging the moral or political virtue or value of the act. But apart from anything else, theory which tells us that we ought to understand judgments of legal right by distinguishing questions of fact from questions of value are reminiscent of Canute ordering back the tides. 'Right' as an evaluation of behaviour is profoundly tied, within our culture, to moral right. Positivist thought is not powerful enough to undo those ties. But further, I suggest, it has no real intention of doing so. Fetishism comes in, not as Kelsen thought (Kelsen 1970: 101ff), as the 'ideological fallacy' of interpreting the right here as an expression of absolute value, but because in legal discourse the right *is* an absolute value. That is to say, positivist Jurisprudence is itself mistaken in saying that this valorisation of human law is a 'mistake' of natural law or natural rights theories. Legal positivism prescribes the wrong cure on the basis of an inadequate diagnosis. Natural law theory does not make a mistake when it interprets the legal ought as tied to an absolute value. Rather it gives expression to an actual social phenomenon, rights fetishism.

When some thing, some token for some other object of desire or veneration is fetishised, it acquires qualities and properties which it lacks outside the social relations and practices which constitute the fetish. It acquires active capacities which appear as part of the thing itself. Thus the Constitution acquires genius. Warning an accused of his or her right to silence acquires the capacity to validate a police interrogation even when it is known that the accused, coming from a culture which lacks the concept of the right to silence, does not understand the warning and responds to the interrogation according to quite different customs (Coldrey 1987). Underlying these apparent pieces of nonsense are the ideas that the Constitution ought to be obeyed and that people ought to understand the right to silence. It can be argued that the 'ought' in question is properly interpreted as an hypothetical ought rather than a categorical one: that is, that we should understand these ideas as elliptical ways of saying that if we want peace, then the Constitution ought to be obeyed; and that if people want protection from police interrogation, then they need to understand that they have a right to silence. But what does this argument have to do with a social reality in which out-dated Constitutions reproduce social relations, the progressive phase of which has been and gone, and within which people are punished following procedures which, in application to them, are ritual rather than rational?

This, then, sketches the idea of rights fetishism to be fleshed out. My starting point is to take rights seriously, not in general, but at two specific levels. First, we should listen to the claims being made by subordinated people. The claims of Australian Aborigines to recognition of their sovereignty as a nation of people (Tasmanian Aboriginal Centre 1988), to land rights, and to compensation for past and present injury, are claims of right. The claims of women to security for their bodies on the streets and in homes are claims of right. The claims of progressive trade unions to take industrial action outside guide-lines agreed to by corporatist bureaucrats on issues of pay, safety at work, productivity and job security, are claims of right. The claims of social welfare recipients to privacy from intrusive social workers, to respect from arrogant officials and to freedom from state and media led campaigns of criminalisation and denigration ('dole cheats', 'security fraud', 'welfare scams', 'dole bludgers') are claims of right. Strategies for securing the recognition and enforcement of these rights raise other questions. Law reform of the kind with which we are familiar might not be the answer. But cognisance of the inability of established constitutional and institutional arrangements to meet these needs should not find expression in denunciation of rights as lies and illusions. Listening to the claims being made is a step in envisioning a form of political community which we do not presently have.[1] Supporting them as

144

claims of liberal ideals of liberty, equality and democratic community, or of justice or human rights or whatever is, I suggest, a matter on which it is wrong to legislate. There are too many possibilities of a coming together of diverse ideologies that are yet too fragile to be ordered about. That said, my analysis eschews such politico-moral notions and construes these rights as claims made by people bearing the heaviest burdens of our way of life, which express resistance to the established order of things.

Implicit in this reflection is the second level at which we should take rights seriously. Rather than supposing that those who believe that our present legal system and its mechanisms of rights are instruments for the progressive realisation of liberal ideals are *merely* apologists for the status quo, we should try to work out the strength of their convictions. There are two points for consideration here, the first political, the second moral. The political point is that in a society structured by materially unequal social relations, people on the down-side of these relations would be worse off without law than they are with law. This observation seems to hold even if it is the case that legal practices and institutions reproduce established social relations. This is Thompson's and Reynolds' point. The legal systems of the countries in which I write, rely for their effectivity on being accepted as legitimate, as well as on the use of coercive force. This acceptance has to be supported by the imposition of constraints on the arbitrary use of governmental and bureaucratic power. Economic power is less effectively controlled by law. But even here, law has been the means of implementing welfare policies and varying degrees of market intervention. The moral point is still the Kantian perception of the ethical value of equal concern and respect for individuals. There is nothing at all to be said for slavery, bondage or other status structures that deny it.

However, generalisation of the political value of law to an assertion that law is a necessary if not sufficient means of protecting individuals or subordinated groups from those with more power, rests on the assumption that unequal social relations are an inevitable feature of the human condition. There is no doubt that recorded history is overwhelmingly a history of societies with such structures. But first, that is no ground for saying that it always will be. Slavery remained an institutional feature of American and, effectively, Australian society, well into the nineteenth century. An argument that slavery always has been and always will be part of the human condition could have been made then and it would have been the same argument. It is obviously false. Second, there is some evidence of sex–gender relations in traditional Australian Aboriginal society that suggests that these were both economically and culturally basic to that society, and that they were relations of economic, political and spiritual equality (Rose 1987; Bell 1987). At least so far as the heuristic concepts of political theory are concerned, there is no reason to confine our possibilities to unequal social relations with or without law. There is the possibility of imagining real equality.

With the moral point, as I have indicated, the problem is surely not the defensibility of equal concern and respect as a moral postulate. It is rather that the limits of this concern and respect are set by the antithetical concept of individual–social. It is the law or the government or the state which is thus enjoined to accord equal treatment. By contrast, not to prefer one's self and one's own in private life is thought to be something of a moral failure. Finnis' and Dworkin's derivation of political obligation from personal, associative obligation modifies the antithesis at the practice level. Since, if we are decently rounded people, we have family, friends, business partners, union brothers, academic colleagues and leisure associates as well as quite unknown fellow citizens, we work out responsibilities appropriate to each role and thus through reasonable practice get the right balance. Even so, he who single-mindedly pursues his business or career, avoids paying his taxes and shows no concern for any living thing outside his immediate family is not so reprehensible as she who neglects her children for the picket line or protest camp. The former lacks a dimension of balance in his life but the latter has got the whole thing wrong.

If we take the view that both these stereotypes of adversarial argument have in equal measure got the whole thing wrong, the bias of the abstract organising individual–society concept becomes evident. Nonetheless, there is a universality to the postulate of equal concern and respect that must be regarded as the real strength of natural law and rights based Jurisprudence. The trap which too dismissive an attitude to rights falls into is to dismiss ethical individualism for the wrong reasons.

The idea of empowering people to do what they want to do with their own lives and insisting that they each take responsibility for their own acts is a single idea and a good one. It is contradicted by forcing people to act in accordance with norms set by an alienated authority. Telling people what they ought to do might be justified by reference to some desired social order, or some supposed hierarchy of merit or desert, or moral sensibility or a supposed split between reason (good) and passion (evil). But in the lack of any such actually desired order such justifications cannot but deny the contradiction involved. Ethical individualism thus constitutes an exemplary instance of Poulantzas' idea of ideology (above: 13). The horizon constituted by it constructs the autonomous moral subject and, in place of its lived relations with others, hands it back rights. As part of this same process of thought the norm (objective right) is constructed as the ground of this relatively coherent discourse. The legal version of this justificatory process might well be termed the rites of rights and is part of their fetishisation.

GRASPING AT CONTRADICTION: THE BENEFITS AND BURDENS OF RIGHTS

In order to take rights seriously at the levels at which I have suggested we should, and in order to defend ourselves against traps which an uncritical belief in the political and ethical value of rights sets up, I want to introduce a distinction, drawn from Marxian economic thought, between a good and a commodity. A good is a thing that is produced for the purpose of satisfying the wants or needs of its producer. Its value is what Marx calls use-value. A commodity, on the other hand, is a thing which is produced not for the purpose of satisfying the wants or needs of its producer, but for exchange. No one would want to buy a thing that had no use-value for them. So a commodity has use-value. But a commodity also has, in addition, exchange value. For example, a coat, ten pounds of tea, forty pounds of coffee, one quarter of corn, etc. are all equated to twenty yards of linen or, in the money form, to 2 ounces of gold (Marx 1938: 35ff). This relation of equality gives the exchange value of the various commodities. When exchange becomes a regular practice within a society, the exchange value of a commodity is its equivalence to all other commodities. As the universal equivalent form of value in such societies, exchange value is referred to simply as value. How goods get to be converted into commodities with contradictory forms of value is a question of political economy that need not concern us. The contradiction in the forms of value that are a product of this process, is a contradiction between a concrete and an abstract form of value.

The notions of goods, commodities, use-value and exchange

value are contextualised by classical political economy and are not directly translatable to Jurisprudence. Indeed, as we shall see in Chapter 6, any such translation is interrupted, precisely as a consequence of rights fetishism. In moral, legal and political philosophy there is little precision in the use of the notion of value. In the philosophy dictionary I use, the article headed 'value' begins: 'A theory of value is a theory about what things in the world are good, desirable, and important' (Flew 1984: 365). The central questions of such theories are said to be concerned with the necessity, or otherwise, for an external justification of morality and the relation between things having extrinsic or instrumental value and intrinsic value or worth. Any theory of value, the article concludes, must propose some things that are good in themselves or a method for assessing claims that a thing is such a good. Fortunately there is no need here to try to sort out the confusion of terms (ideals, values, virtues, basic goods, etc.) and the variable uses of these terms in Jurisprudence. The points relevant here are, first, to note the distinction between economic value and ethical or universal value; second, to note that whatever form of value a good is thought to have, its characterisation as a good, in the context of moral, legal and political philosophy and Jurisprudence, constructs a unitary thing with a property – value. Obviously, an overall negative evaluation of the thing is excluded by this construction. But more significantly, where complex social phenomena such as law or rights are concerned, an inquisitorial stance on the value of the thing, based on the perception that the thing has contradictory aspects, is also excluded. It might be admitted that the thing has a potential to be put to bad use, or has some undesirable features. But whatever negative moments the thing may have – burdens, dangers, constraints or what have you – the judgment made is that these are either justified or outweighed by its positive ones.

We must lift the assumption that rights are goods (benefits, choices, requirements of justice, fairness or integrity) if we wish to question their value for subordinated people, but we need neither replace it with an assumption that they lack value of any kind, nor pretend a non-evaluative or 'objective' point of view. By analogy with the notion of commodities, we can conceive rights as embodying contradictory forms of value – one form or kind of value for those individuals who have them and another form of value for all. This assumption is not inconsistent with the framework within which rights are thought to exist. On the contrary it reflects the person/society antithesis embedded within the framework of legal thought. The contentious thing about it is the supposition of a contradiction within the notion of rights. Here it must be kept in mind that ideology extends into logic; that classical logic with its axiom of non-contradiction is the dominant but not the only system of formal, mathematical logic. There are also systems of dialectical logic within which contradictions are differently treated.[2] Still, having introduced this idea of a contradiction within rights by an analogy and in abstract terms, I want to give it an intuitively recognisable context, by moving to a more mundane level – the benefits and burdens of rights, and to dismantle the Jurisprudential representation of these as non-contradictory.

The benefits and the burdens of rights are inseparable. They can be observed at the most mundane and obvious levels. Refusing police, unarmed with a search warrant, entry to one's home, returning faulty or misdescribed goods to a shop, having an opportunity to speak in defence of one's liberty or property or life, being able to appeal against the decision of a biased or incompetent official or tribunal or magistrate, being able to join with others in public protest – these are all rights conceded within the legal systems of which I write. Asserting these rights does not always work out in the way the text books would have it. That shows a discrepancy between the theory and practice of law. Where the empirical evidence is that it is women, children, people of colour, people without, or with badly paid, work for whom rights do not work, there are grounds for thinking that legal practices and institutions are systemically skewed against subordinated groups. Neither the discrepancy nor its skewed incidence, however, make it sensible to deny the benefits of rights when they do work.

The price of rights is obvious when it has been necessary to get legal advice or assistance and the bill comes in. It is profoundly important to the question of access to the beneficial mechanisms of the legal system. But it is derivative rather than basic as a burden. The real burdens of rights are not quantifiable in monetary terms. They are the burdens of domination by official and bureaucratic authority and of alienation of capacities to control one's own life, and they are imposed by the state's monopoly of physical force and the legal profession's monopoly of safeguards on its use. You must be deferential to the official who has the job of recognising and enforcing your rights; take your hands out of your pockets as you stand before the magistrate and show proper respect for the police.

However you perceive your case, if you want assistance from the profession and the courts, it must be placed within a doctrinal legal framework. This may make it incomprehensible to you. It may make an unhappy but hitherto non-adversarial relationship into a bitterly adversarial relationship. It will also determine what is factually relevant to your dispute or difference, over-riding your own perceptions of what is important and significant in what has happened to you. Your lawyer, knowing the idiosyncrasies of judges and juries, may not let you into the witness box. Having your say in court, expressing your frustration or anger or sorrow at something gone wrong, speaking in your own words to the political dimensions of your case, will only harm your chances.

To put it mildly, Jurisprudence does not invite us to make a critical analysis of what we hand over for having enforceable rights against others. The idea that rights have ethical value rules that out. It is not that burdensome aspects of life in our legal societies is denied. Nor does law, like a fairy godmother, concern itself only with benefits. The concept *correlative* to rights is obligations, and obligations place constraints on liberty. This concept, in Jurisprudence, is certainly not contradictory. As Hohfeld's analytic schema assures us, the contradiction of rights is no-rights (Hohfeld 1916). Burdens then are just the other inevitable side of the coin of benefits and are distributed amongst the population by law. Necessarily or contingently, depending on the concept of law being defended, these obligations are coercively enforced. If legal obligations thus place constraints on liberty, they do so in accordance with the requirements of at least formal and procedural justice and, in the ideal case, with substantive justice as well. The question that arises now, is whether the burdens of prescription and punishment which are identified but justified in Jurisprudence concern the same practices as those which I have identified as involving domination and alienation.

I believe that they do and that their Jurisprudential representation is fetishised. Dworkin's demonstration example of how rights discourse can resolve a conflict between justice and integrity illustrates the point (Hunt and Kerruish 1991).

Human legal systems share human fallibility. Laws, even the laws of a true community, may be unjust. Given justice as an interpretive heuristic of liberal legalism, it will very often be the case that such injustices can be interpreted out of the system. But this may not always be possible. We can get situations in which principles of justice and of law as integrity are in head-on conflict. To illustrate such situations Dworkin gives us a fable of a dutiful daughter. We are asked to imagine a society that is a true community, but which has a traditional rule that daughters must marry the man of their fathers' choice. The rule is discriminatory since sons are not so constrained. The community, however, being a true community, meets the reciprocity condition that individuals are entitled to equal concern and respect. The problem here is one of paternalism. 'The culture accepts the equality of sexes but in good faith thinks that equality of concern requires paternalistic protection of women in all aspects of family life ...' (Dworkin 1986: 205). The family in this community is not in any other respect a seriously unjust institution. Its paternalism is its only unjust feature. But since it is an institutional feature of the society, this is not an isolated instance of an unjust law or practice that can be interpreted out of the culture by liberal judges. 'Now' says Dworkin

> the conflict [between justice and law] is genuine. The other responsibilities of family membership thrive as genuine responsibilities. So does the responsibility of a daughter to defer to parental choice in marriage, but this may be overridden by appeal to freedom or some other ground of rights. The difference is important: a daughter who marries against her father's wishes, in this version of the story, has something to regret. She owes him at least an accounting, and perhaps an apology, and should in other ways strive to continue her standing as a member of the community she otherwise has a duty to honour.
>
> (Dworkin 1986: 205)

The daughter, on Dworkin's analysis, has an abstract and general obligation to obey the law (giving her father an abstract right that his daughter marry the man of his choice) but a concrete right to choose her own spouse. The concrete right overrides the abstract obligation but does not annul it. The abstract obligation spawns concrete obligations (to account, perhaps to apologise, and to obey and honour in all other respects), the burdens of these obligations being borne by the daughter. The daughter *may* claim her right, but *must* do so regretfully, apologetically and as the subject of further liabilities. It goes without saying, since rights are things individuals have that she can claim this right only on her own behalf. She is entitled by self-interest to make this claim for herself, but constrained by her obligation to obey the law of her true community to do so deferentially and in isolation from other women facing similar problems.

There are three clear lines of objection to the moral of this fable. First, the individual right is, from a feminist standpoint, an insufficient remedy. Second, in its exclusion of the propriety of civilly disobedient political action for legislative change, it is undemocratic. Third, Dworkin's resolution is androcentric. The remedy is insufficient from a feminist standpoint because it is offered to all women only abstractly, only in theory. The concrete right is vested in one, isolated woman. The theoretical availability of the right to all women takes no account of the differences between women so far as their actual capacities to claim this right are concerned. The dutiful daughter, it would seem, has had the benefit of an education in liberal legalism and knows of her concrete right; or perhaps she has luckily come upon some feminist literature. Moreover, it would seem that she is not going to be beaten and ostracised for insisting on her rights. Not all women in her society will find themselves so lucky. The undemocratic aspect of Dworkin's resolution of this problem lies in confining the dutiful daughter's entitlement to disobedience of the single offensive law. Civil disobedience is a political strategy of resistance to established social practices or laws. Dworkin denies dissidents the right to plan their own strategy! The logic of his argument would justify polices bursting in on a gathering of feminist women, men and children planning a campaign of generalised civil disobedience and ordering them to disperse. The only political community that Dworkin recognises is that of the nation state. This political community can justifiably repress alternative political communities – communities of solidarity between people on the down-side of social relations. The androcentrism of Dworkin's fable lies in his insensitivity to the magnitude of the wrong to women, his placement of the burden of accounting and apologising on the woman, and his sublime neglect of the fact that the dutiful daughter and her father speak different languages. If the father, in good faith, believes women are in need of protection from their own choices, what can change his mind? Whatever the daughter says will be interpreted as confirming the belief. Androcentrism, like ethnocentrism, precludes perception of the value of different approaches to and ways of life. Dworkin has given serious consideration to questions of civil disobedience (Dworkin 1978: 206; 1985: 104). We can safely suppose that he would admit and defend the limits he places on it. But it does not seem to have crossed his mind that his resolution of the dutiful daughter's dilemma is seriously problematic as a devaluation of women. There is a blindness here that cuts much deeper than the conservatism of his position on civil disobedience and, like Hart's unawareness of his ethnocentrism, this is no endearing innocence.

Up to less than two decades ago, welfare authorities in Australia, acting on a policy of assimilation regularly endorsed by the white population in democratic elections, took Aboriginal children from their parents and institutionalised them or fostered them in white families. The grief and protest of the parents went unheard over generations. The psychological and cultural harm to the children saw their regular progression from orphanages and missions to gaols and doss-houses. Unless Dworkin can find a convenient distinction between good faith sexism and good faith racism, the moral of his fable is that Aborigines had an obligation to account for demanding their right to bring up their own children, perhaps an obligation to apologise for insisting on that right, and a duty to honour and obey the law of white Australia in all other respects. This is not just, in his terminology, 'unattractive'. It lacks any awareness of and concern with the question of how someone whose sexual or cultural identity has been repressed or dislocated finds a sense of self at all. He is unaware of it, I suggest, because of rights fetishism.

RIGHTS FETISHISM AND COMMODITY FETISHISM

The difference between the Jurisprudential representation of the benefits and burdens of rights and my own, is a difference of standpoint. This difference cannot be reduced to one of truth value (they are wrong and I am right) or to moral and political values (liberal versus socialist and feminist values). Truth value and politico-moral values are more complexly woven into these inter-pretations of ways of life and of law of and for them. From the standpoint of empowered classes the Jurisprudential repres-entation of punishment and prescription is perfectly sensible. Their and their agents' exercise of repressive and coercive power is, for them, rightful. It is an exercise of rightfully constituted authority. Their belief in expert and professionalised knowledge, perception of the need to be deferential to those higher up in the social and professional hierarchy, and conviction that they know what is best for all members of the society, are good faith beliefs and convictions which form the intentional aspect of legal practices. They become part of social reality through those practices. But, in different measure, the repression by, and alienation from, the law of a way of life of and for these empowered classes, is also part of social reality. It is the experience of those put down by law.

No doubt the beliefs and perceptions of empowered classes have experiential bases as well. There is no reason at all to doubt that they value their freedom; that they devoutly believe in a notion of abstract equality that enables them to justify existing social relations despite the persistence of sexism and racism and of inequalities in wealth, opportunity and political power; and that their sense of personal identity and worth is secure within fraternities of empowered white men. The difference is that, in the negative aspect of the ideology appertinent to these experiences and beliefs, they claim that their view is objectively or uniquely true or right. It is right enough to justify the use of physical violence; right enough to destroy other cultures; right enough to devalue women. Again this is, from my standpoint, 'unattractive'. But ethical or aesthetic argument at this point is not my particular concern. The truly odd thing here is that this claim of right finds a basis in our social reality; it cannot be dismissed as irrational or as having no social validity. This then is where we need the notion of fetishism.

Fetishism is an immensely complex social, psychological and ideological phenomenon. On the one hand fetishism in a broad sense involves some thing standing for something else. On the other, in that same broad sense, it has a connotation of irrationality and mysticism. In part, the significance of Marx's idea of commodity fetishism is his identification of fetishism within secular, economic practices. That is where an analogy with secular, legal practices begins. We would, however, misunderstand Marx's idea of commodity fetishism if we understood it in an ordinary language way to mean an irrational reverencing of commodities. If that is a characteristic of capitalist societies (and those concerned for the environment would have little doubt that it is), it is a consequence of commodity fetishism and does not take us far in understanding what commodity fetishism is.

Marx's theory of commodity fetishism is a particular application of an understanding of ideology in both its neutral and negative senses – a particular exercise in tracing the way in which reality appears. Commodity fetishism, Marx argued, is a social process within which inanimate objects, things produced by human labour, acquire an identity independent of their identity as things which have value to human beings as useful objects. This identity is their exchange, as distinct from their use-value. The value of a commodity appears as a thing-like property of it – like its size or weight; a property which gives the commodity a capacity to enter into relations with other things and other people. A chair, for example, is useful as a convenient resting place for human bodies. That is its use-value and it is clearly no abstract or universal value. It has a clear social character and is dependent on ways and technologies of physically resting. But given a system of production in which goods are produced, not for use by the producer, but for exchange on a market, chairs from the moment at which their production begins, indeed, as futures markets attest, even prior to that, have an exchange-value relation with other things and have value for human beings. The exchange-value relation is one within which all commodities, being equated to a single commodity (the universal equivalent), 'appear not only as qualitatively equal as values generally, but also as values whose magnitudes are capable of comparison' (Marx 1938: 36). So we think of a chair, a coat, a book as all being equal to ten dollars. The value of the commodity thus appears as a property of it which enables such commensurations to be made.

The jurisprudential analogy here is with the construction of legal subjects as beings having (the properties of) freedom and reason. It is these characteristics, essentialised so as to become the identity of the subject, by virtue of which such subjects can be conceived as equal.

Marx's discussion of commodity fetishism begins with an analysis of the social processes which give rise to this phenomenon of the appearance of value as a property of objects. For it is, he thought, an odd thing that what in actuality is a social relation between producers of commodities is perceptible to people as a relation between things. Moreover, the appearance of value as a relation between things was not corrected by an appreciation of the labour theory of value – the economic theory which, Marx thought, provided a scientific explanation of the value of commodities. This point is critical to the notion of commodity fetishism. As Marx puts it

The recent scientific discovery, that the products of labour, so far as they are values, are but material expressions of the human labour spent in their production, marks indeed, an epoch in the history of the development of the human race, *but by no means dissipates the mist through which the social character of labour appears to us to be an objective character of the products themselves*. (my emphasis)

(Marx 1938: 45)

The appearance is, in that sense, a real social phenomenon – a part of social reality. It is not an illusion and does not, in any straightforward sense, involve cognitive defect, mistaken perception or the like. It is the way commodities really do appear to be. This contradiction, then, between the reality and the appearance of economic value, was what Marx explained in terms of fetishism.

It was, he thought, a consequence of the fact that things are produced by individuals or groups of individuals working independently of each other. The social character of each producer's labour, that is its character as labour *for others*, only shows itself, therefore, in the act of exchange. In Marx's words

... the labour of the individual asserts itself as part of the labour of society, only by means of the relations which the act of exchange establishes directly between the products, and indirectly, through them, between the producers.

(Marx 1938: 44)[3]

When exchange has acquired such extension as a social practice that goods are produced for the purpose of exchange, a new concept becomes thinkable. This is the notion of abstract labour, or, in Marx's theory, abstract human labour power. Abstract labour power is what every worker has and is devoid of all particular characteristics and skills. It is distinct from concrete labour power which will be a capacity to do labour of a particular kind – bricklaying, or tailoring, or soliciting, or teaching. The producer's labour thus acquires 'socially a two-fold character'. On the one hand, as a definite kind of labour, it must satisfy a definite social want and has, in that case, use-value. On the other hand, it can satisfy the wants of the producer him or her self only so far as all useful private labour is mutually exchangeable and thus ranked equally. This latter character of labour appears as the common quality of different products – their value.

Clearly the idea of commodity fetishism is heavily dependent on the labour theory of value, and the objection that it stands or falls with Marx's version of the labour theory of value needs to be addressed. Prior to this, however, I want to extend the analogy I have begun between commodity fetishism and rights fetishism. There is a parallel between abstract legal personality and actual lived identity and the notions of abstract and concrete labour power. At one level the parallel is obvious. Abstract legal personality is personality devoid of all particular social and psychological characteristics. It is the capacity for having rights and is 'personality' only, as Salmond puts it, because

> The prime case of a person is a human being, and personality *would seem to entail* the possession of those characteristics belonging peculiarly to mankind, i.e. the power of thought, speech and choice. (my emphasis)
>
> (Fitzgerald 1966: 298)

The analogy between legal personality and labour power, however, holds in virtue of the suggestion that equal concern and respect for individuals, insofar as that is embedded in our legal systems, is a moral good. In this respect, I agree with Dworkin that a theory of the ethical value of law which best fits and most coherently justifies legal practices will find the source and measure of that value in the basic good of equality. This does not commit me to thinking that Dworkin's theory of the ethical value of law is the best theory of the value of law. It would do so only if I agreed that a theory of the value of law has to have ethical value as its bottom line, and I do not agree to that. This raises a question as to the relation between different forms and contexts of value which I address in the next chapter. For the moment my point is that theories of the value of law and/or rights need not be theories of ethical value.

With just a shift in focus now, we can fill out the earlier suggestion that rights, like commodities, have contradictory forms of value. What is analogous to the use value of a right is the value, to someone making a claim, of having that claim recognised and enforced. That value may be economic, political, or psychological. In any case it will make sense only within a given social context. On the other hand, the idea that rights have ethical or political value is analogous to the exchange value of a commodity. It is an abstract, universal form of value and it appears as a property or quality of things, namely, laws and the rights they confer. It is that by virtue of which different individuals are commensurable or equal; their 'essential humanity', their capacity for 'thought, speech and choice' or their freedom and reason.

I am calling this appearance a fetish. Hart, Finnis and Dworkin would deny that. The appearance, they would say, is the reality of rights and of law. To go further here we must go back to commodity fetishism. Smith and Ricardo, Marx thought, went far enough beyond the appearance of value as a property of commodities to understand that its quantitative determinant lay in the amount of labour expended in its production. But, he thought, classical economics never once asked the question of *why* labour is represented by the value of its product and labour-time by the magnitude of that value. It lacked, in other words, a significant philosophical dimension; or perhaps, to put that around another way, it had a philosophical dimension which closed out this inquiry. On the quantitative determination of value made in classical economy, all kinds of labour are reduced to their common character of being the expenditure of *human* labour power. This, for Marx, is a wrong reduction. Marx wants rather to say that the equality of every kind of particular human labour, which is of course a relative equality, consists in its being *social* labour – labour for others, rather than what it appears as, private labour for the production of social things. Unless, then, we understand that commodities are fetishised, we will misunderstand value.

Marx argues that the form of value itself is complicit in this misunderstanding. This, he thought, explained Smith's and Ricardo's failure to go beyond a quantitative analysis of value and ask *why* labour is represented by the value of its product.

> It is one of the chief failings of classical economy that it has never succeeded, by means of its analysis of commodities, and, in particular of their value, in discovering that form under which value becomes exchange-value.
>
> (Marx 1938: 52)

This remark is difficult, the difficulty centring on interpretation of the notion of form. It makes sense, I suggest, not as a reference to the concept of value, but as a reference to the phenomenal manifestation of economic value in the commodity and the appearance form of that commodity. This appearance form, Marx thought, is misleading because, while it is a true expression of the universal form of economic value *in commodity-producing societies*, it is not a true expression of the universal form of economic value. We are misled,

he thought, because philosophy and social science begin *post festum*
– after the event – when an historical process of social change has
stabilised into 'natural, self-understood forms of social life' and
'man seeks to decipher, not their historical character, for in his eyes
they are immutable, but their meaning' (Marx 1938: 47). As a
consequence, classical political economy treats exchange value, not
as the universal equivalent form of value *in commodity-producing
societies*, but as the universal form of value.

Now I do not think this analysis commits Marx to affirming the
existence of a universal form of economic value and so falling back,
self-inconsistently, into a kind of Platonic realism or Hegelian
idealism. On the contrary, Marx makes a sociological assumption
here: that work, conceived as the production of objects having
use-value, is 'the normal activity of living beings' (Marx 1938: 14
n.1). Adam Smith, he thought, overlooked this in seeing only the
negative moment of work as 'the mere sacrifice of rest, freedom and
happiness' (Ibid.). But this oversight too was understandable, and
in much the same terms. Smith had only the wage labourer in mind,
conceived work only in its alienated form as wage labour, and so
misunderstood its relation to the production of exchange value –
its social character and its potential as a means of self-realisation.
What Marx tried to do was counteract these misunderstandings by
emphasising the historical and material limits on the universality of
the concept of value. Specifically this means that Marx did not think
there was any such thing as a universal form of value.[4]

We can come back now and complete the analogy between rights
fetishism and commodity fetishism. Concepts of justice, practical
reasonableness, fairness, utility and integrity are conceptualisations
of universal or ethical forms of value which, in Jurisprudence, are
said to be embedded in our legal system. Which values are embedded in our legal system and the ways in which they are embedded are differently explained. For Finnis, human law is a
derivation and determination of the natural law. For Hart, on the
one hand, formal and procedural justice are a matter of rule
following and are necessary if not sufficient conditions of justice as
fairness. On the other, legal, as distinct from pre-legal, forms of
social regulation and control are justifiable on utilitarian grounds.
For Dworkin, law is integrity in pursuit of justice, fairness and due
process. These beliefs conceal and contribute to rights fetishism.
But they are neither lies and illusion, false consciousness or practical
ignorance, nor the materiality of rights fetishism. They are ideo-

logical forms of legal, professionalised and institutionalised practices of determining particular cases by reference to general rules, of coercively enforcing these determinations and of justifying them in terms of legal and moral 'truths' which deny the incompleteness of lawyers' ideas of law.

My question is what is the social reality, in normative terms, the need, for the justification of legal prescription and punishment in terms of ethical, universal value? Perhaps there is a legitimation need here, a need which, in being met, minimises the use of coercive force. But its cost for classes and groups who are on the down-side of the social relations which law secures, makes it absurd to say that law is, for them, an unqualified good. It seems more promising then to stay with rights fetishism and find the social reality of this justificatory hype in legal practices.

PROBLEMS AND OBJECTIONS

My suggestion then is that, just as Marx grasps at commodity fetishism within the social process of the abstraction of particular concrete labour to abstract social labour, and does so in order to develop an adequate theory of economic value, so a notion of rights fetishism, located in legal practices constructing abstract legal personality, can help us to understand the value of law for those who are put down by it. This is not *just* a matter of a theory of the value of law that seeks to come to terms with the perplexity manifest in the socialist, feminist and critical debates. There are practical, political consequences of rights fetishism which are harmful and hurtful to working people, women and people of colour, and there are practical, political questions concerning law reform, law teaching, legal practice and use of the courts in political struggles that an understanding of rights fetishism may help us to address.

There are many anticipated objections to this suggestion. The whole question of value in Marxist thought is deeply controversial and that comes on top of the total rejection of his approach by non-Marxist thinkers. Moreover, I am aware that the approach I have taken runs the risk of slippage and confusion between economic and other kinds of value.

Four inter-related questions seem to constitute a nerve centre of contention.

1   Is value a non-redundant category in economic theory and, if

so, is there a measure of economic value extrinsic to market transactions?

2 How are the various – economic, social, psychological, ethical, etc. – categories of value related?

3 Is Marx's account of commodity fetishism an account of an actual social phenomenon or is it a convoluted and pseudo-scientific critique of the morality of capitalist ways of life?

4 Is there, in any case, a normative dimension in Marx's notion of commodity fetishism and what is it?

I shall deal with the first of these questions in the remaining part of this chapter. It is relevant to the objection that the whole idea of commodity fetishism stands or falls with Marx's version of the labour theory of value. Since my idea of rights fetishism is constructed by an analogy with commodity fetishism and involves the claim that fetishism is an actual phenomenon of secular social practices, it is vulnerable to this objection. It is not moreover an objection confined to economic theory. It is a specific application of a broader, in principle, objection to theory within which fetishism can be identified as a problematic aspect of our social reality. This broader objection goes to working with concepts of reality, actuality and appearance and proposes discursive values and practices, and in some cases, conditions of existence, in their place. The objection insists that scientific realism continues an Enlightenment superstition – the idea of scientific knowledge – and that Marxism is incorrigibly flawed at that level.

The other questions are compendiously dealt with in the next chapter. They bring us onto ground so far only touched on – the relation between neutral and negative ideology. My argument is that the exclusion of standpoint in Jurisprudence is central to its negatively ideological aspect and that the notion of rights fetishism helps us to get a firmer grip on exclusionary practices and the conditions of their effectivity. This argument will take us into an exploration of the normative aspects of the notions of fetishism. Without it the explanation of rights fetishism (and indeed of commodity fetishism) is incomplete. But we should deal with the in-principle objection first.

Marx's view, that the value of a commodity is a matter of social relations of production, is fundamental to his notion of commodity fetishism. It is the idea that economic value is a matter of social relations that underlies his perception of an oddity that needs to be explained – namely, an incongruity between the appearance and the reality of value. And it is the idea that the social relations in question are relations of production, rather than those of consumption, that is basic to his version of the labour theory of value. This view then places him within, on the one hand, a particular philosophical tradition and, on the other, a particular tradition of economic theory.

Against a modelling by MacCormick of Whig (classical and neo-classical political economy owing much to the thought of Adam Smith) and Marxist legal theory, which proposes a thesis–antithesis relation between the two (MacCormick 1982: 8ff), it should be noted that the philosophical and economic traditions in question were not confluent and that Marx's critique of classical political economy involved rather more than a different moral evaluation of capitalist society (cp. MacCormick 1982: 6ff). On the philosophical side, Marx's tradition was that of classical German idealism. The Kantian critique of Locke and Hume, followed by Hegel's critique of Kant had, by the time Marx wrote, already made this a distinct tradition from that of the empirically minded Scottish Enlightenment intellectuals, Hume and Smith (Callinicos 1985, Ch.1). On the economic side, Ronald Meek points out that two 'quite distinct and rival traditions in nineteenth-century economic thought', identified by Maurice Dobb, both derived from Adam Smith and diverged, on the one hand, into the work of Ricardo, on the other, into the work of Malthus (Meek 1977, Ch.VIII). MacCormick, predictably, proposes his version of liberalism as the long awaited synthesis of his models. The important point here is not to refute this grandiose claim, but to resist, by pointing out the Jurisprudential strategy of broad brush classification to produce polarised models, and the persistently bad habit of interpreting philosophical texts without reference to their tradition. It would seem that the necessity of taking a point of view internal to a system of thought does not extend past law to philosophy!

The philosophical basis of Marx's view is the idea that concepts, such as value or law or capital, have no sense or meaning outside the social relations of a given time and place and are explicable, on the bottom line, in terms of social relations. More formally, it is an idea that involves assumption SR identified above (p.27), as a constitutive assumption of a version of scientific realism. The economic tradition that Marx worked within followed the Ricardian line in holding that the social relations relevant to value and price are those of producers. In this society, we are most likely to be familiar with a way of thinking that interprets economic value by reference to how much someone wants a thing and supposes that this value is quantified as a price through a market regulated by supply and demand (Dworkin 1985: 237–66). This way of thinking is a populist form of dominant economic theories. Such theories take supply and demand or consumer relations and activities as basic explanatory principles of price, whereas the Ricardian–Marxian version of the labour theory of value supposes that the explanatory principle for the commensuration of different kinds of thing is to be 'anchored in man's activities and relations *as a producer*' (Meek 1977: 153). These debates are ongoing and fundamental. Their questions, about value, about price and its determination or causation, and about the transformation of value to price, are, outside negatively ideological theories, no more conclusively answered than are questions about the relation between thought and reality raised by the philosophical components of Marx's view. There are simply different traditions in the development of economic thought as there are different traditions and frameworks of philosophical thought. Moreover, the Ricardian–Marxian tradition has recent and contemporary exponents, most notably Sraffa, who, while recognising the explanatory and predictive flaws in Marx's version of the labour theory of value retain its explanatory principle (Meek 1977, Ch.V, VIII).

This is sufficient to answer the objection that the dependence of Marx's idea of commodity fetishism on his version of a labour theory of value, is a conclusive argument against it. There is no non-dogmatic argument against the view that value is a non-redundant category in economic theory or against the view that its explanatory principle may be extrinsic to market transactions. Flaws in Marx's version of the theory will not do the job of proving a category mistake. Indeed, I am not at all clear how a category mistake could ever be proved in a logical sense, except from an assumption of universally *a priori* categories of thought *and* a specification of what they are. Marx's perception of an incongruity between the appearance and the reality of the value of commodities, and his recognition of the social reality of the appearance, is certainly dependent on his metaphysical and epistemological views; but then, whose perceptions and conceptualisations are not?

That answer does not conclude all issues of contention surrounding deployment of the notion of fetishism in secular, social practices.

If it did we would be left with incommensurable knowledges and reduced in our theoretical endeavours to edifying conversations. On Marx's own account there are questions of 'the reality and power, the this worldliness' (Marx 1976: 6) of a theory. So far as economic theory is concerned, such an assessment is beyond my competence. But we are, I think, over one threshold objection that would be damaging to my idea of making such an assessment in respect of fetishism in legal practices. The economic theory, in its substance, without doubt relies on both a contentious choice of explanatory principle and a contentious assumption concerning work. But again, for a confutation of the substance of labour theory of value to be so complete as to destroy the notion of commodity fetishism developed through it, it would have to be proven, at least to the satisfaction of all economists, that production relations are irrelevant to price, and that work is without any form of value for human beings. The first condition is not met. The second could only be asserted by someone who thought that human life can be sustained and reproduced without any form of productive activity. This, I think, is rather too strong a claim! Whatever else we may be, I do doubt that we are, in all ways, like the lilies of the field. Of course, we can be dogmatic here and say that work has to be shown to have ethical value in the sense of being a basic and universal good, before a theory of value can take it into account. But this, for reasons to be explored in the next chapter, is again merely dogmatic.

Marx is no canonical or judicial 'authority' who, once shown to have been wanting in his grasp of absolute truth, falls into dust or disrepute. It is rather the regimes that fetishised his own thought that have done that. We can be glad to see them go without thinking that their demise proves that the history of social thought comes to an end with various versions of the principles of liberalism. Modification of some of the ideas that fed into Marx's perception of commodity fetishism, particularly those ideas that facilitate reductive or essentialist interpretations, far from rendering fetishism obsolete as a category for social and legal theory, enable its further development. We come back then, on this question, to one of my introductory comments. Theories offer us ways of living within the world. Whatever their field they are normative; they argue that we ought to understand things thus and so, with various meanings of the kind of ought involved and for various supporting reasons (above: 12). I leave it to others to argue that we ought not to accept the notion of rights fetishism because it is a false idea based on a false economic theory and a false metaphysics. The further task for this work is to explain the sense in which, I think, we ought to take the idea of fetishism in our secular legal practices seriously.

6

AGAINST JURISPRUDENCE: THE EXCLUSION OF STANDPOINT

NORMATIVITY AND COMMODITY FETISHISM

The normative dimensions of theory

We have yet to explore what I have called the *normative dimensions* of an account of fetishism in secular economic or legal practices. Exploring the normative dimensions of accounts of fetishism is exploring the point or purpose of characterising social practices in this way and the reasons for thinking the characterisation adequate to reality. These dimensions can therefore only be authoritatively explained by those who do perceive the fetish character of the practices. It is, clearly enough, by virtue of a particular framework of thought, that fetishism is perceived as a phenomenon of social practices. It is also the case that the very notion of a fetish is such that the fetishist's account of what he or she is doing will contradict the theorist's account of the practice. Fetishism is the substitution of one thing for another – a departed lover's shoe for the departed lover, a symbol for an actuality – together with a loss or lack of awareness, a forgetting, that the substitution has taken place. The fetishist and the theorist cannot agree about the practice in question.

This consideration of normative dimensions is a necessary task in social theory for it is an exploration of the limits of thought. For those who do not recognise standpoints, these limits are the foundations of knowledge or horizons of interpretation. For those who do, these limits are just what we are seeking to transcend. Not for some further abstraction. Not for a mystical rush of blood to the head which makes us think we have apprehended the transcendental form of knowledge or truth or goodness, but for the very practical and down-to-earth purpose of finding out how to join with others with different but still subordinated standpoints for the purpose of ending our subordination.

This can be put another way. Exploring the normative dimension of the idea of fetishism in secular practices is an undertaking concerned to avoid the accretion of negative ideology of which neutral ideology is a condition. This is one of the most important tasks for emancipatory theory in general and for a theory of rights fetishism in particular. So we must review the most basic ideas of the approach being taken here. Our perceptions are mediated by our conceptions and our way of conceiving social reality. But not only by our practices of thought and language. Also by our practical activity. It is not thought alone that is active. Bodies are too. We do things and in action we engage with other things and other people. Intentionally for sure, but what we intend to do is not always what we actually do. This is where standpoint comes in. The ideas of standpoint and of the relativity of thought to standpoint recognise that acting, thinking subjects are located within social relations and ideologies, and that how the world appears to such subjects and how they represent it in thought and language will differ. How, as active, thoughtful subjects we conceive ourselves and others, what we want for ourselves and others, how we feel about ourselves and others, how we think we should go on in various social practices, and how we think we should go about satisfying felt wants and needs: all these dimensions of consciousness are socially constructed and will differ from subject to subject (Jaggar 1983: 369ff). Standpoint theory, in this realist and relational version of it, assumes social relations to be part of the social reality within which subjectivity is constructed. So active thinking subjects are also agents for groups and classes within social relations. Normativity comes in as ideas of what ought to be done in thought or action, doubly mediated by ideas of how and who we are and ideas of how and who we would like to be.

Normative dimensions of commodity fetishism

The question of the normative dimensions of Marx's account of commodity fetishism asks why Marx perceived this phenomenon and called it 'commodity fetishism'. It is a question about his philosophical framework and method and of the political and moral norms embedded in the account. It is an area of great interpretive controversy within and about Marxism. I take the view that Marx integrates questions of logic, metaphysics and epistemology, and method; and I take this integration to be a thoroughgoing relationalism that extends into the interplay of fundamental philosophical questions and the application of a framework of thought to social inquiry. Here I follow Lenin's comment, made in the course of his study of Hegel, that 'in *Capital*, Marx applied to a single science logic, dialectics and the theory of knowledge of materialism' (Lenin 1976a: 317). Marx adopted Hegel's approach to philosophy and applied it to analysis of the capitalist mode of production in Britain. To take this holistic approach is not to say that for purposes of analysis one cannot distinguish metaphysical assumptions from norms of method, or moral and political from epistemological dimensions. But it is to argue against interpretations that suppose a hierarchical relation between these questions such that there is one set of questions which provide the foundations of the theory. In particular, I argue against the view that there are moral and political foundations to Marxist thought that are comprehensible independently of the Hegelian notion of dialectics and the approach to social theory known as historical materialism. Finding a beginning then for this interpretive question poses a problem. But Marx did not separate passion from reason and so I begin from what seems to me to be a concern central to his perception of fetishism as a strangeness, a weirdness, in capitalist social formations.

The concern relates to the dilemma of *The Magician's Apprentice*; the apprentice who, having used one of his master's spells to get bucket and broom to do his chores, forgets how to control them and is held witness to their destructive power as they repeat their cycle 'again, again and quicker' (Goethe 1862: 101). This theme is of general significance in Marx's work.

> Modern bourgeois society with its relations of production, of exchange and of property, a society that has conjured up such gigantic means of production and of exchange, is like the sorcerer, who is no longer able to control the powers of the nether world whom he has called up by his spells.
>
> (Marx and Engels 1952: 49)

In the context of commodity fetishism it is expressed as concern with '... the action of objects, which rule the producers instead of being ruled by them' (Marx 1938: 46).

While Marx relies here on an analogy with religious ideologies, so that the idea of commodity fetishism is articulated to his critique of religion (Marx 1938: 51; 1975: 146), the point he is making is that the domination of human beings by inanimate objects and processes which they themselves have made and set in motion, is *not* confined to fairy stories and religious regimes. This is only an analogy, not a perception of identity. But those, blinded by a humanist conceit of the European Enlightenment, who think that fetishism is a characteristic of unenlightened 'primitive' or religious ways of life, will miss this. So the transformation of the secular to the sacred goes on into the construction of new religions of scientism, positivism, legalism and consumerism.[1]

These secular practices, so far as commodity fetishism is concerned, are practices of the market exchange of commodities; practices which take place within capitalist relations of production and give rise to a particular appearance form of value, exchange value. Marx thought that it was the lack of an understanding of the phenomenon of commodity fetishism that disabled Smith and Ricardo from getting through its neutrally ideological barrier to an adequate theory of economic value. But we are not yet into negative ideology. Marx considered classical political economy as a flawed but good faith attempt to investigate 'the real relations of production in bourgeois society'. Negatively ideological economic theory is what he calls 'vulgar economy' which

> deals with appearances only, ruminates without ceasing on the materials long since provided by scientific economy, and there seeks plausible explanations of the most obtrusive phenomena, for bourgeois daily use, but for the rest, confines itself to systematising in a pedantic way, and proclaiming for everlasting truths, the trite ideas held by the self-complacent bourgeoisie with regard to their own world, to them the best of all possible worlds.
>
> (Marx 1938: 53)

The complicity of negative ideology in the reproduction of political domination is strongly emphasised by critical and hermeneutic theorists (Thompson 1984). I do not disagree. But to look only at ideology in the negative sense is a little like closing the stable door after the horse has bolted. The more practical thing to do is to ask how these negatively ideological theories are produced and credentialed. What comes together here is commodity fetishism as a consequence of certain kinds of economic practice and a failure in classical political economy to comprehend it. This no more adds up to negative ideology than comprehending commodity fetishism, as Marx thought he had, makes it go away. But on the other hand, embedded in Marx's analysis of commodity fetishism is a concern for how, given this phenomenon, we can avoid being misled into representations of our selves and our societies that, by attributing active capacities to inanimate things, contribute to our being ruled by them. This is where classical political economy did not help, due, Marx thought, to the limitations of the 'bourgeois intellect' (Marx 1938: 53).

We can look at this in a down-to-earth way. How could and why should the bourgeoisie have conceived itself as lacking control over a social order which its economic and legal practices were getting into place? How could and why should it not have conceived itself as in possession of enlightened, scientific knowledge, when its way of life was destroying feudal relations of status (within which the bourgeoisie were subordinated to clerics and aristocrats), and when its knowledge and understanding was assisting this process? And then, when the European bourgeoisie is fairly securely in power, when it has possession and control of the means of production, when it is drawing the entire world into the ambit of its market and its culture, why should it perceive itself as being ruled by things? This is just where contradictory views of social practices will come in and, with them, epistemological and methodological questions.

The problem with 'the bourgeois intellect' which Marx emphasises is its preoccupation with the meaning of concepts. All symbolic forms of representation, whether in language or not, are part of a process whereby human beings objectify their perceptions and conceptions and then use these produced objects in various ways. Marx thought the method of science and philosophy that fails to take sufficient account of practical activity within this process, that is, the practical activity that forms the conditions of the representation and the use made of representational things, to be one sided. That, in my interpretation, is the most significant sense in which Marx is a materialist philosopher. He was equally critical of ahistorical understandings of a given social reality – that is, understandings that neglect the long process of development of social phenomena and treat them as 'natural, self-understood forms of social life' (Marx 1938: 47).

Accordingly, in constructing his theory of (economic) value,

Marx thought it quite wrong to begin from a concept of value, that is, from an idea of value in general: of what is good for us, what satisfies our wants and needs, and so forth (Marx 1976a: 213ff). The commodity, he insisted, was the subject of his analysis. It is the commodity that is on the one hand a use-value and on the other a value. The point is one of method emerging from a background theory of reality, social reality and human practices of thought and representation: that one should not try to understand economic value from the concept of value in general but from its most concrete, phenomenal form within a social formation, in capitalist social formations, the commodity.

It is important to understand that Marx was *not* saying that the practices constitutive of commodity fetishism were morally or politically bad *because* they gave rise to strange and misleading appearances. One would not call the refraction of light 'morally or politically bad' because it gives rise to misleading appearances, and the point, so far as commodity fetishism goes, is similar. It is also important to this interpretation, to insist that an abstract concept or law of value drawn from an analysis of the accumulation of capital is not a point from which we can understand commodity fetishism. The formation of capital by the extraction of surplus labour is not part of the problematic of commodity fetishism. The problem here is the possibility of being misled by the appearance form of value because of the lack of an adequate understanding of it. There are moral and political ideas embedded in Marx's theory of commodity fetishism that come from his concern about people's being ruled by things, and certainly this concern was our way in to the normative dimensions of the account. Equally the substance of Marx's economic theory stands behind the account. But origins are not ends and the idea of fetishism in secular practices will be misconstrued if, in the grip of another ideological formation of capitalist social relations, we treat these moral, political or economic ideas as bottom lines of his analysis. We should let Marx speak for himself on this point, and what he insisted on was that it is the contradictory values of the commodity, its use value and its exchange value, that is the appropriate beginning point for an understanding of capital. This other ideological formation is the legal, political and moral thought of the bourgeoisie and, I add, of empowered white men. It brings us back to rights fetishism.

171

THE NORMATIVE DIMENSIONS OF RIGHTS FETISHISM

Silencing and closure

Doctrinal legal discourse functions by silencing. This is ground we have already covered. One has to take a point of view internal to the discourse to comprehend it, and within the discourse law's truths are what count as truth, and legal meanings are the exclusively relevant meanings. Those who are committed to the ethical value of law, claim that this silencing is of all, equally, in the interests of some universal moral ideal – justice or integrity or utility. What is interesting about silencing is that those who participate in it (in various discourses; legal doctrine is certainly not alone here) do so in the names of knowledge, of freedom of speech, and of political pluralism. They are either sublimely unaware of this contradiction between their practice and their theory, or they justify it as necessary to achieving their goals.

A contradiction at the heart of ways of thought that value rationality as coherence or consistency should be very damaging to their plausibility. But it is not. The contradiction is 'resolved' in the construction of ethical principles. If all, equally, are silenced to law's truths, then none may complain. Ethical or moral norms, as Kant perceived, not only have a universal form. In content they must satisfy the criterion of universalisability (Kant 1909; Flew 1984: 360). In the 'moral law', then, there is said to be that unity of form and content that makes it the perfect form of practical reason. Of course, in the application of this perfect form of reason, much turns on inclusion and exclusion from the class of 'moral persons'. Children, 'native inhabitants' of British colonies, women and lunatics, for example, have historically been excluded or given subordinate status within the class. However that may be, the universal form and universalisable content of ethical norms makes them the most perfect form of a norm.

If norms are seen as the objects of knowledge of law, then whether or not law is disassociated from morality, it participates in the form of the universal ethical norm. Rights now, abstract or concrete, being a product or ground of law, share this ethical dimension and are thought of as goods: things having at least the form, if not the content, of moral value. 'Individuals', moral or legal persons, have rights and rights have value. I have suggested earlier (above: 148) that we must lift the assumption that rights are goods

172

in this universal sense if we wish to understand the value of law for persons occupying subordinated standpoints. We can go further now into the reasons for this suggestion. The problem with thinking of rights as goods, is that it may make us forget that a right is not what we want or need. As the response of the Aboriginal elder to an injunction ordering a government authority to desist from harming a sacred site illustrates (above: 17), there is a difference between being respected, and winning a court case which establishes entitlement to respect in a specific instance. The action would not have been necessary were the respect accorded.[2]

What more can the law do? Nothing: and nothing because its limitations as a mode of social regulation and control are not acknowledged within its discourses and cannot be acknowledged if its coercive enforcement is to be minimised. Thus, its limited historical significance and the limits engendered by the circumstance that it is the law of and for a way of life that requires social relations of material inequality, are denied. By giving voice to this denial, Jurisprudence becomes an exemplary instance of negatively ideological thought. Thought, that is, which is unaware of its incompleteness, its imperfection, its inevitable one-sidedness; thought that has closed out the possibility of finding a better practice of social regulation and control than the practice of which it is part.

It will be objected that this is quite wrong. That the limits of law are recognised in Jurisprudential discussion of its relations with morality and political power, and institutionalised in the separation of powers between the legislature, the executive and the judiciary. The degree of truth in this objection refutes overly generalised, radicalist claims that rights are just 'lies and errors'. It is sufficient to make legal action a useful tool in a political struggle. In deciding whether and how to deploy it, however, we should have it in mind that the limits to law which are set out in Jurisprudence are not the limits which a theory of law which takes legal practices and institutions back to social relations, rather than stopping at norms as objects of knowledge of law, reveals. The limits of law which a relational and realist theory reveals, are its historical finiteness and the actuality of what it can deliver within a society whose social relations are the conditions of existence of the dominant legal form. We do not escape this in the existence of other, non-classical forms of legal regulation and control, though theorists who point to the diversity of such forms do well to remind us of this diversity

(Cotterrell 1984: 171ff; De Sousa Santos 1985: 299). But Jurisprudence takes its model from the classical legal form identified by Weber (1978: 654ff) as formal rational law and, as enthusiastic responses to Dworkin's work attest, has considerable success in promoting the idea that this form places us on the only road to progress. This ideological message inhibits the implementation of ideas of socialist legality and feminist initiatives at legislative and administrative levels (Purdy 1989).

The message relies on a closure which is negatively ideological. It happens in thought. It happens with the construction of norms as objects of knowledge of law in general. The appearance of rights as goods with a simple, uncontradictory property of value is the flip side of this coin. My question is why and how does it happen. It is in answer to that question that I suggest that legal practices of deciding particular cases by general rules, of coercively enforcing the judgments, and of justifying them in terms of legal or moral 'truths' which deny the incompleteness of lawyers' ideas of law, constitute rights fetishism. Jurisprudence finds its basis in the social reality of this fetish.

The legal alienation of subjectivity

The normative dimensions of this account of rights fetishism concern the point and purpose of characterising legal practices in this way, given a recognised dependence of the characterisation on a framework of thought. I make no claim to universality for this framework. These reasons are relative to my standpoint. Further I make no claim to epistemic or moral superiority for these views. In this, my version of standpoint theory is different from standpoint *epistemologies* whether feminist or liberal or socialist. But we shall come back to this later. We should look first at these normative dimensions.

Rights fetishism is subtle. It involves a demand, as a *quid pro quo* (literally, a something for a something) from all who want a share of the benefits and protections of law, that they adopt a pre-fabricated identity and alienate their very sociability – capacities to get along with each other and deal with problems of conflicting interests and desires – to professional experts, officials and agents of the nation state (Duncanson and Kerruish 1986). Socio-legal theorists have demonstrated that this demand is commonly refused. Stuart Macaulay's classic study of contract law (Macaulay

1963; see also Beale and Dugdale 1975) shows that business people have developed modes of dispute resolution that avoid legal action. But that is not to say that the demand is not made; only that some people are in a position to refuse to pay the price of legal forms of regulation and control. More pertinent are studies suggesting that alternative modes of dispute resolution (informal justice) may give groups on the down-side of a power relation a worse outcome than formal legal proceedings (Abel 1981). Against use of such studies to legitimate law as the best possible means of dispute resolution between materially unequal parties, however, we should place Cain's work on informal justice and her arguments for committed legal practice (Cain 1985). For the point here is that in a committed legal practice the clients are participant in legal proceedings in a much fuller sense. At this level, my concern is with the price of rights; the costs to us of alienating our subjectivity and becoming 'legal persons'.

We need to come back to the way doctrinal legal discourse silences in order to see the necessity of this price; in order to appreciate, in other words, that this is nothing that can be given up within legal modes of social regulation and control, and moreover, that it cannot be given up because it is what justifies the silencing. It can best be explained by reference to the right to be heard.[3] We do not take listening to both sides of an argument seriously if we understand what one party is saying but not the other; and this question of understanding goes beyond use of the same language. It extends into world views in the broadest sense. The artificiality of doctrinal legal discourse, together with a professional class of expert operators of it, may then be thought to provide a solution to the problem of discursive difference between parties.

There would be something to be said for this idea of doctrinal legal discourse as a meta-discourse were it ideologically neutral, were the services of the legal profession actually equally accessible to all, and were it the case that arguments within this discourse were guided by, but were not about, its own technical peculiarities. None of these conditions for the effectiveness of the solution hold however. Nor can they hold given materially unequal social relations, a private, substantially self-regulated legal profession which offers its services and gets its rewards on a market in which all are welcome but few can buy, and a whole set of considerations inclining the discourse toward technicism.[4] Dworkin's idea, to admit the ideological character of doctrinal legal discourse and to engage in

175

purposive interpretation that will keep the discourse on line toward its utopian goals, concedes that the first condition is not met and so tries a different justification. This justification only works, however, if we think that liberal ideology retains progressive potential and signally fails to address the other two problems. Nonetheless, by giving a more ambient context to the alienation theme with which we began, Dworkin reveals a parallel, in normative dimensions, between commodity fetishism and rights fetishism. Marx's concern was with the action of objects which rule their producers; with the exchange-value form of value giving rise to the appearance of commodities as having active capacities to enter into relations with each other.

Can we voice such a concern in relation to human legal systems? The difficulty we confront is voicing concern at human laws ruling our lives when this is just what laws are meant to do, and when alternatives seem either reactionary or impossible. This difficulty is met, however, by making the concern more precise. It is focused on a disjunction that goes to the very heart of legitimating strategies in Jurisprudence – the disjunction of the rule of law from the rule of men. The claim here is that this metaphorical expression of the impartiality of the law is a metaphor whose value is spent. The rule of law is the rule of men and it is high time that was recognised. This, from a feminist standpoint, is to deny the authority of present law to rule us. From both socialist and feminist standpoints it is to refuse it respect by virtue of its form. It is to begin to say that we will respect the law only insofar as its content, its institutions and its professional operators earn that respect in our eyes. Perhaps then the questions should be: how can we *not* voice this concern, why should we not make this demand on our judges, our lawyers, our public servants and our politicians? For the demand is not new. The bourgeois jurists of the seventeenth and eighteenth centuries made it against the functionaries of the *ancien régime*. Bentham made it with his attack on Blackstone (Bentham 1977; Hart 1982: 21). Dickens made it in *Bleak House*. Critical, feminist and socialist legal theorists are making it today.

But the demand is still too abstract. There are further questions. How we can make the demand with a resonance that will sound through the centuries of silencing in which judges and legislators, and bureaucrats and legal practitioners of various kinds have participated, and participated in good faith? For the participation goes on, in many instances, still in good faith. Another question goes to the detail of the demand or, perhaps better, of the translation of an abstract demand into specific ones. These are political and research questions for concerted thought and action in relation to particular cases and problems. But the theory of knowledge and method that makes rights fetishism visible in the first place can guide our thought about them. We begin then to ask how Jurisprudence, as a negatively ideological discourse based on rights fetishism, maintains its credibility, and why its protagonists are blind to rights fetishism.

Configuration and exclusion of standpoints

I suggest that normative aspects in Marx's account of commodity fetishism can be understood only in terms of standpoint, though his actual reference is to 'the bourgeois intellect'. Relevant to rights fetishism we should take account of a comment in a Preface to *Capital* that uses the term 'standpoint' albeit in quite a different context.

> To prevent possible misunderstanding, a word. I paint the capitalist and the landlord in no sense *couleur de rose* [the colour of the rose]. But here individuals are dealt with only in so far as they are the personifications of economic categories, embodiments of particular class-relations and class-interests. My standpoint, from which the evolution of the economic formation of society is viewed as a process of natural history, can less than any other make the individual responsible for relations whose creature he socially remains, however much he may subjectively raise himself above them.
>
> (Marx 1938: xix)

In the context of the discussion of commodity fetishism Marx, assuming differences between reality, social reality, and phenomenal appearances, distinguishes scientific from vulgar political economy, and explains commodity fetishism as a phenomenon which both conceals the social reality of economic value and, despite discoveries within classical political economy, continues to inhibit comprehension of it by the bourgeois intellect, that is, in the context of the text and its place and time of production, from the bourgeois standpoint. In the context of his Preface, Marx refers to his own standpoint, as a theoretical or neutrally ideological position, to make the point that moral criticism of individuals for the existence of capitalist social relations is not intended and is indeed inconsistent with his theory of social and historical change. These points come together in relation to rights fetishism. Its fetish character explains the contradictory views on legal practices and institutions that are presented in this book. The place in history of those practices makes moral criticism of individuals engaged in them otiose.

But political criticism is in no way otiose and this gives rise to a problem. It is not only difficult to hold political and moral questions apart, it is misleading to do so. Within the Western tradition of political philosophy, the idea that ethics is above politics, rather than a branch of it (cp. Aristotle 1955: 26) is a late-comer that may be seen as an impoverishment of practical reason (MacIntyre 1981). Nonetheless, there are differences between morals and politics which conflations, such as Dworkin's politico-moral principles, elide, and which consideration of only political questions avoids. That said, the modern ethical and meta-ethical thought of empowered white men need detain us only briefly. Insofar as it affirms a principle of individual responsibility and worth it is empowering. Insofar as its conception of the 'individual' disconnects human subjects from each other and insofar as the human 'individual' is located outside the ecology of living systems, it is a disaster. What I want to bring out here is a way in which the two indications from Marx of the relevance of standpoint to social theory, can be linked together as normative dimensions of rights fetishism by reference to social relations of sex–gender and race.

The premises of this argument are, first, that relations of production are not only and not primarily the social relations from which social reality is constructed. Social relations of reproduction are equally basic. Second, that questions of moral and political value, as well as questions of the scientific values, are different *kinds* of questions to questions about economic value; as different as questions about chemical valencies. The first premise has, I think, been established by feminist and black action. The second is more contentious and more difficult precisely because its truth is concealed by fetishes – scientism and economism on the one hand, rights fetishism on the other. But the very degree of controversy surrounding questions of value, both in economics and in moral and political philosophy is, I think, evidence that value is an 'essentially contested concept' (Gallie 1955–6).

While Marxist thought is distorted by economistic, positivistic or scientistic interpretations of it which make a mechanical inversion of the classical liberal idea that value is *essentially* subjective and 'fact' is *essentially* objective, these interpretations of Marx's thought were encouraged by its sociology of basic social relations. Once we move, however, from economics to law, we move to a discourse which wears its morally and politically normative dimensions on its sleeve. And once we critically analyse a discourse which, in its own terms, is concerned with relations of ruler and ruled, social relations of sex–gender and race assert their relevance. Thus even within Pashukanis' application of classical Marxist theory, which does suggest a single law of value located in relations of economic production, we find, in the context of his discussion of law and morality, a recognition of sexual as well as, and as distinct from, class determination of difference; differences which are excluded by the universality of normative discourse (Pashukanis 1978: 153).

Once relational social theory becomes aware that social relations of sex–gender and race are not reducible to class, an epistemological question arises as to how knowledge and understanding gained from one standpoint, say a socialist standpoint, is related to knowledge and understanding gained from another, say a feminist standpoint (Cain 1990). We will come back to this. The point here is that rights fetishism excludes *all* standpoints. Consequently Jurisprudence and mainstream moral and political theory is untroubled by this problem. But this is no gain. It is a lack. It is a circumstance, I suggest, that helps to explain the stagnation of mainstream Western moral, political and legal thought. The abstract, universal, moral norm is as abstract, as static and as lifeless an idea as one can imagine and its paralysing effect on thought extends into other discourses that construct norms as their objects of knowledge or that take values, including the political values of various traditions, as their bottom line of explanation.

It will be objected here that this whole argument overlooks two things. First, that Kantian ethics does not dominate the field of contemporary moral, political and legal thought, is just the classical statement of one of various schools of thought to which Hart and Finnis, for example, owe very little. Second, that in fact Western moral, political and legal thought has not stagnated; that there is a thriving debate on justice and human rights which has its practical conditions and effects in the institutions of the United Nations and non-governmental organisations which are concerned with human rights abuses and aid to poor countries.

There is truth in both these objections. I am not, however, claiming that Kantian ethics is dominant in mainstream ethical thought. I do not have a point of view internal to this discourse and have no interest in making any such judgment. It would seem that Aristotle and Hume, Locke and Rousseau are alive and well in its ethics and politics, and Hobbes too. I notice a return to various versions of neo-Aristotelian thought in protestant and republican traditions, as well as continued assertion of its Aquinian development. John Rawls, whose influential theory of justice *is* neo-Kantian, acknowledges his debts to Hart in developing the idea of justice as fairness (Rawls 1973). The syntheses and arguments go on; flourish, indeed. I claim only that Kant took a line of thought, very consistently, to a particular stagnant end, and that the force of this moral logic is still with us, though contemporary exponents, such as Rawls, actually take much of their 'inspiration' from the institutionalised legal form of it. The second point only counts as an objection if it is assumed that the vitality of contemporary concern for human rights and social justice derives from the mainstream of Western ethical thought. This I deny. I do not deny that this tradition is informed by the experience of those who have fared well in life and who thus have an understanding of certain of life's goods. Nor am I concerned to denigrate whatever good is done by institutions which organise practical activity consistently with that thought. But it is socialists, feminists, environmentalists, black thinkers and fighters and liberation theologists who are engaged on the active side of changing moral and political awareness.

These then are the people who have the trouble of relating different knowledges from different standpoints and what now, after traumas of sectarianism, is becoming clear, is that there is no cause to be threatened by the plurality of representations of reality if the denial of difference is no part of our ideology. It is threatening only for those who seek to impose their world view on others; and that seems to be pretty much in the same measure as the idea of objective knowledge has been deployed as a strategy of power. But against the flourishing pragmatism of our era, and against the fear of a heart of darkness in Western masculinity,[5] or of making the same mistakes again, I think that a theoretical project aimed at finding things out for the purpose of emancipating subordinated groups and classes and preventing the destruction of our physical environment, is no occasion for supposing that truth is what we say it is, or what works for us, or that we can do without it.

Practice again

We need, in this project, to come back to practice as the *actuality and goal* of our enquiries (Lenin 1976b: 212ff). Not practice, as the pragmatists would have it, as a mode of verification of our theses; and not a concept of practice that in being specific to human activity, falls into another humanistic conceit and down-grades the non-human world to human production (Marx 1964: 106ff). This is where feminist and environmentalist modes and conceptions of practice are necessary (Mathews 1989) and where Western thought must defer to the relationship that indigenous people in Africa, America and Australia have with the non-human environment. It is a context in which a tough notion of caring suggested by Grimshaw (1986) can be developed. Practice, simply as intentional human activity that changes the world, is what we have. There is not, thus far, much cause for complacency, and the celebrated unity of theory and practice can as well describe the way of thought of the successful lawyer or careerist academic as the socialist exemplar of what is to be done. In the context of this book, practice as the goal of our inquiry, is intentional human activity that changes the world by bringing about the end of materially unequal social relations. It is a strictly non-Utopian goal. It is what we do in the present in taking up the personal and political challenge of finding ways of making and sharing standpoints with others.

On one level, as Cain (1990) has pointed out, this is a matter of actually choosing and changing our relationships. On another level, there is a task that comes down to working out who is on 'our' side and in what way. The other side of that coin is working out, personally and politically, who 'we' are. One thing, surely, that we do know here, is that we are the most numerous and the resonance that is sought will come from our coming together. In aid of this, I want to look more closely at standpoint, as an actuality of the being of active thoughtful subjects, and point of view as commitment to the normative dimension of a way of thought. The barrier constituted by ideology in the neutral sense is what is in issue here. I think we stumble over it if we conflate standpoint and point of view.

POINT OF VIEW AND STANDPOINT

Point of view and perspective (e.g. internal/external) are ideas that are used to support and justify knowledge claims as either privileged or practically interested judgments. They are in that sense purely epistemological and methodological notions. Standpoint on the other hand has epistemological and methodological *relevance* deriving from a desire to find out, but it is not, in the understanding of this book, a purely epistemological notion. Standpoint here is an actual position of active thoughtful subjects within the social relations of a given society and, at the same time, a position within ideology (above: 25ff). It is a political, sociological and a philosophical concept, and in its latter aspect it is contextualised by the Hegelian–Marxist philosophical tradition.

Point of view and standpoint in
Jurisprudence and legal theory

Point of view is purely epistemological because it is concerned with the intentional or purposive aspect of social practices. We can say that it is a critical reflective attitude to a standard of behaviour as normatively (legally, in Hart's case; morally in Finnis') correct. In that case point of view is a concept that helps us to understand reasons for action. Alternatively, we can say, like Dworkin, that it is the point of view taken by participants in an interpretive practice on which propositions are correct and why. Again the notion goes to reasoning. Thus a solicitor may say to her client, for example, that from a legal point of view it is not correct to say that promises, all other things being equal, ought to be performed. The law, she will explain, takes account only of certain kinds of promises: then she or he may go on and explain which and, from a legal point of view, why. The notion of perspective, comes in with recognition that an object of inquiry will 'look' different according to the relationship between the observer and observed. In Jurisprudence it is at home in debate about whether a social theory of law should be written from an external or an internal point of view.

There is no reference to standpoint as distinct from point of view and perspective in any of the texts we have examined. We find it, however, in Pashukanis' *Law and Marxism* and in sociological Jurisprudence.

The critique of bourgeois jurisprudence from the stand-point of scientific socialism... must, above all, venture into enemy territory. It should not throw aside the generalisa-tions and abstractions elaborated by bourgeois jurists, whose starting point was the needs of their class and of their times. Rather by analysing these abstract categories, it should demonstrate their true significance and lay bare the histori-cally limited nature of the legal form.

(Pashukanis 1978: 64)

This is a reflection on method, and Pashukanis can be interpreted here as saying that there is a point of view internal to the bourgeois jurists' ideas of law, and that it is necessary to understand this point of view – to see how the system of thought fits together and functions, to understand its intentionality – if one is to understand law. But he himself speaks from a standpoint. In terms of his metaphor we can put it this way. As persons with a standpoint for the working class we do not change our standpoint when we go onto enemy territory and look at the terrain from the enemy's point of view. Pashukanis, however, did not, I think, have a clear grasp of the difference between point of view and standpoint; a lack of clarity attributable to his idea that a single law of value based in economic relations of production governed all forms of normat-ivity. So we must go on from here.

In American sociological jurisprudence the term 'standpoint' is used by Pound (1959: 129–32), largely to draw attention to the relevance of social roles (law-maker, individual subject, judge, etc.). In a more analytical mode, Twining and Miers attempt a clarifica-tion of 'standpoint' and 'role'. They suggest that the notion of standpoint is relevant to the task of predicting *only* in terms of 'ultimate consequences'; that is to say, without reference to moral or political considerations or, one might say, to intentions (Twining and Miers 1976: 24ff). To remove the notion of standpoint, how-ever, from the traditions of Hegel, Marx, and Gramsci, each of whom might be thought to have worked with the notion (Harding 1986: 26; Cain 1990: 1) is to change the meaning of the term and link it to the liberal idea of a standpoint that is outside the world; the celebrated Archimedean point from which all may be seen and known. Within the Hegelian–Marxist tradition, standpoint links a social actor's knowledge and understanding to his or her position within social relations. Hegelian origins of the notion are linked by

Harding to Hegel's thinking about the relationship between master and slave; Marxian origins, whether in Marx or Gramsci, to the class character of knowledge. To link standpoint to an amoral approach to predicting, as Twining does, is not inconsistent with a dimension of the notion within the Marxist tradition (Marx 1938: xix); but to disconnect standpoint from social relations and interests changes it beyond recognition. Within understandings of society that conceive social relations in terms of social roles, Pound's 'confusion' of standpoint and role is closer to the notion within the Hegelian–Marxist tradition, than is Twining's and Miers' attempt to distinguish analytically distinct concepts of standpoint and role.

Standpoint and feminist standpoint epistemologies

The shift in the meaning of 'standpoint' that occurs when it is taken out of a relational and sociological theory and relocated in a sociologically informed but dominantly analytic tradition of Jurisprudence, is replicated in feminist theory with the construction of feminist standpoint epistemologies. The shift, I suggest, again occurs under the influence of the dominantly analytic tradition of English language philosophy. According to Sandra Harding's sympathetically critical account of feminist standpoint epistemologies, their most general point is to suggest that 'women's subjugated position provides the possibility of more complete and less perverse understandings'. Standpoint is for her 'a morally and scientifically preferable grounding for our interpretations and explanations of nature and social life'. She cites Jane Flax, Hilary Rose, Nancy Hartsock and Dorothy Smith as exponents of this standpoint approach (Harding 1986: 26). Curiously she neglects to acknowledge Alison Jaggar's very comprehensive and clear discussion of radical and socialist feminist conceptions of the standpoint of women (Jaggar 1983: 369ff). Jaggar locates the notion of standpoint within epistemology and develops it in relation to the problematic of arriving at an adequate representation of reality. She thus begins with a contrast between the liberal epistemologist's conception of an Archimedean standpoint 'somewhere outside the reality that is being observed' and the Marxist disavowal of such a standpoint. She insists on a structural identity between traditional Marxist and social feminist epistemology which, combined with insistence on the

... special social or class position of women ... gives them a special epistemological standpoint which makes possible a view of the world that is more reliable and less distorted than that available either to capitalist or to working class men.

(Jaggar 1983: 370)

I do not suppose Jaggar to make an historical mistake in linking liberal and Marxist notions of standpoint. Some will claim a sense in which a standpoint within and a standpoint wholly outside social relations are the same kind of idea. However, I doubt the emancipatory value of that approach. The theoretical practice of justification of a theory or a thesis as epistemically or morally superior by reference to the standpoint from which it has been formulated is inconsistent with an emancipatory point of view.

This is why I want to clarify the difference between the two notions. Epistemic and ethical justifications are theoretical practices not wholly unlike the legal practice of justifying a decision as objective or objective and right or uniquely right. They produce their own forms of fetishism from which the negative ideologies of scientism and ethical rationalism have emerged.

Of course, Marx considered that the critique of the bourgeois standpoint in classical political economy, made through his explanation of commodity fetishism, enabled him to develop a more adequate theory of economic value. Likewise I think that rights fetishism has to be understood if the value of law for people on the down-side of social relations is to be adequately assessed. But methods of argument and reasoning come in here, and Marx would not have separated his standpoint from his logic, his metaphysics and his ideas of method in social science, to justify this belief by purely epistemological argument.

> The question of whether objective truth can be attributed to human thinking is not a question of theory but is a practical question. Man must prove the truth, i.e., the reality and power, the this-worldliness of his thinking in practice. The dispute over the reality or non-reality of thinking which isolates itself from practice is a purely scholastic question.
>
> (Marx 1976: 6)

Again then, we come back to practice. If epistemology could only mean that special branch of philosophy and social theory that is concerned with justifying beliefs, then I would agree with the anti-epistemologists that we should give it up. But what distinguishes my position from theirs is that I do not understand truth as justified belief. There are all manner of beliefs that are justified in all manner of ways. Beliefs in the *Rechtsstaat* as the institution that emerges at the end of history for example! Epistemology is the theory or science of knowledge, and a different conception of knowledge and of truth entails a different conception of epistemology.

There are other problems with standpoint epistemologies which Harding identifies which reinforce the view that justifying one's knowledge and understanding as epistemically or morally superior is inconsistent with an emancipatory point of view. They are ably summarised by Cain (1990: 18–19) and involve the elision of differences between women, problems of essentialism, ethnocentricity and the false valorisation of the repressed.

Working backwards through that list, the first point to be made is that when it comes to actualities, materially unequal power relations harm, hurt and damage. We come back here to the difference between an experience of suffering a particular form of oppression (say racial discrimination) and a consciousness that others are suffering this, and to the limited potential of thought, even thought proceeding from the experience of some other form of oppression (say sex discrimination) and representation to bridge that gap. On the latter count, if we are academics, students or intellectuals, male or female, black or white, we are confronted by the privileged position of the mental over the manual labourer within the division of labour maintained in our societies. The tendency of this division of labour is to separate us further from those actually experiencing the grossest forms of harm, hurt and damage of materially unequal social relations. Theory cannot but elide some differences, but in my judgment this is not a difference that should be elided.

An equally profound difficulty is that knowing and understanding in the Western tradition of which many socialists and feminists are part, are modes of containing other knowledges and penetrating other ways of life.[6] Essentialism and ethnocentrism are very much in issue here and the question is how are we not being essentialist and ethnocentric if we claim epistemic and moral superiority for the knowledge produced from a particular standpoint? If we try to avoid that by speaking more generally of a single standpoint for subordinated people and use this formulation to legitimise our theory, this starts to look like an inversion of the single Archimedean point.

Standpoints are particular. Active thoughtful subjects each have positions within social relations. But standpoints are positions within social relations and within ideologies. They are therefore identifiable only where an ideology in the neutral sense which is of and for a class of a particular social relation has emerged. We can speak of the standpoint of empowered white men as a standpoint which is opposed to a feminist standpoint, and the standpoint of the bourgeoisie as opposed to a socialist standpoint. From philosophy of science and social science and from this analysis of Jurisprudence, we can specify a standpoint of empowered white men as relevant to the production of knowledge that represses, silences and is used destructively. It is a standpoint which women and people of colour may opt for, and it is a standpoint which may in fact be occupied by theorists who claim to have gone beyond its classical eighteenth century epistemology. For point of view comes in here too, and what we are looking for, in the normative dimensions of a theory, is an emancipatory point of view.

FORM, CONTENT AND UTOPIAN GOALS

Jurisprudence, I suggest, now, but not during the seventeenth and eighteenth centuries when bourgeois jurists elaborated their desired social order, is a form of negative ideology analogous to, and consistent with, vulgar economy. It deals only with appearances and with meanings, rather than with the real social relations of our legal systems.

When thought about ways of life, from and for a given standpoint, consolidates its products, a more or less complete theory emerges within which there is a point of view which explains the normative dimensions of the theory – its norms of method, politics and morals and its propositions about how we ought to understand the world, ourselves and others. Legal doctrine is a highly stylised and dogmatic form of such a theory. It is articulated as general norms to be applied to particular disputes, imposes its meanings on all participants in legal practices and claims truth for itself so as to justify its coercive enforcement. This form, I suggest, is a form of the thought of empowered white men. Historically, a dominant legal form appropriate to the rule of the bourgeoisie emerged from the regulation of social relations of possession, ownership, control and alienation of land and commodities. There are other forms of legal relations. Relations of status within family and political community, and relations emerging from what is conceived to be wrongdoing are examples. They have a different and longer history. But the bourgeoisie's accession to political power was intimately tied to its economic strength. This strength lay in the emergence of a capitalist mode of production with its characteristics of private ownership of the means of production, socialised labour (that is, labour for others), commodification and market exchange.

The content of norms regulating and seeking to secure possession, title, control and alienation of land and commodities, in tending to further the interests of property and commodity owners, was (and is) part of the dynamic of the production of legal forms. Forms and content of law and laws about production relations thus emerge configuratively with forms and content of law and laws maintaining social relations within which one class or gender or racial group is dominated by the other. Since the rule of the bourgeoisie in dissolving status ties inconsistent with capitalist production was relatively liberatory, it incorporated an emancipatory point of view.

A point of view involves commitment to various moral, political, methodological and epistemological norms. It can only be emancipatory if these norms are informed by the experience of subordinated people and are aimed at ending that experience. To the extent a theory helps subordinated groups and classes to achieve this aim it has value for them. For the bourgeoisie, a class formed from people who had lacked political power within the *ancien régime*, this value became, in theory, absolute.

But in practice, it was never the case that the bourgeoisie, as an homogeneous fraternity of persons committed to freedom, equality and reciprocity, ruled with absolute security over all. The church and the aristocracy hung on to some of their power and their privilege. Diverse forms of capital and diverse methods of capital accumulation bring factions of the bourgeoisie into competition with each other. On the other hand, in different measure at different times and places, there is an ongoing resistance from workers, peasants and indigenous peoples. Further, institutionalisation of bourgeois rule within the nation state is no precision instrument or apparatus of checks and balances between legislature, executive and judiciary. There are both traditional rivalries between organs of government and diverse sites and lineages of power which make its operation far less predictable (Carson 1981; Foucault 1977). In practice then, the bourgeoisie moves with only relative security into the position of a ruling class. The absolute, unquestionable value of its science and its law is thus set against a social reality of rivalry and tensions within, resistance to, and questioning of, its capacity to rule. Belief in that absolute, unquestionable value is sustained now by further and further abstractions of thought from the day-to-day actuality of materially unequal social relations and the practices which maintain them. What begins, perhaps, as genuine and well-founded optimism in having found a liberatory way, turns up now as the points of view of various discourses of and for orthodoxy. The various legal points of view are just that.

They are taught and learned and operated with, still for the same goals of the ascendant bourgeoisie – liberty, equality and fraternity – but goals that have now become Utopian; goals which will never be achieved. An abstract, watered down version of them is instantiated in the law, but this very instantiation turns into a barrier to maximum freedom, material equality and political community that is not of and for white men because legal points of view exclude the relevance of standpoint as a condition of their own effectiveness.

A feminist standpoint, for example, comes from an awareness of unequal power relations and cannot be understood from a legal point of view. Nor can a socialist one. Standpoint as explained here has as a consequence the standpoint relativity of knowledge whereas law's truths are absolutes.

But now we should notice a turn. A legal point of view can be taken by someone with a feminist standpoint, it is just a matter of choosing to participate in legal practices. She or he can learn what propositions count as true and false within doctrinal legal argument and why. Moreover, difficult as this enterprise may be, it can be an effective mode of feminist practice. A committed feminist practice will challenge the politically and, from subordinated standpoints, morally compromising legal ethic of pretending impartiality and acting as a hired gun for whoever can pay.

This in turn hinges on the fact that legal practices and institutions are modes of and venues for political action. Consequently the *content* of doctrinal legal rules is a fully social product which mounts constant challenge to their static normative form. Repressive laws are resisted in multiple ways; progressive ones are fought for by persons occupying subordinated standpoints; are negotiated and compromised by ruling classes and groups. Without doubt the legislators and public servants, the judges and the lawyers, who have had most to do with the verbal and textual formulations of these laws have been white men who belong to or who serve the ruling classes. But modern legal practices of social regulation and control are not reducible to domination of a population or class by a sovereign or other class. This, as an ideological message of Hart's *The Concept of Law,* encoded in the distinction between active officials and passive citizens, is, however qualified, its most disempowering point (Skillen 1977; Edgeworth 1989). There is participation in legal practices that goes across classes, sex–gender groups and races and that is not just because the politically naive get 'sucked in' to the idea that they have rights as some American Critical Legal Theorists seem to think. Political action for the legislative change and legal action pressing new claims of right on the courts are modes of participation in legal practices. They have limited success, reflected in the content of the laws, albeit contained by their form and compromised by forensic procedures.

So far as law's content is concerned, 'we', as exploited and devalued and oppressed people, need to understand our own part in the making of the legal system. We need to struggle against the forces that tend to confuse and devalorise our contribution by refusing the demand of rights fetishism and asserting a subjectivity that is ours. Here, I suggest, it helps to appreciate the interplay of the emancipatory point of the view of classical liberal thought as a point of view coming from the standpoint of an ascendant bourgeoisie, and the devaluation of everything that is outside the fraternity of empowered white men and those whom they choose to join them. This devaluation is inherent in thought which is of and for the standpoint of empowered white men. It appears to be no part of liberal ideology because of the centrality of abstract equality to that way of thought. This appearance, however, is not more than a refusal to recognise the realities of material inequality and the value of socialist, feminist and anti-racist thought. The configuration of thought from bourgeois and empowered white male standpoints in the forms of legal practices, doctrines and institutions, and the contradiction between the once emancipatory point of view of classical liberal thought and the devaluation of 'the other' that is inherent in the point of view of empowered white men, goes some way to explaining the complexity of law as an ideological formation.

These complexities are difficulties in the way of working out the value of law for those who are put down by it. Part of the work of standpoint theory, therefore, is to work out the degree of truth within theories developed from an opposed standpoint or, relevant to our inquiry, the value that law has for those with whom we share or seek to share a standpoint. That is why we need to hang on to an idea of truth. It is also why we cannot understand the value of law in terms of universal judgments of its beneficence or otherwise.

The important thing, now that a variety of basic social relations have been identified, and now that the difference between point of view and standpoint has been explained, is to be clear that emancipatory points of view can be shared by people with different standpoints. Claiming an emancipatory point of view as 'our' point of view, given different standpoints, brings us back to questions of who 'we' are. Standpoint reclaims political communities from the homogenised community of nationalist political thought. But locating our political identity within basic social relations is not just a matter of adopting an 'emancipatory point of view' and even participation in class, sex–gender and race politics is insufficient. We must constitute our agency for subordinated classes and people by more than good intentions and need to be very wary of supposing that our practice has done that, or if it has at one time, will continue to do so.

This brings us, I think, to a need to recognise and be careful of *all* the normative dimensions of an emancipatory point of view. There is no established tradition that has a monopoly on it. At particular times and places there will be political movements that consistently act in accordance with such a point of view. Liberalism was once an emancipatory theory and is now, at best, a theory that tries to hold some of the ground won by socialists and feminists and black thinkers and actors against its own neo-classicist wing. Socialism has become complacent and corrupt where it has assumed its own rightness or virtue and lost sight of its dialectic, and feminism can be essentialist and ethnocentric. Nonetheless, it is from socialism and feminism, with deference to black standpoints, and with remembrance of liberal contributions, that some practical reflections on the normative dimensions of a legal theory can be offered.

1. I think that we, as people trying to construct and maintain emancipatory points of view from a variety of subordinated standpoints, need to counterpoint our moral to our political thought in ways *we* find harmonious. On that score, an ethical discourse that has consistently devalued women, people of colour and working

people – people of action as opposed to contemplative people – is dissonant indeed. This is the good sense of the Marxist rejection of rationalist ethics.

2. An emancipatory point of view can be found within knowledges of different standpoints at different places and times. But its normative requirements, political, epistemological or methodological, cannot be allowed to become the bottom line of our thinking. The basis for an emancipatory point of view, within a society structured by social relations of material inequality, must lie within an active struggle against alienation, devaluation and oppression. It cannot be carried over into principles for maintaining existing social relations so long as any form of subordination and inequality remains inscribed in those relations. For when that happens, once-progressive thought, no less than doctrinal legal thought, loses itself in its own product, its normative requirements. It thus falls prey to its own forms of fetishism.

3. The real difficulties in knowledge and understanding are the multiple centricities of thought – ethnocentricity, androcentricity and gynaecocentricity, not to mention the narcissism of finding within one's own thought the model of pure rationality.[7] Here, on the positive side, I find Lenin's idea of dialectic as

> living, many-sided knowledge (with the number of sides eternally increasing), with an infinite number of shades of every approach and approximation to reality (with a philosophical system growing into a whole out of each shade).
> (Lenin 1976c: 360)

helpful. It leads him to liken human knowledge 'to a curve, which endlessly approximates a series of circles, a spiral' (Ibid.: 361). One could go on: a series of spirals. But spirals of thought and theories of practice are, again, very abstract. In the meantime, there is the problem of coping with differences in standpoints and their consequences for knowledge and understanding. I do not think this can be done pragmatically. It must be done in a principled way and this brings us back to the oppressive potential of telling others, even others with whom we share a standpoint, of what they ought to do and how they ought to think. I have found an analogy between authors and prisoners throwing messages over the wall that encloses them, to be helpful here. We can only hope that the message will be picked up and acted on by others but have no means of knowing whether or not it will be. This, it seems to me, is how it is so far as our identities as authors and thinkers are concerned. Our endeavour must be to get those messages over the barrier of our inevitably, but neutrally, ideological thought, not to persuade our fellow prisoners either that it is impossible or that we know what messages will secure our release.

4. But authors, prisoners of our own thought, is not all that we are. There is a materiality of things and an experience of living that enable us to know that we cannot think ourselves out of our prison though we may be able to think ourselves into accepting it, or into believing that we have no choice but to accept it, or even that it is a cell, which, in keeping us safe from the world and its ways, enables us to contemplate the forms of truth and goodness. Alternatively we could just get to like it in there and think, with a horribly misconceived generosity, that everyone else really ought to join us. This, it seems to me is where negative ideologies begin. So we must keep it in mind that the barrier of neutral ideology is neither insurmountable nor wholly opaque. It has its materiality in the practices of and for particular ways of life of which legal practices are an example, and in our own preparedness to accept the authority of those who think that these practices are for the good of us all. We must then resist that imposition of thought and confront, within ourselves, the bases of that preparedness. For that task, far from being problematic, the multiplicity of subordinated standpoints is a valuable thing from which we can gain wider social and deeper self-knowledge. Standpoint specific research on law and laws, then, is the norm of method that emerges.

7

BY WAY OF A CONCLUSION: STANDPOINT RELATIVITY AND THE VALUE OF LAW

I have argued in this book that Jurisprudence is a negative form of ideology. The material inequality of social relations in the societies in which I write cannot, in my view, be justified. They are a condition of our legal system and are maintained and reproduced by it. In justifying the legal maintenance of the existing order of things, Jurisprudence justifies that order.

My purpose, however, is not only to articulate this critical perception of legal practices and institutions and the representations of them that we find in Jurisprudence. It is more significantly an epistemological concern: a desire to understand and to trace the way in which reality appears to persons having different and opposed standpoints. So I have asked how it is that men, in good faith, can come up with the idea that those who are put down and kept down by law have obligations to respect or obey it. Asking this question has brought me to rights fetishism and to rights as having contradictory forms of value. By way of a conclusion, I want to draw together various strands of the arguments of this book concerning the value of law for people on the down-side of social relations.

1. *Rights fetishism*. Legal practices of deciding particular cases by general rules, of coercive enforcement of those decisions, and of claiming that such judgments and their enforcement are objectively or uniquely right, constitute rights fetishism. Rights fetishism, most generally, is a phenomenon of active thoughtful subjects losing themselves in and to their own product: their thought and their laws. So the rule of law is disjoined from the rule of men and so, in Jurisprudence, we are invited to subscribe to ideas of law as an objective system of rules or principles, removed from the partisan desires and concerns of human subjects by its professional admin-

istrators, and provisional of the best possible means of social regulation and control.

There is here both an alienation of subjectivity and a disclaimer of responsibility for the repressive and coercive aspects of legal practices and institutions: a claim for the impartial innocence of law. But having noticed that, the question that arises is how does this happen? In particular, when, with an historical perspective, we acknowledge the emancipatory point of view embedded in the thought of the bourgeois jurists of the seventeenth and eighteenth centuries, there are questions about why and how and to what extent this point of view turns into a conservative one.

2. *Rights and rights talk.* A perception of rights fetishism constituted by legal practices, while it only begins this inquiry, does go some way to explaining the views on rights addressed in the previous chapters. On the one hand, writers such as Edward Thompson in England and Henry Reynolds in Australia, mindful through their historical research of the benefits of the rule of law accorded to or withheld from working or Aboriginal people, come up with claims for law as an unqualified good or as having a pure, uncorrupted form. On the other, critical theorists with a sceptical view on that side of things seem to be telling those who do claim their rights, that they do not know what is good for them. Both positions, I suggest, lack an analysis of the form of legal norms as products of the reason of empowered white men, and have insufficient regard for the extent to which that reason is limited. It does not participate in any universal form of rationality and is inappropriately deployed in telling women and black and working-class people what to do. On the other hand, this gives no occasion for wholesale denigration of that reason and its products. Such denigration tends to deny its own ideological limits: the limits of thought that condemns. It is rather to say that, because social relations and practical activity of human subjects of those relations are integral to thought and reason, the very moment of understanding some thing about our selves and our social reality, is a moment of change.

3. *Neutral ideology and negative ideology.* I have therefore been concerned to argue that although our jurists' views of law are negatively ideological, they are not merely false or mere illusion. There is a basis in social reality for their ideas of law. We should consider ideologies – more or less complete systems of thought – as neutral where they are simply standpoint relative understandings of social

reality. They become negatively ideological subsequently, on account of neglect of standpoint and the standpoint relativity of thought. People are not stupid. There has to be some basis in social reality for an ideology to be powerful. It has to make sense of some experiences of life to find its grip. A legal system is not just fashioned from and for the standpoints of the bourgeoisie and of empowered white men. What happens is that with some sense of this, but with too much arrogance or complacency or fear to inquire into the contribution of subordinated people to the emergence of legal forms, and to legislative or adjudicative reforms of the substance of the laws, jurists taking up dominant standpoints understand and represent law as divinely inspired, or as natural necessity, or as the genius of a culture.

Reality is otherwise. The process of the production of modern legal systems is part of an ongoing production of social life. A country's jurisprudence is a specific representation of a socially constructed order of things – a construction that is not the prerogative of ruling classes or of men, but which is struggled for, negotiated, compromised and redirected every step of the way. Doctrinal legal discourse contributes to this process a more or less complete theory of a desired and, for some, desirable social order. It formalises and structures a very wide range of social relations, converting them into legal relations – relations between legal persons who are bearers of rights and obligations.

4. *Jurisprudence as neutral ideology*. The forms of these relations are various and the character of the legal subject is, likewise, not uniform. Philosophical Jurisprudence, however, takes as its model a classical bourgeois form of legal relation – a relation between abstractly equal legal persons. The equality of legal persons inheres in their being conceived as autonomous actors with a capacity to make reasoned choices as to their rights and obligations. The reality of the material inequality of social relations, as well as the actual identities of people living within them is left behind in this abstract representation. Our actual being as members of and agents for classes or groups constituted by social relations, the exploitative, repressive or oppressive character of our basic social relations, and the differences between the range of choices actually available to people occupying different positions in an hierarchical social structure, are thus no part of law's 'truths': not, at least, within this classical form of the law of obligations in contract, property and tort

from which Jurisprudence takes off. And while, as I have commented, this is not the only form of legal relation, it remains sufficiently instantiated within the legal system for the legitimating purposes of Jurisprudence. For those purposes, what the jurists say and, we must assume, believe, is that the ethical ideal of equal concern and respect for individuals is a basic principle of the law and that this is a consequence of liberal and bourgeois enlightenment.

5. *Jurisprudence as negative ideology*. Leibniz is said to have commented: 'I have found that most sects are right in a good part of what they propound, but less so with regard to what they reject' (Colletti 1973: 35). The remark can be applied to Jurisprudence as a closed and dogmatic (sectarian) way of thought. It is true that the principle of equal concern and respect informs much doctrinal legal discourse. It is also true that the form of legal relations representable in terms of this principle are, paradigmatically, relations between owners of and dealers in a classically bourgeois form of wealth, commodities. But what is left out in the suggestion that all this is attributable to the good ideas and practical reasonableness of the masters of capitalist social formations, is history, and the contribution to progressive social and legal change of the thought and action of people having subordinated standpoints. The negatively ideological character of Jurisprudence rests in these exclusions.

Explaining this peculiarly selective understanding of social reality brings us back to rights fetishism as a forgetting that rights to this or to that are not the this or the that. A condition of their existence and of their value for people is a way of life within which people are *not* accorded equal concern and respect and are *unequal* in matters of everyday life. A condition of their practicality as a means of protecting and empowering those on the down-side of social relations is their enforceability. When we look to the legal point of view we find the closure that embeds this forgetting into legal ideology – the exclusion of standpoint; the belief in the objectivity and utility, or unique rightness of legal resolutions of social problems.

6. *Threatening instances and questions*. A closure within a system of thought does not determine courses of events, and however well funded its propagation may be, is but an obstacle in the way of the practical activity of classes and groups whose thought and awareness is different. So there are ongoing problems for the jurists.

Much as Jurisprudence would have us believe that we live in the best of all possible worlds and that our jurisprudence contributes the ground rules of and for this lucky arrangement; and much as this is truth for those with a standpoint for empowered and enriched groups and classes, legal and political actions by subordinated people and their servants and agents in the professions and elsewhere, are a constant and threatening reminder of a social reality of inequality. In the problem of unjust laws and legal systems, in the tie between law and coercion, and in the failures of the legal system to deliver what it promises – access to justice, control of exploitative and environmentally destructive practices by 'private' corporate enterprises, and protection of citizens from the depredations of police, prison officials and bureaucrats – the problematic nature of the whole enterprise of deciding particular cases by general rules and coercively enforcing the decision, keeps on asserting itself. What the jurists pass off as authority, as the rightful exercise of power, is questioned and challenged. Rightful according to what standards, whose standards? Obligation imposing, respect deserving on whom, from whom? On 'us' whose labour power is the source of their profit, whose thought and being is devalued by these standards, whose cultures and ways of life and bodies have been trampled and beaten? How? Why?

7. *A question of value*. The response is that this is the best that can be done in an admittedly imperfect world. Central to questions of the value of law, then, is the relation between this material or actual inequality in matters of wealth, health, opportunities and power, and the abstract equality between persons that is presupposed within doctrinal discourse. Abstract equality, equality in some respects, would seem to be better than none at all. It becomes the best possible option with the jurists' authoritative ruling that material equality is impossible. Progress towards social justice, however, so they tell us, can be achieved if, with a preferred set of Utopian goals in mind, we just continue on with the legal practices of the past few hundred years.

8. *Legitimation and the value of law*. If abstract equality, used as the basis for this justificatory argument, gives a legitimating purchase to law, that is nothing of which to complain. It is not, in my view, a sufficient reason for denouncing law as valueless or worse. It is up to progressive theorists and political movements to open up prospects for human emancipation. Complaining that conservatives do

not see these possibilities misconceives the reality of political and ideological struggle. It also, I think, fails to take sufficient account of rights fetishism as an actual phenomenon of our social formations. It fails to appreciate the reality of the forgetting and the sense of righteouness in the silencing. It fails to consider how human imagination is captured and stifled by ritual and tradition. And it fails to understand that alienated identities are creative only in a struggle for a sense of self and other that challenges the conditions of that alienation.

9. *Abstract equality and unmet needs*. Here then is a reason for taking rights and the value of equal concern and respect for individuals – abstract equality – seriously. It is the strength of the moral and political convictions of our jurists. But if, at the same time, we listen to the claims made by subordinated people, and watch to see how these claims fare in the courts and on the floors of houses of parliament, and count how rarely these claims get through to there, we will begin to understand how very thin this equality is. Moreover, when we observe the forces of reaction that emerge when a claim is conceded, we begin to understand its fragility. The petty bourgeois white male supremacist and his complicitous woman are not, as Jurisprudence implies, phenomena of aberrant 'wicked' legal systems like those of the Third Reich and South Africa. They are on the streets of the countries of which I write as well. Our jurists may turn away from them in horror. What they are blind to is the extent to which such people are products of social relations which the jurists justify.

If then we take up a standpoint that is of and for subordinated groups and classes, we will ask how we can make this thin and fragile equality more substantial. We will reject the complacent and ahistorical belief in steady progress towards Utopian goals, and delve into why a once-progressive innovation turns against us, lets us down and tends to keep us down. That, it seems to me, is the really important question about the value of law.

10. *Living with contradiction*. As a matter of method it seems clear that research work to be done on this question has to be done on particular doctrines and from particular standpoints. My hope for this work is that an understanding of rights fetishism as an actual and pervasive social phenomenon will reveal rights as having contradictory forms of value. They have a value, like the use-value of commodities, that is a value for whoever has the right. And they

199

have a value that appears as universal and absolute, but is, in actuality, limited and relative. I suggest that once we grasp this, we can feel quite comfortable with scepticism as to the latter form of value and commitment to fighting with subordinated people for the rights they claim. Recognition of this contradiction, to put this another way, enables us, without being inconsistent, to claim particular rights, without having or pretending to have the moral or political commitments of a legal point of view. Our moral and political commitments lie elsewhere. The reasons that we have for claiming a right, may not be reasons that the law acknowledges. Their validity will be standpoint relative and their normative force will derive from an emancipatory point of view. With professional understanding of the legal point of view, however, we can undertake to translate them into reasons that are acknowledged within legal argument.

Is this a scandalous attitude? Some will say so. A matter, they will say, of demanding the benefits and refusing the burdens of the rule of law. They are right. This is precisely the claim because the benefits and burdens are skewed. In the meantime there are theoretical and political questions we need to address that are more serious than scandalising. There are limits to translatability, and, while progressive legislative and adjudicative innovations can extend these limits, the effects of the division of mental and manual labour, and the hostility of professional expertise to other ways of knowing, are serious difficulties. As legal professionals and academics, constituting our agency for subordinated groups and classes, we face all the difficulties of fracture within and between them, and all the difficulties of our own fractured identities. Were doctrinal legal discourse our only means of pursuing material equality, we could be sure that such equality would be a Utopian goal. Fortunately, however, that is not the case. Legal practices and theory are just one incomplete way of pursuing it; possibly a relatively insignificant way. We should not, in a vulgar inversion of legal professional self-importance, lose sight of that.

Always there is that double barrier of ideology that keeps moving into place against our advances. If there is one aspect of that barrier which is peculiarly difficult to avoid in philosophy and general theory of law, and is, for that reason, a particularly important object of inquiry for such work, it is that, as a consequence of rights fetishism, normative constructs of human reason cast loose their moorings as deliberately formulated standards for human action and float off to constitute a realm of the sacred. Other people, other cultures, have beliefs in sacred realms of which I do not speak. Within the realm that is constituted by rights fetishism, however, reason is divorced from passion. Its prescriptions as to how we ought to act and to be, express only those feelings of moral and political superiority that persuade people that they know and have a right to tell others what to do.

So I must insist that I am not suggesting that legal practices are 'bad' or 'wrong' because they give rise to rights fetishism. My point is rather to explain and hopefully avoid the barren reaches of thought of which rights fetishism is a condition. In particular, I have sought to explain and avoid forms of moral and political normativity that give expression to ideas of what is good for 'us', where 'we' are an homogeneous moral or political community. That community might be all moral persons, or the national community of free and equal citizens, or the working class, or women, or subordinated people. Whatever it is, in this way of thinking, differences are elided or, if they will assert themselves, are hierarchically evaluated.

All theory is normative, and norms, as ideas about what ought to be done or how we ought to understand our selves and our world, have a necessary generality. They represent the limits of our understanding of self and other, not the foundations. They must be constituted and understood in ways that avoid their turning against us as barriers of negative ideology.

NOTES

INTRODUCTION

1   I developed the idea of taking this approach from reading Sumner (1979), though I am not certain that it conforms to what he intended.
2   The work of Jeremy Bentham, in particular, *Of Laws in General* (Bentham 1970), is an important exception to this tendency in the production of Jurisprudence. However, it was John Austin's lectures in Jurisprudence, delivered at the University of London, 1828–32 (Austin 1879) of which *The Province of Jurisprudence Determined*, published in 1832 (Austin 1955), is a prefatory part, which brought Bentham's work into mainstream professional legal culture.
3   Robert Bropho, Spokesperson for the Fringedwellers of the Swan Valley, personal communication, 10 March 1990.

CHAPTER 1

1   These models of different conceptions of ideology are far too simply drawn to be attributed to any particular theory or concept of ideology. The first model is taken from the positivist tradition in philosophy of science and social science – a tradition which is represented in both mainstream and Marxist philosophy; see further Larrain 1979. The second model is taken from the rationalist, natural law tradition (Finnis 1980) and again finds its way into Marxist philosophy; see further McCarney 1980: 147 n.1, 153 nn.226 and 229. The third model is taken from social and political theory; for the neutral sense, see further the theories of Seliger and Gouldner discussed in Thompson 1984; Lenin 1947; McCarney 1980; for the negative sense, see Thompson 1984.
2   This is a tendency in an oeuvre of North American feminist theory within which the concept of standpoint has received very significant development; see Jaggar 1983. It has recently been reviewed and critiqued by Harding 1986. The notion of standpoint sketched here, draws more on Cain 1986, 1987, 1990, who clearly locates it within a realist ontology. A comparison of point of view and standpoint is

202

undertaken in Chapter 6. I argue there that a notion of standpoint as distinct from point of view, escapes much of Harding's critique.

3 Samuel Johnson is said to have kicked a stone as a refutation of Berkeley's idealist philosophy (Sayers 1985: 146). Bhaskar presents a philosophy of transcendental realism. He asks the question, 'what must be the case for [scientific practices] to be possible?' and argues that in this degree philosophy must continue to travel the Kantian road (Bhaskar 1979, Ch.1).

4 This approach is translated into particular requirements of method in, for example, Cain 1987 (comparative research), Hope 1987 (trans-cultural analysis).

CHAPTER 2

1 See, for example, David Hope's use of the concepts of sovereignty, social relations, and relations of the secular and sacred (reference to the different meanings of the concepts in Pitjatjantjarra and white Australian culture) to find a transcultural viewpoint for social analysis (Hope 1987). In a different context, see Pashukanis 1978, Introduction.

2 There is a problem of consistency in Hart's text between his first identification of different kinds of rules (obligation-imposing and power-conferring rules) and his second and more substantially deployed classification of rules into primary and secondary rules. See Cohen 1962.

3 Finnis has a second justification of private property: a rule of human experience that private enterprise is more productive and more careful of resources than public enterprise. Human beings, he argues just *are* more concerned with private advantage, just *do* prefer 'their own', and a theory of justice must articulate with the world as it is (Finnis 1980: 170).

4 In particular, Finnis deals with the Hohfeldian classification (Hohfeld 1913) and the lawyer's two-term analysis of rights as a relationship between persons and things (see e.g. MacCormick 1974; 1977: 188), and with the long-standing debate between benefit and choice theories of rights (Hart 1983: 162; MacCormick 1982: 154). His stance on these debates, which mainly take place between analytic or positivist jurists, is largely external – that of the critical commentator rather than the committed protagonist of a particular view.

5 Two important Realist texts are Frank 1930 and Llewellyn 1962. On the Realist movement, see Hunt 1978: 37–59; Rumble 1968; Twining 1973b; for a recent re-thinking of it, Ackerman 1984. American Legal Realism has significant similarities with and, possibly, a substantial debt to the German School of Free Law; see Weber 1968: 897; Herget and Wallace 1987.

6 At the conclusion of his Preface to *The Philosophy of Right*, Hegel wrote:

The teaching of the concept, which is also history's inescapable lesson, is that it is only when actuality is mature that the ideal first appears over against the real and that the ideal apprehends this same real world in its substance and builds it up for itself into the shape of an intellectual realm. When philosophy paints its grey in grey, then has a shape of life grown old. By philosophy's grey in grey it cannot be rejuvenated but only understood. The owl of Minerva spreads its wings only with the falling of the dusk.

(Hegel 1967: 13)

CHAPTER 3

1 In general, Finnis' support is pre-modern. He cites sixteenth century English lawyer, Christopher St Germain in dealing with the relationship between human law and natural law, and Sir John Fortescue's *De Laudibus Legum Angliae* ('In Praise of the Laws of England') (about 1470) and *De Natura Legis Naturae* ('Of the Nature of the Law of Nature') (about 1463) in his discussion of the need for authority. These topics are central to his work. Hart and Dworkin are both modern theorists. Dworkin, however, as a liberal rights theorist, has ties back to pre-Benthamite (seventeenth and eighteenth century) theory, whereas Hart's ties are more strongly with the late eighteenth and nineteenth centuries – periods which saw a widespread acceptance in England of utilitarian theory and which were the heyday of positivism.

2 Dworkin argues that when people disagree about whether a particular (P) falls within a general term (T) it is not necessarily the case that P is, as Hart would have it, a penumbral case of T. P might be a paradigmatic case of T for one person and a paradigmatic case of not-T for another. The example he uses supposes disagreement over whether photography is or is not a form of art (Dworkin 1986: 41–2). For a clear defence of Dworkin's position here against Hart's, which makes use of Gallie's idea of an 'essentially contested concept', see Waldron 1985.

3 Bhaskar gives a valuable schema of social theories which he summarises as follows:

Table 2.1 Four Tendencies in Social Thought

	Method	*Object*
Utilitarianism	empiricist	individualist
Weber	neo-Kantian	individualist
Durkheim	empiricist	collectivist
Marx	realist	relational

Bhaskar 1979: 39; and see above, Ch.1

4 The reference is to Yeats' poem 'The Second Coming'

> Turning and turning in the widening gyre
> The falcon cannot hear the falconer;
> Things fall apart; the centre cannot hold;
> Mere anarchy is loosed upon the world.

(Yeats 1950: 210)

and to the post-war managerialist and 'death of ideology' theses which

204

argued that class antagonisms had been overcome in contemporary capitalism and that power had shifted to a new class of managers who acted to balance the interests of different social groups; see Westergaard 1972.

CHAPTER 4

1 When this fraternity is seriously challenged by theorists committed to challenging the inevitability of material inequality, the going gets quite a lot rougher. Dworkin provides the best illustrations because he writes at a time when such challenges are growing stronger. Thus, despite the very open political allegiances of North American Critical Legal Theorists, he asserts that they 'move toward a new mystification in service of undisclosed political goals' (Dworkin 1986: 274; and see further at pp.440–4). When he comes to the discussion of utopian political theory as part of Jurisprudence, he links Marxists with fascists as unqualified for participation in these arguments (Dworkin 1986: 408). While I agree that Marxist political theory is not Utopian, Dworkin makes a serious mistake here, contradicting his own commitment to due process, by a thoughtless attempt at establishing guilt by association. Were he seriously concerned to reflect on the problems of his own culture rather than to celebrate it against the deficiencies of others, particularly of German culture (pp. 101ff, 173), he would realise that linking Marxism with fascism has more to do with McCarthyism than anything else.
2 A legal fiction is an allegation of fact which is known to be untrue but which cannot be contradicted. An example is given by Salmond (Fitzgerald 1966: 74). 'He who desired to enforce in the English courts a bond executed in France was permitted in his pleadings to allege a bond executed "at a certain place called Bordeaux in France in Islington in the County of Middlesex".' This allegation was not allowed by the court to be contradicted (see further Fuller 1931).
3 I owe this point to Eric S. Hayward.
4 'To recognise reason as the rose in the cross of the present and thereby to enjoy the present, this is the rational insight which reconciles us to the actual ...' (Hegel 1967: 12). The rose is the symbol of joy. As I understand him, Hegel uses the metaphor to convey the idea that, however bad the world may seem to be, it is, in essence, a realisation of reason. Philosophy's task is to apprehend the world as it is and, by understanding its rationality, become reconciled to it. Where, as in *The Philosophy of Right* one aspect of the world being considered is the state, the task may be seen as one of legitimation *par excellence*.

CHAPTER 5

1 I owe the idea of envisioning in this context to Eric S. Hayward.
2 I pretend no competence in formal, mathematical logic and owe this point to Graham Priest and Uwe Petersen; see Priest 1987. The point

has to be made against Dworkin's global dismissal of 'the infertile metric of contradiction'.

3   It may be noted that it is for this reason that Pashukanis considered the legal form to be most directly related to relations of exchange rather than relations of production. This point is controversial within Marxist legal theories; see Fine 1984; Hirst 1979; Warrington 1981. The question of the significance of Marx's idea of commodity fetishism to legal theory is central to the controversy.

4   It might be objected here that Marx takes work as a basic good and use-value as a universal form of value appertinent to it. This objection is unsustainable. Marx is not an Aristotelian or neo-Aristotelian philosopher and what is characteristic of use-value is just its social and concrete nature. It should, however, be noted that assumptions about normality are dangerous things which have been used by white male philosophers and scientists to devalue women and people of colour. Furthermore, it should never be forgotten that the work ethic of capitalism found one expression as an inscription on the gates of Dachau and Auschwitz 'Arbeit macht frei' (Work makes you free) and continues to find expression in racist stereotypes of non-Northern Europeans as, in varying degrees, lazy and irresponsible. These points caution against an uncritical espousal of Marx's thought. Nonetheless, a distinction between work as productive, caring or creative activity and labour as alienated work is important here. It is labour as wage slavery that is valued in capitalist ideology, and concentration camp slavery that was justified by fascism. And it is wage labour against which the unpaid work of women and the work of people whose culture is part of non-capitalist modes of production is devalued.

CHAPTER 6

1   We can abstract concepts of alienation and mystification as vices of a way of life from this concern. Alienation in particular, as Bertell Ollman's excellent work shows (Ollman 1976) is an important notion in Marx's thought and can certainly be treated as central to it. But it is a very abstract concept which has perhaps lost some of its power in indiscriminate use and needs now to be followed through work on its phenomenal occurrence at specific sites.

2   This analysis is borne out by events. At the time of writing the Fringe-dwellers of the Swan Valley are again seeking legal aid to restrain a further desecration of a site of significance at and around Bennett Brook, this time by a private developer, but again with the concurrence of the Western Australian government and again without consultation.

3   This is a right given within the rubric of administrative law in the United Kingdom and Australia (Hotop 1985) and within the constitutional requirement of due process in the United States.

4   See Edgeworth 1989 for a political contextualisation of Hart's *The Concept of Law* and problems of technicism in law. Edgeworth's approach makes much more sense of the tendency than the mainstream

jurists' conventional, complacent and non-explanatory metaphor of the pendulum swinging endlessly through time, between certainty and generality on the one hand and discretion and flexibility on the other. The problem of excessive technicality (technicism) tends to be linked to the formalist side of the swing (Atiyah 1983: 94), but as Edgeworth suggests, there is an excess of technique in the managerial and bureaucratic modes of legal regulation and control too.

5 The reference is to Joseph Conrad's novel *Heart of Darkness* and to postmodernist reluctance to engage with logic and dominant ideas of rationality beyond deconstruction.

6 Peter Fitzpatrick first made me aware of the importance of this point; and see Fitzpatrick 1987.

7 The reference is to the Greek myth of Narcissus – a handsome youth who fell in love with his own reflection.

BIBLIOGRAPHY

Abel, R. L. (1981). 'Conservative Conflict and the Reproduction of Capitalism: The Role of Informal Justice', *International Journal of Sociology of Law*, 9, 245–67.

Ackerman, B. A. (1984). *Reconstructing American Law*, Cambridge, Mass.: Harvard University Press.

Aristotle (1938). *Politica* in *The Works of Aristotle*, vol.10 (W. D Ross ed.), Oxford: Clarendon Press.

Aristotle (1955). *The Ethics of Aristotle: Nichomachean Ethics*, (trans. J. A. K. Thompson), Harmondsworth, Middlesex: Penguin.

Ashworth, A. (1987). 'Belief, Intent and Criminal Law', in *Oxford Essays in Jurisprudence*, 3rd series (J. Eckelaar and J. Bell eds), Oxford: Clarendon.

Atiyah, P. S. (1983). *Law and Modern Society*, Oxford and New York: Oxford University Press.

Austin, J. (1879). *Lectures in Jurisprudence*, 4th Ed., London: John Murray.

Austin, J. (1954). *The Province of Jurisprudence Determined*, London: Weidenfeld & Nicolson.

Austin, J. L. (1956). 'A Plea for Excuses', *Proceedings of the Aristotelian Society, New Series*, vol. LVII, 7.

Baker, J. H. (1985). 'English Law and the Renaissance', *Cambridge Law Journal*, 44, 46.

Barker, M. (1985). 'Kant as a Problem for Marxism', in *Radical Philosophy Reader* (R. Edgley and R. Osborne eds), London: Verso.

Barrett, H. and Yach, D. (1986). 'The Teaching of Jurisprudence and Legal Theory in British Universities and Polytechnics', *Legal Studies*, 5, 151–71.

Bartholomew, A. and Hunt, A. (1990). 'What's Wrong with Rights', *Journal of Law and Inequalities* (forthcoming).

Beale, H. and Dugdale, T. (1975). 'Contracts between Businessmen: Planning and the Use of Contractual Remedies', *British Journal of Law and Society*, 2, 45–60.

Bell, D. (1987). 'Aboriginal Women and the Religious Experience', in *Traditional Aboriginal Society: A Reader* (W. H. Edwards ed.), Melbourne: Macmillan.

BIBLIOGRAPHY

Belsey, A. (1986). 'The New Right, Social Order and Civil Liberties', in *The Ideology of the New Right* (R. Levitas ed.), Cambridge: Polity Press.

Bender, L. (1988). 'Feminist Theory and Tort', *Journal of Legal Education*, 38, 1.

Bentham, J. (1970). *Of Laws in General* (H. L. A. Hart ed.), London: Athlone.

Bentham, J. (1977). *A Comment on the Commentaries by Jeremy Bentham* in *A Comment on the Commentaries and a Fragment on Government* (J. H. Burns and H. L. A. Hart eds), London: Athlone.

Benton, T. (1984). *The Rise and Fall of Structural Marxism: Althusser and his influence*, London and Basingstoke: Macmillan.

Bernstein, R. J. (1983). *Beyond Objectivism and Relativism: Science, Hermeneutics and Praxis*, Oxford: Basil Blackwell.

Bhaskar, R. (1978). *A Realist Theory of Science*, Sussex: The Harvester Press; New Jersey: Humanities Press.

Bhaskar, R. (1979). *The Possibility of Naturalism: A Philosophical Critique of the Contemporary Human Sciences*, Brighton, Sussex: The Harvester Press.

Blake, W. (1966). *Complete Writings* (G. Keynes ed.), Oxford, New York, Toronto, Melbourne: Oxford University Press.

Bottomore, T. (ed.) (1983). *A Dictionary of Marxist Thought*, Oxford: Blackwell.

Bourdieu, P. and Passeron, J-C. (1977). *Reproduction in Education, Society and Culture* (trans. R. Nice), London and Beverley Hills: Sage Publications.

Burt, F. (1987). 'The Moving Finger or the Irremovable Digit', *Australian Law Journal*, 61, 465.

Cain, M. (1985). 'Beyond Informal Justice', *Contemporary Crises*, 9, 335–73.

Cain, M. (1986). 'Realism, feminism, methodology and law', *International Journal of Sociology of Law*, 14, 255–67.

Cain, M. (1987). 'Realist philosophy, social policy, and feminism: on the reclamation of value full knowledge'. Paper presented to the British Sociological Association Annual Conference, Leeds. Available in mimeo (1988).

Cain, M. (1990). 'Realist Philosophy and Standpoint Epistemologies *or* Feminist Criminology as a Successor Science', in *Feminist Perspectives in Criminology* (L. Gelsthorpe and A. Morris eds), Milton Keynes: Open University Press.

Callinicos, A. (1985). *Marxism and Philosophy*, Oxford and New York: Oxford University Press.

Campbell, T. (1983). *The Left and Rights: a Conceptual Analysis of the Idea of Socialist Rights*, London: Routledge & Kegan Paul.

Carson, W. G. (1981). *The Other Price of Britain's Oil*, Oxford: Martin Robertson.

Cohen, L. J. (1962). Critical Notice of *The Concept of Law* by H. L. A. Hart, *Mind*, LXXI, 395–412.

Coldrey, J. (1987). *'Aboriginals and the Criminal Courts'*, in *Ivory Scales: Black Australia and the Law* (K. M. Hazlehurst ed.), Kensington: University of New South Wales Press.

Colletti, L. (1973). *Marxism and Hegel*, London: Verso.

Concise Oxford Dictionary of Current English (1964), 6th Ed., Oxford: Clarendon.

Conrad, J. (1973). *Heart of Darkness*, Harmondsworth, Middlesex: Penguin.

Cotterrell, R. (1984). *The Sociology of Law: An Introduction*, London: Butterworths.

David, R. and Brierly, J. E. (1985). *Major Legal Systems in the World Today: An Introduction to the Comparative Study of Law*, 3rd Ed., London: Stevens.

De Sousa Santos, B. (1985). 'On Modes of Production of Law and Social Power', *International Journal of Sociology and Law*, 13, 299–336.

Dickinson, J. (1929). 'The Law behind Law', *Columbia Law Review*, 29, 113.

Douzinas, C. and Warrington, R. (1987). ' On the Deconstruction of Jurisprudence: Fin(n) is Philosophiae' in *Critical Legal Theory*, (P. Fitzpatrick and A. Hunt eds), Oxford: Blackwell.

Duncanson, I. and Kerruish, V. G. (1986). 'The Reclamation of Civil Liberty', *Windsor Yearbook of Access to Justice*, 6, 3–35.

Dworkin, R. (1978). *Taking Rights Seriously*, London: Duckworth.

Dworkin, R. (1985). *A Matter of Principle*, Cambridge, Mass. and London: Harvard University Press.

Dworkin, R. (1986). *Law's Empire*, London: Fontana Paperbacks.

Eagleton, T. (1986). *Against the Grain: Essays 1975–1985*, London: Verso.

Edgeworth, B. (1989). 'H. L. A. Hart, Legal Positivism and Post-War British Labourism', *University of Western Australia Law Review*, 19, 275–300.

Edgley, R. (1985). Introduction in *Radical Philosophy Reader* (R. Edgley and R. Osborne eds), London: Verso.

Fine, B. (1984). *Democracy and the Rule of Law: Liberal Ideals and Marxist Critiques*, London: Pluto.

Finnis, J. (1980). *Natural Law and Natural Rights*, Oxford: Clarendon Press.

Finnis, J. (1983). *Fundamentals of Ethics*, Oxford: Clarendon.

Fitzgerald, P. J. (1966). *Salmond on Jurisprudence*, 12th Ed., London: Sweet & Maxwell.

Fitzpatrick, P. (1987). 'Racism and the Innocence of Law' in *Critical Legal Studies* (P. Fitzpatrick and A. Hunt eds), Oxford: Blackwell.

Fitzpatrick, P. and Hunt, A. (eds) (1987). *Critical Legal Studies*, Oxford: Blackwell.

Flew, A. (ed.) (1984), *A Dictionary of Philosophy*, London: Pan Books.

Foucault, M. (1977). *Discipline and Punish: The Birth of the Prison* (trans. A. Sheridan), Harmondsworth: Penguin Books.

Frank, J. (1930). *Law and the Modern Mind*, New York: Brentano's.

Fuller, L. (1931). 'Legal Fictions', *University of Illinois Law Review*, 25, 363, 513, 877.

Fuller, L. (1958). 'Positivism and fidelity to law – A Reply to Professor Hart', *Harvard Law Review*, 71, 630–72.

Fuller, L. (1969). *The Morality of Law*, New Haven and London: Yale University Press.

Gabel, P. and Kennedy, D. (1984). 'Roll over Beethoven', *Stanford Law Review*, 36, 1–55.

Gadamer, H. G. (1975). *Truth and Method*, London: Sheed & Ward.

Gallie, W. B. (1955–6). 'Essentially Contested Concepts', *Proceedings of the Aristotelian Society*, LVI, 167–98.

Goethe, J. W. von (1862). *Poems and Ballads* (trans. W. E. Aytoun and T. Martin), Edinburgh and London: William Blackwood & Sons.

Griffin, S. (1982). 'The Way of all Ideology' in *Feminist Theory: The Critique of Ideology* (N. O. Keohane, M. Z. Rosaldo and B. Z. Gelpi eds), Chicago: University of Chicago Press.

Griffiths, J. A. G. (1985). *The Politics of the Judiciary*, 3rd Ed., London: Fontana.

Grimshaw, J. (1986). *Feminist Philosophers: Women's Perspectives on Philosophical Traditions*, Brighton, Sussex: Wheatsheaf.

Habermas, J. (1984). *The Theory of Communicative Action* (trans. T McCarthy), Boston: Beacon Press.

Hacker, P. M. S. (1977). 'Hart's Philosophy of Law' in *Law, Morality and Society*, (P. M. S. Hacker and J. Raz eds), Oxford: Clarendon.

Harding, S. (1986). *The Science Question in Feminism*, Ithaca and London: Cornell University Press.

Hart, H. L. A. (1958). 'Positivism and the Separation of Law and Morals', *Harvard Law Review*, 71, 593–629.

Hart, H. L. A. (1961). *The Concept of Law*, Oxford: Clarendon Press.

Hart, H. L. A. (1982). *Essays on Bentham: Jurisprudence and Political Theory*, Oxford: Clarendon Press.

Hart, H. L. A. (1983). *Essays in Jurisprudence and Philosophy*, Oxford: Clarendon.

Hazlehurst, K. M. (ed.) (1987). *Ivory Scales: Black Australia and the Law*, Kensington: University of New South Wales Press.

Head, B. W. (1985). *Ideology and Social Science: Destutt de Tracy and French Liberalism*, Dordrecht, Boston, Lancaster: Martinus Nijhoff.

Hegel, G. W. F. (1967). *Philosophy of Right* (trans. T. M. Knox), London, Oxford, New York: Oxford University Press.

Herget, J. E. and Wallace, S. (1987). 'The German Free Law Movement as the Source of American Legal Realism', *Virginia Law Review*, 73, 399.

Hindess, B. and Hirst, P. (1977). *Modes of Production and Social Formation: an Auto-Critique of Precapitalist Modes of Production*, London: Macmillan.

Hirst, P. (1979). *On Law and Ideology*, London and Basingstoke: Macmillan.

Hirst, P. (1980). 'Law, socialism and rights' in *Radical Issues in Criminology*, (P. Carlin and M. Collinson eds), Oxford: Martin Robertson.

Hohfeld, W. N. (1913). 'Fundamental Legal Conceptions as Applied in Judicial Reasoning', *Yale Law Journal*, 23, 16–59.

Holmes, O. W. (1897). 'The Path of the Law', *Harvard Law Review*, 10, 457.

Hope, D. (1987). 'Policing in Aboriginal South Australia: a transcultural problem' in *Ivory Scales: Black Australia and the Law* (K. M. Hazlehurst ed.), Kensington: University of New South Wales Press.

Hotop, S. D. (1985). *Principles of Australian Administrative Law*, 6th Ed., Sydney: Law Book Co.

Hunt, A. (1978). *The Sociological Movement in Law*, London: Macmillan.

Hunt, A. (1985). 'The Future of Rights and Justice', *Contemporary Crises*, 9, 309–26.

Hunt, A. (1988). 'The Role and Place of Theory in Legal Education: Reflections on Foundationalism', *Legal Studies*, 9, 146–64.

Hunt, A. and Kerruish, V. G. (1991). 'Gender Discrimination in *Law's Empire*', *Reading Dworkin Critically* (A. Hunt ed.), Providence, Rhode Is., Oxford, U.K.: Berg Publishers (forthcoming).

Hutchinson, A. (1987). 'Indiana Dworkin and Law's Empire', *Yale Law Journal*, 96, 637.

Ignatieff, M. (1984). *The Needs of Strangers*, London: Chatto & Windus.

Ilyenkov, E. V. (1977). *Dialectical Logic: Essays on its History and Theory*, Moscow: Progress.

Jaggar, A. (1983). *Feminist Politics and Human Nature*, Totowa, NJ: Rowman and Alanheld; Sussex: The Harvester Press.

Kairys, D. (1982). *The Politics of Law: A Progressive Critique*, New York: Pantheon Books.

Kant, E. (1909). *Fundamental Principles of the Metaphysic of Morals* in *Kant's Critique of Practical Reason and Other Works on the Theory of Ethics*, 6th Ed. (trans. T. K. Abbott), London: Longman.

Keat, R. and Urry, J. (1982). *Social Theory as Science*, 2nd Ed., London: Routledge & Kegan Paul.

Kelsen, H. (1970). *The Pure Theory of Law*, 2nd Ed. (trans. M. Knight), Berkeley: University of California Press.

Kennedy, D. (1981). 'Critical Labor Law Theory: A Comment', *Industrial Relations Law Journal*, 4, 503.

Keohane, N. O., Rosaldo, M. Z. and Gelpi, B. C. (eds) (1981). *Feminist Theory: A Critique of Ideology*, Chicago, Ill: University of Chicago Press.

Kerruish, V. G. (1985). 'Systematically Misleading Theory: Legal Positivism on Law and Legality', *Law in Context*, 3, 75.

Kerruish, V. G. (1987). 'Epistemology and General Legal Theory' in *Social Theory and Legal Politics* (G. Wickham ed.), Sydney: Local Consumption.

Kerruish, V. G. (1988). 'Coherence, Integrity and Equality in Law's Empire: A Dialectical Review of Ronald Dworkin', *International Journal of Sociology of Law*, 16, 51–73.

Klare, K. (1981). 'Labor Law as Ideology: Toward a New Historiography of Collective Bargaining Law', *Industrial Relations Law Journal*, 4, 450–82.

Larrain, J. (1979). *The Concept of Ideology*, London: Hutchinson.

Law Reform Commission (1986). *Report No.31: The Recognition of Aboriginal Customary Laws*, vol.1, Canberra: Australian Government Publishing Service.

Lee, S. (1988). 'Law's British Empire', *Oxford Journal of Legal Studies*, 8, 278–92.

Lenin, V. I. (1947). *What is to be done?* Moscow: Progress.

Lenin, V. I. (1976a). 'Plan of Hegel's Dialectics (Logic)' in *Collected Works*, vol.38 *(Philosophical Notebooks)* 315. Moscow: Progress.

Lenin, V. I. (1976b). 'Conspectus of Hegel's Book *The Science of Logic*' in *Collected Works*, vol.38 *(Philosophical Notebooks)* 85. Moscow: Progress.

Lenin, V. I. (1976c). 'On the Question of Dialectics' in *Collected Works*, vol.38 *(Philosophical Notebooks)* 357. Moscow: Progress.

Levitas, R. (ed.) (1986). *The Ideology of the New Right*, Cambridge: Polity Press.

Llewellyn, K. (1930). 'A Realistic Jurisprudence – The Next Step', *Columbia Law Review*, 30, 431.

Llewellyn, K. (1931). 'Some Realism about Realism', *Harvard Law Review*, 44, 1222.

Llewellyn, K. (1962). *Jurisprudence: Realism in Theory and Practice*, Chicago: University of Chicago Press.

Macaulay, S. (1963). 'Non-contractual Relations in Business', *American Sociological Review*, 28, 45.

McCarney, J. (1980). *The Real World of Ideology*, Brighton: Harvester Press.

MacCormick, N. (1974). 'Law as Institutional Fact', *Law Quarterly Review*, 90, 102.

MacCormick, N. (1976). 'Children's Rights: a Test Case for Theories of Right', *Archiv für Rechts- und Sozialphilosophie*, Bd. LXII/3, 305–16.

MacCormick, D. N. (1977). 'Rights in legislation' in *Essays in Honour of H.L.A. Hart* (P. M. S. Hacker and J. Raz eds), Oxford: Clarendon Press.

MacCormick, N. (1978). *Legal Reasoning and Legal Theory*, Oxford: Clarendon.

MacCormick, N. (1981). *H. L. A. Hart*, London: Edward Arnold.

MacCormick, N. (1982). *Legal Right and Social Democracy: Essays in Legal and Political Philosophy*, Oxford: Clarendon.

MacIntyre, A. (1981). *After Virtue: a Study in Moral Theory*, London: Duckworth.

Marx, K. (1938). *Capital*, vol.1 (trans. S. Moore and E. Aveling; F. Engels ed.), London: George Allen and Unwin.

Marx, K. (1964). *The Economic and Philosophic Manuscripts of 1844* (D. J. Struik ed.), New York: International Publishers.

Marx, K. (1974). 'Critique of the Gotha Programme' in *The First International and after* (D. Fernbach ed.), London: Penguin.

Marx, K. (1975). 'On the Jewish Question' in *Karl Marx and Frederick Engels Collected Works*, vol.3, 146. London: Lawrence and Wishart.

Marx, K. (1976). 'Theses on Feuerbach', (F. Engels ed.) in *Karl Marx and Frederick Engels Collected Works*, vol.5, 6. London: Lawrence and Wishart.

Marx, K. (1976a). 'Marginal Notes On Wagner' in *Value: Studies by Marx*, London: New Park Publication.

Marx, K. and Engels, F. (1952). *Manifesto of the Communist Party*, Moscow: Progress.

Mathews, F. (1989). 'Attentive love: an epistemology of interconnectedness'. Paper read to Eco-Politics IV, Adelaide, South Australia 1989.

Meek, R. (1977). *Smith, Marx, and After*, London: Chapman & Hall.

Moles, R. N. (1987). *Definition and Rule in Legal Theory: A Reassessment of H. L. A. Hart and the Positivist Tradition*, Oxford: Blackwell.

Moulton, J. (1983). 'A Paradigm of Philosophy: the Aversary Method', in

Discovering Reality: Feminist Perspectives on Epistemology, Metaphysics, Methodology, and Philosophy of Science (S. Harding and M. B. Hintikka eds), Holland: Dordrecht.

O'Hagen, T. (1984). *The End of Law?* Oxford: Blackwell.

Ollman, B. (1976). *Alienation*, 2nd Ed., Cambridge: Cambridge University Press.

Olsen, F. (1984). 'Statutory Rape: A Feminist Critique of Rights Analysis', *Texas Law Review*, 63, 387–432.

Outhwaite, W. (1987). *New Philosophies of Social Science: Realism, Hermeneutics and Critical Theory*, London: Macmillan Education.

Pashukanis, E. B. (1978). *Law and Marxism: A General Theory* (C. Arthur ed., trans. B. Einhorn), London: Ink Links.

Phillips, R. (1982). 'Law Rules O.K.?' in *Theoretical Strategies* (P. Botsman ed.), Sydney: Local Consumption Publications.

Poulantzas, N. (1973). *Political Power and Social Classes*, London: New Left Books and Sheed & Ward.

Pound, R. (1959). II *Jurisprudence*, St Paul: West Publishing Co.

Priest, G. (1987). *In Contradiction: a Study of the Transconsistent*, Boston: Martinus Nijhoff.

Purdy, J. (1989). 'Women, Work and Equality: The Commonwealth Legislation', *University of Western Australia Law Review*, 19, 352–79.

Rawls, J. (1973). *A Theory of Justice*, London, Oxford, New York: Oxford University Press.

Raz, J. (1970). *The Concept of a Legal System*, Oxford: Clarendon Press.

Reynolds, H. (1986) *The Law of the Land*, Ringwood, Vic.: Penguin Australia.

Rorty, R. (1980). *Philosophy and the Mirror of Nature*, Oxford: Blackwell.

Rose, F. G. G. (1987). *The Traditional Mode of Production of the Australian Aborigines*, Sydney: Angus & Robertson.

Rumble, W. E. (1968). *American Legal Realism: Skepticism, Reform and the Judicial Process*, Ithaca, NY: Cornell University Press.

Ryle, G. (1963). Introduction to *The Revolution in Philosophy*, London: Macmillan.

Sayers, S. (1985). *Reality and Reason: Dialectic and the Theory of Knowledge*, Oxford: Basil Blackwell.

Schauer, F. (1987). 'The Jurisprudence of Reasons', *Michigan Law Review*, 85, 847.

Scheman, N. (1983). 'Individualism and the Objects of Psychology' in *Discovering Reality: Feminist Perspectives on Epistemology, Metaphysics, Methodology, and the Philosophy of Science* (S. Harding and M. B. Hintikka eds), Dordrecht: D. Reidel.

Skillen, A. (1977). *Ruling Illusions*, Sussex: The Harvester Press.

Smart, C. (1990). *Feminism and the Power of Law*, London: Routledge.

Sophocles, (1947). *Antigone* in *The Theban Plays* (trans. E. F. Watling), Harmondsworth, Middlesex: Penguin.

Stanner, W. E. H. (1987). 'The Dreaming' in *Traditional Aboriginal Society: a Reader* (W. H. Edwards ed.), Melbourne: Macmillan.

Stein, P. and Shand, J. (1974). *Legal Values in Western Society*, Edinburgh: Edinburgh University Press.

BIBLIOGRAPHY

Summers, R. S. (1970). *Essays in Legal Philosophy*, Oxford: Basil Blackwell.

Sumner, C. (1979). *Reading Ideologies: An Investigation into the Marxist Theory of Ideology and Law*, London: Academic Press.

Tasmanian Aboriginal Centre (1988). 'A Nation of Aborigines', paper presented by M. Mansell, 6th Australian Law and Society Conference, La Trobe University, Melbourne.

Taylor, R. (1983). *Metaphysics*, 3rd Ed., Englewood Cliffs, New Jersey: Prentice-Hall, Inc.

Thompson, E. P. (1975). *Whigs and Hunters: The Origin of the Black Act*, Harmondsworth, Middlesex: Penguin.

Thompson, J. B. (1984). *Studies in the Theory of Ideology*, Cambridge: Polity Press.

Tur, R. S. (1976). 'Jurisprudence and Practice', *Journal of the Society of Public Teachers of Law*, 14, 38.

Tur, R. and Twining, W. (1986), *Essays on Kelsen*, Oxford: Clarendon.

Tushnet, M. (1984). 'An Essay on Rights' *Texas Law Review*, 62, 1363–1403

Twining, W. (1973a), 'The Bad Man Re-visited', *Cornell Law Review*, 58, 275.

Twining, W. (1973b). *Karl Llewellyn and the Realist Movement*, London: Weidenfeld & Nicolson.

Twining, W. and Miers, D. (1976). *How To Do Things With Rules*, London: Weidenfeld & Nicolson.

Van Caenegem, R. C. (1987). *Judges, Legislators and Professors: Chapters in European Legal History*, Cambridge, New York: Cambridge University Press.

Waldron, J. (1985). Critical Notice of *Essays in Jurisprudence and Philosophy* by H. L. A. Hart, *Mind*, 94, 281–96.

Warrington, R. (1981). 'Pashukanis and the commodity form theory', *International Journal of the Sociology of Law*, 9, 1–23.

Waters, D. M. (1988). 'Where is Equity Going: Remedying Unconscionable Conduct', *University of Western Australia Law Review*, 18, 1.

Weber, M. (1978). *Economy and Society: An Outline of Interpretive Sociology*, vol.2 (G. Roth and Claus Wittich eds), Berkeley, London: University of California Press.

Westergaard, J. H. (1972). 'Sociology: the Myth of Classlessness', in *Ideology in Social Science: Readings in Critical Social Theory* (R. Blackburn ed.), Glasgow: Fontana/Collins.

Williams, R. (1976). *Keywords: A Vocabulary of Culture and Society*, London: Fontana Paperbacks.

Winch, P. (1963). *The Idea of a Social Science and its Relation to Philosophy*, London: Routledge & Kegan Paul.

Wittgenstein, L. (1958). *Philosophical Investigations* (trans. G. E. M. Anscombe), Oxford: Blackwell.

Yeats, W. B. (1950). *Collected Poems*, London: Macmillan.

Zweigert, K. and Kotz, H. (1987). *An Introduction to Comparative Law*, 2nd Ed. (trans. T. Weir), Oxford: Clarendon.

INDEX